After Stumps Were Drawn

After Stumps Were Drawn
The Best Of Ray Robinson's Cricket Writing

Selected by Jack Pollard
Foreword by Sir Donald Bradman

© the estate of Ray Robinson, 1985; and
© for this selection: Jack Pollard, 1985
First published in 1985 by William Collins Pty Ltd, Sydney
Typeset by Post Typesetters, Brisbane
Printed and bound by Dominion Press — Hedges & Bell

National Library of Australia
Cataloguing-in-Publication data:

Robinson, Ray, 1905–1982.
After stumps were drawn.
ISBN 0 00 216583 X.
1. Cricket — Addresses, essays, lectures. I. Pollard,
Jack, 1926- . II. Title.
796.35'8

Acknowledgements

The stories in this book come from *Between Wickets*, published by William Collins in 1946, *From the Boundary*, published by William Collins in 1951, *The Glad Season* (appeared in some countries as *Green Sprigs*), published by William Collins in 1954, *The Wildest Tests*, published by Pelham Books in 1972, *On Top Down Under*, published by Cassell in 1975, *The Cricketer* magazine published in London since 1921, *The Australian Cricketer*, published in Melbourne, *Sporting Life* magazine, published in Sydney, the Sydney *Sun* and the Sydney *Sun-Herald*. The editor and publisher would like to sincerely thank the publishers and editors of these publications for permission to reproduce Ray Robinson's articles for this special commemorative edition of the work of a much-loved cricket writer.

The photographs used come from the *Daily Telegraph* (Sydney), the *Sun-Herald* (Sydney), the *Age* (Melbourne), the *Herald* (Melbourne), the *Courier-Mail* (Brisbane), and Jack Pollard's collection.

Publisher's Note

Cricket and cricketers' statistics and records have been left as originally written.

Contents

Foreword
by Sir Donald Bradman

The name Ray Robinson conjures up for me mental pictures of three men. The most famous of them was known to me only by reputation. I refer of course to 'Sugar' Ray, renowned for his pugilistic skill and the man generally acknowledged to have been, pound for pound, the greatest boxer of all time.

Perhaps the least famous of the three was the Australian Test cricketer who died in 1965 at the age of 51. This frail cricketing genius represented his country against England at Brisbane in 1936 scoring 2 and 3 (c Hammond b Voce each time), never to be selected again. Jack Pollard in his famous book *Australian Cricket* had this to say of him: 'An outstanding right-hand batting stylist whose lack of judgement off the field ruined a career rich in promise. Yet only a handful of Australians have handled a cricket bat with such culture. His timing and elegance of stroke-play were comparable only to that of Trumper, Jackson and Kippax. Often when you watched him in the nets you felt that he was a class above the others.' That was an apt description.

The other Ray Robinson, the subject of this book, bore no resemblance to his namesakes. He was a quiet, meticulous, studious individual, extremely shy and self-effacing, but he died with the reputation of being the finest sporting journalist and writer that Australia has produced.

Journalists occupy a peculiar place in our lives. Essentially they must ferret out information, try to obtain 'scoops', and convey to the

11

public what they have gleaned. Prior to the advent of radio and television the daily press was virtually the only source from which people could find out what was happening. Inevitably each journalist has to try and prise out valuable snippets to enable him to steal a march on rival journalists. Such an occupation frequently brings about nasty confrontations between the journalist and his subject because things are said over a glass of ale, or by way of an informal conversation, which a sportsman understands to be confidential but the journalist does not. Many a player has been put in an invidious position by an indiscreet disclosure, or worse still by a false interpretation of what he said, or meant. It is because of this special relationship that misunderstandings occur, sometimes to the extent of completely ruining a friendship.

In the case of Ray Robinson I can truthfully say that throughout his long journalistic career, during which cricket became his absorbing interest, never once did I hear a player utter an unkind word about him or complain about something he had written. Because of the implicit trust one could place in him Ray therefore was frequently privy to a great deal of confidential background information which enabled him to write balanced and mature articles on events of the day. Although the face of Ray Robinson was seen at most of the world's leading cricket grounds, where he was kept busy sending back dispatches to his editors, his restless and active mind spurred him to write books. From his pen came *Between Wickets*, 1946, *From the Boundary*, 1951, and *Green Sprigs*, 1954. They were all excellent books and placed him in the forefront of Australian sporting writers. In 1975 came his wonderful *On Top Down Under*, a book devoted to Australian cricket captains. I was the fortunate recipient of an advance copy and still have in my file the correspondence between us. I wrote and thanked Ray for the copy and went on: 'We have here a gem of the first water. After reading only the first three chapters already I am fascinated and enthralled by the incredible amount of absorbing detail which you have produced, obviously after long and diligent research. Your book should sell like Woolworths' pantyhose.' In his reply Ray said: 'I probably wore out five pairs of shoes trudging into libraries in Sydney, Melbourne and Adelaide trying to check on things. From imagining I was writing the book I discovered that the book had taken charge of my life. By the time the last difficulties were disposed of and swept under the carpet I'd lost half-a-stone weight. Your letter helps make me feel it was all worth the effort.'

In a work of such magnitude there just had to be some errors and I politely pointed out a couple to Ray, adding that the typesetter perhaps didn't keep his mind on the job. But he wouldn't blame anyone else. He simply said: 'Some errors are all my own work — unaided. At page proof stage I must have been punch drunk.'

On Top Down Under is unique, and thoroughly merited being chosen in 1976 as the book of the year by the Cricket Society of England. Ray was the first Australian cricket writer to achieve this distinction, and he was followed in 1983 by Jack Pollard, the compiler of this book. I think Ray regarded his trip to England to receive this cherished award as the highlight of his life, which was understandable because he was now ranked alongside such great English writers as Sir Neville Cardus, E. W. Swanton and A. A. Thomson.

If I might be pardoned for intruding a somewhat personal note, let me refer to a revelation he made in *On Top Down Under* which was a real surprise. I had always believed I was the only Australian cricketer offered or awarded a knighthood. However, in his chapter on Australia's first Test cricket captain, Dave Gregory, Ray had this to say: 'When the States formed the Australian Commonwealth, he (Gregory) was offered the post of head of the Federal Treasury together with a knighthood. He declined. Acceptance would have meant going to live in Melbourne and he could not bear to leave Turramurra — not even for Toorak.'

As for Ray's style I can do no better than quote what Alan Ross said in one of his *Playfair* productions: 'For apt phrases describing players in unforgettable ways, Robinson was second only to Sir Neville Cardus. A typical example is that when speaking of Keith Miller's bumpers he said, "Batsmen find it hard to understand Miller's bowling. Much of it is over their heads." And again, "Bradman's position at the top of the batting averages was as changeless as alphabetic order."' So one could go on picking out golden threads from the stream of writing which came from his pen.

Although *On Top Down Under* was by far his greatest and most consuming work, Ray produced books of lesser magnitude, and perhaps understandably, of lesser merit.

In the last couple of years of Ray's life it became clear to his many friends and admirers that his eyesight and health had deteriorated alarmingly. They wondered how his frail body could cope with the travel and the enormous work load he shouldered. Finally the end came, and so passed to the beyond a man who, as far as I know, left behind not a single enemy but many enduring memories of the finest of all Australian sporting journalists and a thorough gentleman. Much of his work will give pleasure to people yet unborn.

Introduction
by Jack Pollard

At his best Ray Robinson was among the finest writers on cricket from any country, and was only challenged by Jack Fingleton for supremacy among Australian cricket writers. He never attempted the dramatic prose of Neville Cardus, nor the racy, self-confident, scalpel-like commentaries of Fingleton. He built his portraits of players painstakingly and it was the final mosaic that lingered in memory rather than the brilliance of his phrase-making. John Arlott called him the most underestimated of all cricket writers; Cardus called him 'X-ray Robinson'.

He was probably the most meticulous notetaker in sportswriting. He left a house full of notebooks and stray pages reminding himself of the habits and style and eccentricities of hundreds of cricketers. He left, too, hundreds, of letters from Test players in which they answered his queries about how they held the bat, why they licked only one finger before bowling, how they developed a characteristic routine in taking block. I remember driving him home not long before he died when he apologized for keeping me waiting. 'I've just confirmed with Imran Khan that Richard Hadlee was barred from bowling under the intimidatory law halfway through the Pakistan–New Zealand Test at Karachi in 1976,' said Robbie. 'It was the only time in any country umpires have invoked that law.' He was like a small child who had just discovered Santa Claus.

To the end of his life he kept querying delegates to meetings that decided some of cricket's most contentious issues on how they had voted. It took him 25 years to discover how the selectors decided to omit Don Tallon from Australia's 1938 tour of England. It seldom took him long to discover that an apparently trustworthy administrator had lied to him about what had happened behind closed doors. All of his discoveries went into his notebooks, which became a vast storehouse of cricket's past for use in one of the thousands of articles he wrote for magazines and newspapers around the world.

The miraculous thing was that for all his factual accuracy, he remained on friendly terms with everybody in cricket, for he had a way of taking the barbs out of his criticisms. The late Jack Fingleton was often cruel in his criticisms of Ray Robinson, claiming he could not possibly write well about cricket because he lacked experience as a Test player. Robbie refused to retaliate. 'Fingo always has something interesting to say on the game,' he would say. 'And Fingo has written some of the game's finest books.' Always fair, never overawed, Robbie kept trying to find good qualities in cricket's villains.

Raymond John Robinson was born on 8 July 1905, the eldest of three sons of a butcher who conducted his business from a shop in New Street, Brighton, Victoria. One of his brothers, Frank, also became a butcher, but Ray and his younger brother Andrew ('Drew') went to work for the Melbourne *Herald,* Ray as a copyboy and Drew as a compositor. Ray attended the Brighton State School and was regarded as a model student. He played a lot of junior cricket and dabbled in golf, squash and Australian football. He originally planned to become a teacher but fell ill while he was sitting for the entrance exam and failed.

The founder of this Robinson clan migrated from Surrey in England, arriving in Fremantle on the *Palestine* in 1852 to take up a position as overseer for Sir George Shenton. Over the next two generations the family spread from Perth to Kalgoorlie to Melbourne. Ray and many of his uncles played for the Brighton Cricket Club. All the Robinsons were right-handed batsmen who liked to thump the ball hard, and were dedicated supporters of the Essendon Australian Rules football club. Another uncle, Alec Robinson, captained the Goldfields XI against MCC at Kalgoorlie in 1924–25, and a cousin, Dr George Robinson, captained Western Australia against the 1946–47 MCC team captained by Wally Hammond. Ray Robinson, the Test batsman from Newcastle in the 1936–37 series against England, was not related to Ray Robinson the writer — whose best was the First XI of the Brighton Club in 1925–26.

The Melbourne Robinsons were extremely friendly with their

second cousins, the Bailey brothers, who worked for the *Sporting Globe* newspapers, and when Ray left school one of the Bailey's, E. N. ('Ernie'), got Ray a job as a copyboy on the *Herald*. Ray was given a cadetship and worked through the early 1920s as an Australian football and cricket writer. In 1925, he wrote to Pelham Warner, editor of the authoritative English magazine *The Cricketer*, saying he was horrified by the poor coverage of Australian cricket in the magazine. Warner invited him to submit his own reports on events in Australia and from 1926 until he died Robinson seldom missed an issue of *The Cricketer*.

Initially, Ray had planned to be a cartoonist. Once, travelling home from work on the bus, he sketched the conductress, Ellen Jessie Gilbert, who he learned was from Tasmania. He gave Ellen the sketches as he got off. From this a romance developed and they married in 1927. Ellen Robinson, who preferred to be known by her middle name, Jess, later worked on the *Bulletin*, writing for children under the pseudonym 'Sister Sadie'.

The Robinson's first child, Brian John, was born in 1930 on the day that Phar Lap won the Melbourne Cup. Ray was not present for the birth, he was away chasing Don Bradman for an interview, and his absence started a problem which worsened throughout the marriage. Jess believed that when children were born his place was by her side. But when their second child, Audrey Clarice, was born Ray was in Naples on route to England with the 1934 Australian team.

Ray had worked on the Melbourne *Herald* during the Bodyline series in 1932–33 and he always believed he was the sub-editor who picked up the word 'Bodyline' and made it a headline when Hugh Buggy used cablese to condense 'in line with the body' in a telegram to the *Herald* from Brisbane.

When a group of journalists helped start the *Star* newspaper they immediately recognized Robinson's talents by offering him the cricket writer's job. He went to England with the 1934 Australian team but had to contribute his articles through the London Press Agency and at first was not allowed to travel with the team. His reports of the team's London matches so impressed the Press Agency, however, that he was commissioned to accompany the team for the later matches on the tour. He made further tours to England with Australian teams in 1948, 1953, 1956 and 1961; toured South Africa in 1957–58, the West Indies in 1954–55, and made a number of tours of India and Pakistan for the *Times of India* and *Sportsweek* in Bombay.

He moved to Sydney in 1939 at the invitation of Frank Packer and spent the war years sub-editing for the *Daily Telegraph*, Sydney. When I first met him in 1943 he was part of a brilliant sub-editors' table that included superb journalists like Richard Hughes, King Watson, Peter Gladwin, Forbes Miller, and George Illingworth. When Packer began to produce a supplement for the *Sunday Telegraph* called *Time* he chose Robinson and Jack Paton to edit it. In his spare time Robbie worked on his first book. At the end of the war he showed the manuscript to Neville Cardus, who had worked as a music critic for the *Sydney Morning Herald* through the war years. Cardus sent the manuscript of *Between Wickets* to William Collins in London, urging them to publish it.

Robinson and Paton left the Packer organization together to edit a supplement called *Fact* for the rival *Sunday Sun*, and in 1948 Robinson went to England with Bradman's famous team despite the attitude of newspaper proprietors who regarded good sub-editors more valuable than reporters. He had never been a full-time cricket writer until that tour, although he had ghosted people like Alan Kippax, Bill Ponsford and Bill Woodfull. A major reason for his departure from Packer's newspapers was Packer's preference for ghosted cricket reports by Test cricketers, which Robinson abhorred. He prepared for the 1948 tour by producing an amazing notebook containing minute details on all of Bradman's players, a procedure he followed on all his subsequent tours.

This tour threw him together for the first time on an overseas tour with Tom Goodman, of the *Sydney Morning Herald*. They formed a formidable duo, far superior I always thought to their English counterparts, great all-rounders, neat, polished and reliable in all they did, accurate reporters with a descriptive flair. Sadly, Goodman, who had been with the old *Evening News* in Sydney after World War I, never persevered with book writing.

The publication in 1946 of Robinson's *Between Wickets*, followed in 1951 by *From the Boundary*, established Robinson's international reputation and alerted cricket-lovers everywhere to his exceptional gifts. But Robinson's talents made no impression on the *Sun* organization's chief executive, Eric Kennedy, who like Packer rated him more valuable on the sub-editor's table and persuaded a former Adelaide lawyer, R. S. ('Dick') Whitington to give up law and become the outfit's cricket writer. There were many who believed Kennedy's judgement was at fault, for Whitington was not a trained fact-gatherer and his material was full of errors.

The competition for the cricket writing job and the desire to live up to the big reputation he had won with his books did cause Robinson to stumble, however, and for a time he became slow almost to the point of tedium in producing his copy. He spent far too long working out telling phrases for sub-editors thirsting for copy back at head office. I remember one day when he scratched around for a special effect and finally at the end of the day confided that he had got it: 'Yardley's perfume of batsmanship.' In this period he missed deadlines and was not wanted by afternoon tabloids, a fate he shared with the great English writer R. C. Robertson-Glasgow, whose copy was mercilessly cut by over-zealous Australian sub-editors.

He was saved by the overseas newspapers who were eager to receive his copy. His syndication department always knew they could recoup most of the cost of sending him on tour with the fees he attracted from journals throughout the cricket world. His children did not see much of him because of his touring and Jessie Robinson's ire over his absences increased even after he bought a block of land at Northbridge in Sydney in 1948 and built a house there. His daughter Audrey became a cadet journalist on the Sydney *Sun* after attending the exclusive Wenona School on Sydney's North Shore. His son Brian went to North Sydney Boys' High School, where he was an outstanding student before graduating in science from Sydney University and taking a Ph.D. at Cambridge University.

In 1966, Robinson's Sydney doctors sent him to the Retina Clinic at Boston, Massachusetts, for operations for detached retinas on both his eyes. The New South Wales Cricket Association passed an emergency loan of several thousand dollars to allow him to make the trip which it was believed would fully restore his sight. The operation on the left eye was successfully concluded but before doctors could operate on the right eye Robinson developed a severe gastric complaint.

He was moved to the nearby Massachusetts General Hospital and there it was found that he had an hereditary stomach complaint. He was required to pay at least $3,000 for blood transfusions needed during the stomach operation. He could not afford that amount, but Australian journalists stationed in New York were organized by *Sydney Morning Herald* chief Allan Dobbyn to go to Boston and donate the 15 pints of blood required.

The vomiting associated with his gastric complaint detached the retina of the right eye completely, and no further attempt was made to repair it. Back in Australia his son, Dr Brian Robinson, had to read the final proofs of his father's book, *The Wit of R. G. Menzies*, while Ray was in hospital in Boston. He had just finished the task when he learned that his father was returning home, doomed to a future of failing sight and a worsening stomach disorder.

Robinson retired as a full-time journalist in 1970. He began another

book, *The Wildest Tests,* delving into his notebooks for accounts of
the dramatic events of cricket in the upheaval of the postwar world.

He was then awarded a Commonwealth Literary Fund fellowship
and a grant from the Literature Board of the Council for the Arts. Ray
threw himself into the task of creating a new book on Australia's
cricket captains. He knew his time was short and that there was not
time now for studied phrase-turning and he developed a facility that
made his writing flow in a manner which some of his previous work
had lacked. His wife Jess died in 1973, aged 73, feeling to the end that
cricket had cheated her. Two years later Robinson's finest book, *On
Top Down Under,* appeared — a marvellous piece of fact-gathering
with the pace of a first-rate novel. It won the English Cricket Society's
Literary Award for 1976. He flew to London to accept the award and
was photographed chatting with his friends E. W. Swanton, John
Arlott and the other leading English cricket writers.

Then he returned to live alone in his house at Northbridge
overlooking Cammeray Bay, occasionally enjoying visits from his
grandson Anthony. Every day Ray worked on articles for cricket
magazines and on revisions to his books. Bill Frindall, the English
cricket statistician, stayed with him for a summer, and old friends like
Bill O'Reilly, Bill Hunt and Keith Miller called to see him, but mostly
he was alone, refusing his son's suggestion that he move to a nursing
home or somewhere where people could take care of him; he wanted
to be near his notebooks and files in a place where he could find them
despite near blindness caused by a cataract on his one good eye. In the
cricket season he travelled to grounds on public transport with his
customary large file of notes, as enthusiastic as a junior reporter at his
first big match as he hauled his frail, wizened, grey-haired frame up
the pavilion steps. With little sight left, he peered out at the players on
the field through binoculars, pecking out his pieces with fingers that
had lost all strength.

Most Fridays I took him shopping, stocking up on tins of baby food,
eggs and black currant juice, which was all his stomach would hold. I
was working on a 1200 page cricket book at the time and he told me to
come armed with queries. He was a man who never had any rivals and
shared his remarkable knowledge of cricket eagerly and honestly. You
asked him about Bill O'Reilly and he would tell you of how O'Reilly
fooled great players so badly with his remarkable flight and spin that
they often looked about the field trying to find out where they had
been caught. Talk to him about Jeff Thomson and he would say, 'The
most alarming bowler we have had.'

Bodyline remained a vivid memory. 'It was very disturbing to me because fellows who were friends of mine were subjected to great peril,' he said. 'Nobody was killed but there were some nasty injuries. One time Bill Ponsford had 10 bruises behind the shoulder. Ponsford and Woodfull took some terrible blows.'

He loved to talk about Jack Ellis, the Victorian wicketkeeper in the 1920s. 'The Victorian batting was so strong, with Woodfull and Ponsford opening, that if they won the toss and batted, Ellis used to go and inspect various contracting jobs he and his men were working on around Melbourne.'

Then there was the time Robbie was in the West Indies when a pace bowler named Hilton was sentenced to death for the murder of his wife. A West Indian fieldsman, John Holt, dropped three catches off Australian opener Colin McDonald. Within minutes a macabre banner was erected: 'Hang Holt, save Hilton'.

He wrote five cricket books: *Between Wickets, From the Boundary, Green Sprigs* (published in England as *The Glad Season*), *The Wildest Tests* and *On Top Down Under.* There are wonderful lines for every cricket lover in all of them. Jimmy Burke enjoyed his reference to Jeff Thomson's bouncers: 'In a couple of overs Thomson can turn a thigh pad into Vienna Schnitzel.' Bill Hunt liked: 'Watching Bill Lawry, as you have ample time to do, you sense that he loves batting. If he is not actually wedded to his art everyone can see he is going steady.' John Arlott liked: 'Kippax modelled his stance at the wicket on Trumper's. Cover the heads on photographs of each awaiting the bowler and there are few clues to tell one from the other. The similarity extends even to the shirtsleeves folded halfway up the forearm.' My favourite was his account of how, after World War II had shortened his career, Sid Barnes eliminated all risky shots from his exciting repertoire. 'Often,' wrote Robbie, 'Barnes seems to get bricked up inside his own run factory.'

Ray Robinson was inordinately proud of his son's success as a senior scientist for the CSIRO, involved in the excitement of space age astronomy at the radio telescope at Parkes. He was proud, too, of his granddaughter Anne, an outstanding schoolgirl athlete. Taking a look at the honours on her blazer, he said, 'It looks like the credits for a TV epic.'

Towards the end of June 1982 his son and daughter-in-law, Jill, convinced Ray to spend a while in a private hospital. On the night before he was due to be admitted Ray fell, broke two ribs and punctured a lung. He was rushed to hospital, where doctors found that he was also suffering from an intestinal blockage. For two weeks he seemed to rally under treatment, read the one Dickens novel he had never read, and chatted animatedly with many cricketing friends, drawing on his unlimited store of cricket stories. But the stomach problems could not be solved and doctors put him on morphia to dull the pain of his final day. There was a great sense of sadness that Ray Robbie, who had endured so much, had finally, 'laid aside his pencil'.

When his son went back to Ray's house, he found a half-finished obituary about his mate 'Slasher' Mackay in Ray's typewriter. It was full of the old Robinson magic. 'Not once in an innings of 203 did Mackay justify his nickname; the drone of the bagpipes was still in the background of strokes that rang out with trumpet-like clarity,' he wrote.

Robbie may have endured marital problems, chronic stomach problems, virtual blindness, and a little loneliness, but he never relented in his devotion to his art — cricket writing. I believe his life was a triumph.

Part I
Cricket's Heroes

1 *Handsome Dave*

Silver spoons were scarce in the oddly named colony of New South Wales when Australia's greatest cricketing family was founded. One of the humble portals through which the founder, Edward Gregory, passed as a boy was the drab door of the Male Orphan Institute. His parents had brought him and two infant brothers from London a year before the Battle of Waterloo. After their mother died in 1819 the father returned to England and the three forlorn boys were inmates of the institute until discharged to jobs with tradesmen. The eldest was apprenticed to a shoemaker.

At 22 Edward William Gregory became a schoolmaster and played cricket in Hyde Park when it was a much larger reserve. At 30 he married Mary Ann Smith, sister of a noted Melbourne mayor who became a member of the first Parliament. It was a love match. Among 13 children of this fertile union were seven boys, five of whom grew up to be better cricketers than their father and played for New South Wales. Twenty of the affectionate grandsons represented the State at cricket, football, athletics or sailing.

Governor of the colony in the 1860s was Sir William Denison, whose name is commemorated on maps as Fort Denison, better known as Pinchgut, the convicts' name for the once-fortified island that peers respectfully over the waves at the Opera House. Presenting a medal for meritorious conduct at St James' Church of England School in Sydney, Sir William told the boys that if they

25

obtained good passes there would be jobs for them. Among his hearers was David William Gregory, 15, who had been born at Fairymeadow, 80 kilometres south, on 15 April 1845, while his father was teaching at Wollongong. Awarded the medal in December 1860, young Gregory instantly showed initiative of the kind we all know a Test captain should have in rich abundance. From the school David walked down Macquarie Street to Government House, produced the medal and told His Excellency, 'I've come about that job, sir.' They made him a clerk in the Audit Office at sixteen years.

Aborigines had mia-mias in the trees by the lake in Centennial Park when David and two elder brothers played cricket in the Domain. No proper pitch existed, so they chose the most level strip they could find and made the best of it. Governor Denison and veteran cricket-lovers Bill Tunks and Al Park each gave £5 to lay out a pitch as flat as shovels and a spirit-level could make it, if no more. This technological aid helped Ned, Walter, Dave, Charlie and Arthur Gregory and their National Club mates develop their game in matches against garrison regiment officers and the Currency Lass Hotel teams of colonial-born youths.

None could withstand a trio of Victorian stars, Tom Wills, John Conway and Sam Cosstick, who, in one of their single-wicket triumphs in Sydney, carried off a purse of £100. Wills, a former Rugby School captain, was one of the founders of the spectacular southern game of football, originally designed to keep cricketers fit in winter. Smarting Sydneysiders persuaded three of the Gregory brothers to challenge the victors. Morning after morning, sunrise over the blue Pacific summoned Ned, Dave and Charlie to practise hard for an hour and a half, polishing their form for the great occasion. Talk of the town, the single-wicket contest drew more than five thousand people to the Albert Ground, Redfern, in April 1871. A crowd's demonstration against a Victorian umpire who was no-balling Dave caused an English-born umpire to be substituted (friction that had an unfortunate sequel late in Gregory's career). Trained to the last centimetre, Ned, Dave and Charlie overthrew the Melbourne champions. In the heroes' home suburb, Paddington, north-east of Sydney Cricket Ground, every hotel displayed three cornstalks from which fluttered light-blue ribbons.

Though less dramatic than Stanley's celebrated meeting with Livingstone in the African jungle later in the same year, the meeting of David Gregory and John Conway has had far-reaching consequences extending to the present day, when cricketers of seven countries crisscross the globe to play international matches and eight compete for a World Cup.

When a coach brought Dr W. G. Grace's English team over dusty roads to an upcountry town in 1873, the publican of a primitive hotel apologized, 'Sorry we can't fix you up like they did in the cities, Doc. No bloody baths, you know!' Grace: 'That's all right, my man. We Graces are no bloody water-spaniels.'

By the time James Lillywhite brought the fourth English side out in 1876 for matches against fifteens and eighteens, years of coaching by two voluntary exiles from Surrey, Charles Lawrence and William Caffyn, had upgraded the standard of the colonial cricketers. For the first time it was arranged that they play the All-England team in an eleven-a-side match on the Englishmen's return from New Zealand.

Finding a captain for the first Australian XI was easier than picking a place for the country's national capital. Without wrangling, string-pulling or a casting vote the players had the captain they wanted, Dave Gregory. His last surviving daughter, Pearl (who lived to 92), told me: 'It always pleased father to recall that his fellow-players elected him captain for the first of all Test matches. Yes, the Victorians elected him, as the match was in Melbourne.' She gave a trill of a laugh, as if inter-city rivalries went back as far as her girlhood. Within a few years of separation from the original colony of NSW, the Victorians had precociously built a railway and telegraph before Sydney attempted such ventures.

David Gregory, 31, was a born leader and looked it. His height, 187 cm (6ft 2in.), weight, 90.7 kg (14st. 4lb.), and erect carrriage gave him a commanding appearance. 'Handsome Dave', women of Sydney town called him in days when barques' bows jutted over Circular Quay and the cooling nor'-easter was unimpeded by high-rise office buildings.

Beards today have scarcely kept abreast of the onward march of human progress. Nowhere in Australian cities in the 1970s have I noticed whiskers of such masculine grandeur as those that adorned the chin of Australia's first captain. His full beard was more widely known than any other in the Antipodes except the one on police posters about outlawed Ned Kelly (who was seven centimetres shorter, 17 kilograms lighter and ten years younger).

Gregory's brown eyes mingled the gleam of geniality with the glint of authority. His face had the no-nonsense expression of a man versed in the ways of the world who controlled a staff of public servants. Exceptionally keen sight helped his batting and slip-catching. He wrote the batting order in the large flowing hand of a day when the supremacy of penmanship had yet to be challenged by typewriters. His capital M in Murdoch's name trailed a tail curving like a fishhook.

He smoked a pipe, the masculine vogue of the time, and was a sociable drinker. His daughter never saw him the worse for liquor.

From Caffyn, who had a hairdressing salon in dusty George Street, Gregory picked up much more than how to comb his beard. He freely acknowledged that the ex-Surrey player 'taught me all I really know about cricket'. To methods passed along from the old world he added a fresh outlook calling for more urgent tactics.

To cricket devotees 1877 is as venerated a year as, say, 1066 to the English or 1492 to Americans. It was 23 years after the Crimean War and 23 before the Boer War, tidily spaced by history so that inhabitants of the colonies by the South Seas could give undivided attention to a Combined XI from Sydney and Melbourne playing an all-professional English team. On the Melbourne Cricket Club's ground, amid gumtrees bordering the unpolluted Yarra River, Dave Gregory's toss gained first use of the wicket for his team of six Victorians and five New South Welshmen. Few citizens gave them much chance as Charles Bannerman faced the first ball from Alfred Shaw on a sunny March afternoon. As this Kent-born Sydney batsman headed for the first Test century about four thousand people came from town to watch.

On the second day 12,000 saw Bannerman carry on from 126 to 165. His sorties along the pitch to disturb the control of the professionals caused Yorkshire lob bowler Thomas Armitage to resort to extremes. Before switching to underarm grubbers he tried to land lofty full tosses over Bannerman's head on to the bails. Balls of such pregnant parabola, one reporter estimated, could only have been reached with a clothes-prop. Every Melbourne backyard had one of those, as science had yet to invent the handle-wound clothes-hoist.

Bannerman outlasted seven partners before he retired hurt with a finger split by Yorkshire fast bowler George Ulyett. Admirers subscribed a half-sovereign for each of his runs to reward his astonishing feat. On the rough wickets of the period centuries seemed as scarce as seahorses. Nobody else reached 20, though a stripling of 18 years, Tom Garrett, justified Gregory's judgement in bringing a law student from Sydney University into the team. The youngster coolly made 18 not out toward the total 245. No younger Australian has since played a Test against England. The colonials led by 49 and in the second innings Tom Kendall's left hand bowled them to victory by 45.

The Victorian players' faith in Gregory's capacity to rise above sectional interests was well founded. He gave Melbourne's bowlers 159 overs to 42 by Sydney men and they took 17 of the 20 English wickets. The Victorian Cricket Association had gold medals minted for the victors and appropriately ordered one slightly larger for the skipper.

The immense interest aroused by the Melbourne match demanded that a second be arranged. Gregory and Conway's judgement and willpower had come through a severe trial before the first game. They had not been stampeded by ace bowler Fred Spofforth's ultimatum that he would play only if Murdoch kept wicket — the only man he believed could cope with his bowling. In bringing Spofforth and Murdoch in for the second Test Dave left out his elder brother Ned but insisted that Jack Blackham continue to keep wicket. Again his appraisal was upheld. Standing up to the stumps in Spofforth's third over, Blackham reined in a rising ball and stumped Shaw in a manner hitherto thought impossible.

Gregory lowered himself to tenth place in the first innings of 122. When his side began the second innings 139 behind, he went in first with Nat Thompson and made top score, 43, in an opening stand of 88. Thanks to powerful Ulyett's bold hitting for 63, the Englishmen won with four wickets to spare.

Win or lose, Lillywhite's professionals were receiving £150 for the trip, expenses paid. For eight days' effort the colonials were reimbursed their expenses only. That frugality was augmented by collections around the crowd for Bannerman, Kendall and Blackham, and by the honour and glory. Half a century later another Test player, John Worrall, wrote: 'Dave Gregory's team in 1877 created such enthusiasm throughout the Australian continent that its effects have never really abated'. This still applies.

Sensing it was time to press on with international cricket, Conway suggested that a similar team tour Britain in 1878. Lawrence had already proved this feasible in 1868 with a troupe of Aborigines in whose bags boomerangs were bedfellows with bats. Conway was unable to interest the Victorian and New South Wales Cricket Associations but Gregory strongly supported the proposal. He and Conway, who managed the side, chose five from NSW (Charles and Alex Bannerman, Garrett, Murdoch and Spofforth), four Victorians (Blackham, Frank Allan, Harry Boyle and Tom Horan) and Tasmanian banker-batsman George Bailey.

Though Dave's top score in one innings and his example as a slipfielder had been his only substantial contributions as a player in the first two Tests his initiative on and off the field stamped him as the man to lead the first representative team on a pilgrimage to England, the Holy Land of cricket.

Anyone seeing Australia's first captain sitting among his men could have been forgiven for thinking he held the post of honour by virtue of having the most luxuriant beard. Boyle had a beard to be proud of, but Gregory's beat his by rather more than a whisker. In a photograph of the 1878 team the skipper has the only cravat, blue with white spots, and the only peaked cap, tilted at a rakish angle hardly fitting what was known of his mien as a pillar of the Treasury (which gave him six months' leave). Pork-pie hats balanced somehow on the other players' heads. All wore dark boots.

Each contributed £50 toward tour expenses, three times the fare to Britain. They augmented the kitty by playing 16 preliminary matches against odds of 15 to 22 in Queensland, NSW, South Australia, Victoria and New Zealand. Having no baggageman, they drew lots before each move to decide which would carry the team's bats and pads in a huge canvas bag. It was branded AUSTRALIAN XI in large letters and the players called it the Caravan.

The captain, 33, was the only player over 30. He was a father of three, having married when twenty-one. Most of his men were under 25, with Garrett, 19, already sprouting a semi-circular beard. All the optimism and resilience of youth were needed for 11 players to tackle 37 matches (15 of them first-class) in Britain. They were joined for the first month by William Midwinter, who had returned from Victoria to play for the county of his birth, Gloucestershire, in 1877. Midwinter had changed ready to play with the Australians against Middlesex at Lord's when W. G. Grace and J. A. Bush entered the pavilion. They took him by cab to play for Gloucestershire at the Oval — a hijack they justified by saying he was still under contract.

In their opening match Notts had trounced them by an innings on a freezing day. 'What on earth induced us to come to this country?' Gregory groaned. 'I wish I was back in Sydney with the sun shining on me from a blue sky.'

In London on 27 May the colonials travelled unrecognized in their brake from the Tavistock Hotel, Covent Garden, to Lord's to play a quality Marylebone Cricket Club team. So little was known of them when they entered the field at noon that a Marylebone member exclaimed, 'These can't be Australians; they aren't black!' — a reflected memory of the Aborigines' tour.

Onlookers laughed when Grace hit Allan's first ball to the boundary but England's champion was caught next ball. On a rain-ruined pitch bowlers reaped 31 wickets for 105 runs, 16 of the batsmen for the dreaded duck-eggs. Among them were the Bannerman brothers and their captain. Seven men fell first ball, four were out to the second.

Gregory had a deadlier pair of bowlers — Spofforth 10 for 20 and Boyle 9 for 17 — than the Marylebone Club's Shaw and Morley. Every chance was caught as Marylebone, out for 33 and 19, were beaten by nine wickets in four and a half hours.

For the raw colonial boys to overwhelm a strong Marylebone Cricket Club side was like a war canoe sinking a gunboat. All England took notice. A congratulatory crowd surrounded their hotel. In theatres and music halls actors brought the win into their lines.

The colonials' £50-a-head investment was going to pay off. To see them at railway stations men and women pressed their noses against carriage windows. Players heard such exclamations as, 'Which be Demon?', 'Where be stoomper?', 'They beant black at all!', 'Anyway, that 'un in corner be a half-caste' — a reference to Gregory's swarthy complexion.

Wisden hailed their play as marking the beginning of a new era. London *Globe* spoke of their bowlers introducing a new system. *Home News* said their fielding was admired by all who beheld it. They were praised for breaking away from stereotyped positions and adjusting their places in the field to combat each batsman. Only one century was scored against them.

The new approach by Gregory and his men was taken up by the London *Standard*:

> One of the principal causes of the Australians' success was Mr Gregory's captaincy ... England at present does not possess his equal ... He changes the bowling with promptitude and excellent judgement and varies his field with a quick appreciation of the peculiarities of different batsmen. He realizes that his business is to get the other side out as soon as possible and not to prolong innings by a series of useless maiden overs which, while they gratify the bowler's vanity, weary the field and the spectators. As batsman he hits with great power when well set but is somewhat uncertain and does not keep the ball particularly down. He is a marvellous catch.

With this approach and his oft-expressed statement that 'matches are won by run-getting', Gregory was largely responsible for a new conception of big cricket which won Australia international fame.

Being deprived of all-rounder Midwinter's help complicated his task yet weight of worries never bowed the skipper's broad shoulders. In days when Australia sends 17 players to England it seems almost incredible that 11 men, strangers to English wickets and weather, should have got through 37 matches, finished 25 and won eighteen. The only way Gregory could rest injured, sick or over-tired players was by enlisting outside help to complete the XI in some minor games against odds. Their play pleased Englishmen in every way though there was criticism that they failed to accept adverse decisions with good grace.

Although worn thin at times, Gregory's urbanity mostly stood up to the stresses. Its limit was passed in one of the homewarding team's six games in America. Rejection of three appeals caused the players to believe that one umpire was favouring Philadelphian batsmen, so Gregory withdrew his team to the pavilion. In a heated discussion he refused to play on unless another umpire was substituted. The Australians had already received a cheque for their guaranteed expenses. News of a message to the bank stopping the cheque caused some of the players to waver but Gregory tried to induce them to stick to the principle that they could not continue with an umpire they believed guilty of bias. When the Philadelphian manager told them that to abandon the game would be unfair to 10,000 people who had paid to see the match and thousands more crowding in the gates a majority of the Australians voted to resume. While they were fielding in another game thieves stole many of their belongings. The world tour yielded them £750 each — more than enough to have bought half a dozen choice home sites on Bellevue Hill, Sydney's most exclusive suburb.

The team's triumphal return fanned the sparks ignited by the first win in 1877. Cricket held pride of place among the main colonies' games and cricketers cornered most schoolboy admiration. Within two years a South Australian XI (colloquially Croweaters) tackled Victoria. Near the Swan River at Perth, West Australians (Sandgropers) were sinking a well to water their sandy ground. Within five years Queenslanders (Bananalanders) played their first match against an English team in 1883.

Dislike for Victorian umpires standing in Sydney erupted into the barrackers' riot in 1879, history's blackest mark against an Australian cricket crowd. When NSW's first-innings hero, Murdoch (82 not out, out of 177), was adjudged run out for 10 in the colony's follow-on on the Saturday, smouldering antagonism flared against umpire George Coulthard, whom the Englishmen had engaged in Melbourne to accompany them. Barrackers shouted: 'Go back, Murdoch!' and 'Get another umpire!' Instead of another batsman coming in Gregory appeared at the gate.

Dapper Lord Harris walked to the gate where Gregory told him that in the name of the NSW XI he objected to Coulthard. Asked on what grounds, Gregory said general incompetence (Coulthard had been

accused of two mistakes in the English XI's innings). Lord Harris said
that the home captain afterwards admitted that the objection was
raised because of the decision in Murdoch's case. As a mob was
surrounding the fieldsmen by the wicket Lord Harris returned to
midfield. In defending Coulthard he was struck by a larrikin with a
stick. A. N. Hornby was taking the assailant to the pavilion to be
locked up when he was punched by a would-be rescuer.

Hornby's shirt was almost torn off, though he was flanked by a
volunteer bodyguard from the pavilion. This diversion allowed the
umpire to walk off unharmed.

The climate was as warm as Captain Cook had originally reported,
but nobody could say the natives were friendly — especially when
they thought Emmett had called them 'sons of convicts'. Twice the
field was cleared and the English fieldsmen returned, but the sight of
Coulthard approaching the wicket again brought fresh outbursts by
barrackers demanding his replacement. Lest NSW claim the match on
forfeit, Lord Harris held fast in midfield until 6 p.m. As NSW would
have forfeited if batsmen had not gone in on Monday, Gregory
resumed play. They lost on a sticky strip.

Nearing 34 years, Gregory was then in the last stage of his third
consecutive season in 15 months, involving about seventy matches in
Australia, NZ, England, Canada, USA and Australia again. After a
winter's rest he won the Albert's club batting and bowling averages.
He was almost 36 when he tied for the fielding prize and he continued
to play inter-colonial cricket until he was thirty-seven. For five years
he was honorary secretary of the NSW Cricket Association and
courageous enough to be sole selector. This coincided with his
promotion as Inspector of Accounts at thirty-eight.

His wife, Mary Ann Hitchings, mother of 13, died in 1890. He was 47
when he married Lilies Leslie MacMillian in 1892. A farmer's
daughter, she bore him three children and saw him become Paymaster
of the Treasury in 1897. After her death in 1911 when he was 67 and a
widower of 18 months, he married Ellen Hillier, widow of another
cricketer.

Though he could be as firm on the field as in the Audit Office, his
daughter told me he was a kindly father. Pearl was a curly-haired
brunette nurse when she married a pharmacist Francis Else-Mitchell.
She said:

> My mother, father's first wife, was a daughter of a Singleton
> landholder who ran Sydney's horse-drawn buses in the days before
> electricity. We lived in Paddington, not far from Sydney Cricket

Ground where my Uncle Ned was curator. After mother died we moved across the harbour to Neutral Bay about 1892 and further north to Turramurra about 1895. Though hardly a churchgoer himself, he believed religion was good for his children. Like all the Gregorys he insisted on scrupulous honesty. As a schoolgirl I found a shilling on a North Shore train, enough in those days to pay the return fare from Turramurra to Sydney. I told my father who said, 'Go straight back to the railway and hand it to the stationmaster.'

Next to the cricket, she said, he was fondest of fishing, a tireless walker, liked playing the flute, bred setters and had a fine garden. He and fellow players would often land home with loads of fish. He built his own boats, seaworthy enough to go outside the Heads. He built a small boat for her two children. One of her sons, Jim, was a Sydney University baseball blue and Gordon club cricketer who handled harrowing news in the *Sydney Morning Herald*'s London bureau in World War II. He died at 33, grief-stricken at the slaughter of many of his friends, including Squadron-Leader Keith Truscott DFC — the dashing Melbourne football centre 'Bluey' Truscott. Her other son is a distinguished member of the judiciary, Mr Justice Rae Else-Mitchell, president of the NSW Library Council and of the Royal Australian Historical Society.

When the States formed the Australian Commonwealth, Gregory was offered the post of head of the Federal Treasury, together with a knighthood. He declined. Acceptance would have meant going to live in Melbourne and he could not bear to leave Turramurra — not even for Toorak. When he retired at 60, Premier Sir Joseph Carruthers complimented him on having served ten governors with distinction and having enjoyed the goodwill of every State minister and officer with whom he had worked.

By then Gregory had trimmed his beard until it looked less like Ned Kelly's and more like King Edward VII's. His hair receded but sight and teeth were so good that he went through life without needing spectacles or dentures. It was an uphill walk to his home that brought on a fatal heart attack. He died at 74 on 4 August 1919, a few months before the end of World War I, in which ten of his family served.

2 Wrestler's Grip

Uncanny powers of observation enabled Sherlock Holmes to deduce a man's occupation from his appearance — and give the reasons why. I wonder what Conan Doyle's omniscient detective would have made of the head of Joseph Darling? Photographs of Darling as captain of Australia on three of his four visits to England show a striking likeness to boxer Paddy Slavin. Unretreating dark hair, similar moustaches that never grew limp, blue eyes that did not know how to waver. The jawline denoted the kind of determination needed to withstand the menaces of heavy punching or dangerous bowling. Boxing authority Ray Mitchell tells me that in 1892 — two years before Darling's first Test match — Slavin stood up to West Indian heavyweight Peter Jackson at the National Sporting Club through torrid rounds that were talked about for years. In the Australian dressing-room Joe was inescapably nicknamed Paddy.

No glance to right or left detracted from the resolution of his tread to the wicket. He held his bat full-face to the bowler. Joe could defend as dourly as a later left-hander of Scottish descent, Ken Mackay. When in revolt against his inherited trait, he could drive further than a bigger man, Alan Davidson. Fellow players thought he tended to stonewall unnecessarily and was at his best playing a hard-driving game. Giffen described how Joe jumped in to make well-up balls half-volleys; he knew no Australian whose cuts travelled past point at greater speed.

On one tour of Britain, Rhodes was worrying Darling with a ball the Yorkshire left-hander swung with his arm. Instead of natural spin turning it in to left-handed batsmen, this ball drifted out. When Darling mentioned his difficulty Victor Trumper promised, 'I'll find his arm-ball for you, Paddy.' Before long Trumper described how Rhodes held this ball for delivery. Darling: 'I'll hit him out of the ground next time.' He on-drove it so far out of Old Trafford across Warwick Road that a porter fielded the ball at the railway station.

Fearing a collapse on a fiery Lord's wicket, Darling batted as if the ball was stitched with cordite. His mulish obstinacy almost sent the crowd up the wall of the clocktower. Knowing he could do better, they joined in with a man whistling the Dixie lament 'Poor Old Joe'. Next the head whistler led them into 'We Won't Get Home Till Morning'. Then they changed key and tempo to the 'Dead March in Saul'. The shrill sarcasm upset him — one of the rare occasions when his even temperament was disturbed.

His men were content to follow his directions unquestioningly, believing that his deep understanding of the game and his thorough knowledge of its laws made him as near as could be to having all the answers without creaking of brain cells. No chatterbox, he discussed tactics only with those he thought knew as much about the game as he did. Confidence in him was reinforced by his showing no sign of worry in a crisis: his reaction was to get busy combating it.

Evidence suggests that of all Australian skippers he came closest to being a disciplinarian. Yet the players, choosing their own captain, never looked past him. They were aware of his plain man's aversion to any foppish or showy player. Of staunch Presbyterian parentage, he shunned strong drink as well as tobacco and found over-indulgence in liquor hard to tolerate.

Sixth son of a wheat exporter known as the Grain King, Joe was as Australian as pure Scottish parents could make him. In Parliament his father, John Darling, put through an Act permitting fencing-in of Adelaide Oval in the well-ordered city's northern parklands. Cricket had no place in his plans for Joseph. Prince Alfred College, however, has a way of producing cricketers, as witness the three Chappell brothers generations later. Joe Darling at 15 made 252 against St Peter's College, batting on although both hands were tender with blood-blisters from friction with the bat's cord-bound handle. In the South Australian XI at the age of 16 he shaped well against the 1886 Australian XI's bowlers. As Joe also played Australian Rules football in his teens for an Adelaide premiership side and for Norwood, sport was occupying so much time that his schoolwork suffered.

So John Darling, chieftain of the Caledonian Society, sent his 17-

year-old son to work on wheat farms and learn agricultural management from the hard red ground up. Burying him in the backblocks, Giffen called it. South Australia chose Joe at 19 but his father would not give him leave from the wheatbelt. In days when reapers-and-binders would have been as incredible as flying saucers, hard labour from dawn to dusk built up a farmhand's muscles on Joe's frame, already stocky and athletic. For five years he stuck it, playing Saturday afternoons on rural matting wickets. Within months of marrying a Mundoora farmer's fair daughter, Alice Minna Francis, at 22 he could no longer resist the call of cricket on Adelaide's turf, so returned to open a sports shop in Rundle Street.

Compact as John Edrich, Joe stood 172 cm (5ft 8in.), weighed almost 82 kg (12st. 12lb.) and could handle a bag of cement, a sack of wheat or the most difficult bowling around. Ernie Jones, an ex-miner from Broken Hill, had a high-spirited habit of coming from a shower to wrestle other players naked. Like the champion of a college dormitory, Jonah downed everyone until the day he seized Joe. Locked together, they stumbled around the room until the ex-farmer dumped the ex-miner on his bare buttocks. That was symbolic of the way Darling would never be imposed on.

The first time he faced English bowling he scored 117 and 37 not out for South Australia against Stoddart's team in 1894, but fast bowler Tom Richardson spoilt his Test debut by bowling him for 0. For two days that 0 affronted Joe's eye every time he looked at the Sydney scoreboard while his team scored 586. In the fifth Test at Melbourne his 74 and 50 won him a bat for most runs for Australia, a beaten side. If the cricket world was waiting for a left-hander who could control the desire to swing the ball to leg, Joe Darling was that man. His play on his first tour of England at 25 caused *Wisden* to comment: 'With his upright style and a good straight bat he plays as orthodox a game as a right-handed man.' In fact, Joe was right-handed in everything except batting stance. His 1555 in 32 matches on the 1896 tour set a record for a newcomer to English wickets. They were a reward for farseeing originality in his preparation. For weeks before each of Joe's visits to England the Adelaide Oval groundsman watered a wicket in the nets for him to have long practices as the turf dried through stages of stickiness. As a result, while Clem Hill was honoured as Australia's foremost left-hander on true turf, fellow-players rated Darling best on all wickets because of his resource on sticky tracks. He had the confidence and skill to pick balls he could hit with a kick like one of the horses he left on the farm. The only other batsman I have known to go in for practice on sticky wickets was another of Scottish descent, Archie Jackson. Bowling to him at Birchgrove Oval, Balmain, left-hander Bill Hunt would say, 'Better give it away, Archie, you're getting too knocked about.' Jackson: 'No, Bill, I'll tell you when I've had enough.'

As Joe approached 100 in an Adelaide Test, a leg-hit off Johnny Briggs sailed over the eastern gate into the park. This is the only time a man has raised 100 in Anglo-Australian Tests with a hit right out of the ground. The ball crashed along an ice-cream stall, smashing most of the glasses. At 27 years Darling was the only one before 1900 who topped 500 runs in a series and made three centuries in a rubber. The runaway farmer's batting in the final Sydney Test lifted Australia from a losing position by stopping Richardson bowling so fast and so well. The left-hander's drives had the force to loosen up tight bowling like a heavyweight's right cross loosens teeth. He caused MacLaren to place three outfielders for the fast bowler, yet several shots over mid-off and cover sent the ball scraping up an asphalt cycle-track around the boundary. Darling's 100 is still Australia's fastest Test century against England's bowling — 91 minutes, closely pressed by Trumper's 94 minutes at Sydney in 1903 and Bradman's 99 minutes at Leeds in 1930. When Darling, fourth out, was caught in the longfield off Richardson his 160 contained 30 boundary hits.

As the 1899 team sailed to Britain the players elected Darling captain at twenty-eight. He was capable of flexibility rare in a man of such definite opinions. After Victor Trumper had missed selection Darling saw him make 76 for The Rest against Australia's chosen bowlers in Adelaide. Realizing it would be a mistake to go without a 21-year-old batsman of such potential, Joe called a team meeting. They added Trumper to the side as fourteenth man on half-share (£200). In the twelfth match on tour, Victor's 135 not out in the Lord's Test bore such a stamp of quality that another meeting promptly voted him to a full share of tour profits.

On a morning so wet that play was reported improbable before lunch, half the team went to see through Player's Nottingham tobacco factory. Soon after each had accepted six cigars word came that the match had begun. Hurrying back, they saw Darling, who had lost the toss, fielding with five Australians and five substitutes. The penitent truants were hooted as they ran on the field. A team meeting called by Darling that night fined the culprits £5 each for breach of a tour rule requiring them to be at grounds ready to play at appointed times.

After the eleven and emergency fieldsman were named for each match on tour, the two spare men were freed for three days' sightseeing. Because one player had a fast bowler's thirst — deeper than abstainer Darling thought good for him — the skipper feared he might impair his fitness for a coming Test. To shield him from liquor's lure, captain and vice-captain switched him from the freed list to twelfth man. While the Australians fielded, the bowler left the ground. Asked why, he said he was going to have his three days off whether they liked it or not. After dinner the manager called a team meeting, as the captain was reporting a player for insubordination. Given a chance to explain, the rebel said they could all go to hell. Two players then proposed and seconded that he be sent back to Australia by the next ship. Before a vote, Darling took the man aside, advising him to apologize to the team; once the motion was carried he would see it was carried out. The mutineer apologized and never transgressed again.

Visitors usually regard the general standard of umpiring in first-class matches in England as the best. Yet Darling and his players thought two run-out decisions at Trent Bridge showed that a retired international was emotionally influenced by desire to see his old side win. As Tyldesley was throwing Hill out, they were disturbed to see umpire Barlow jumping with both arms uplifted jubilantly before fieldsmen appealed. On the last afternoon Laver's underhand flick from short leg to wicketkeeper Kelly so clearly ran Ranji out for 30 that the Indian prince jogged on toward the pavilion until Barlow called after him, 'You're not out!' Ranji returned to make 93 not out, enabling England, seven for 155, to escape with a draw. After the Australians reported the incidents to the MCC, Lord Harris told Darling: 'It is evident that this man is unsuitable. He will not umpire any more of your matches.'

When Tom Hayward suffered sunstroke in freakish heat at Old Trafford in 1899 he was replaced in the field by Johnny Tyldesley instead of the listed twelfth man Wilfred Rhodes, who lacked the dash of the Lancashire outfielder. After one over Darling walked on to tell MacLaren he thought the departure from the list was wrong. Agreeing, MacLaren called Rhodes on. The sight of a local hero being sent off caused an angry demonstration. The crowd repeated it when Darling came in to defend for two hours to deny England time to knock off winning runs. When Joe was caught in the outfield by Rhodes the multitude joyfully hailed this as justice coming into its own. At last the Australians were 150 ahead with little more than two hours left. Longing for an exciting finish that would give England a chance, Lancashire secretary A. N. Hornby jokingly offered £250 if Australia would declare the innings closed. Darling said: 'Make it £500 and we'll consider it.' When he did declare with seven out — first visitor to close a Test innings in England — the Englishmen had no hope of making 171 in 65 minutes.

No Australian captain since has allowed himself so little rest as Darling, though for stamina there has been nothing to equal Vinoo Mankad's 1120 runs, 1160 overs and 129 wickets for the Nawab of Pataudi's Indians in 1946. Darling's 1941 runs in 35 games at an average of 41 set a record for an Australian touring England.

The erstwhile wheatgrower's deeds as batsman and captain reconciled John Darling to his son's preference for a cricket career, but the wealthy farmer thought it infra dig for a Darling to run a sports shop. Buying a 4000 hectare (10,000 acre) sheep station, sight unseen, in Tasmania's midlands, he told Joseph to take up the property — or be left out of his will. Then 29 and a father of four, Joe took his family to live on the lonely station, 34 kilometres by rough track from the nearest doctor at Oatlands. While he was toiling to restore it from a run-down state, news came from South Africa of the relief of Mafeking. The Boer War's demands on shipping prevented Englishmen from touring Australia in 1900. The year 1901 opened with a 101-gun salutation to the new Commonwealth of Australia. Cricketers who had brought their country so much to Britons' notice at last had a legally constituted Australia to represent. Instead of blue and white their colours became green and gold.

After two years at grass — as much as the rabbit population left — Darling was persuaded by Melbourne Cricket Club to return to the mainland long enough to lead the team in the first three of five Tests. The first match, Joe's first game of the season, was lost by an innings. Unawed by the green caps, captain Archie MacLaren scored the only century of this Sydney Test and made the Australians follow-on.

Darling's sharpest battle of wits with this clever skipper came as 25 wickets tumbled for 221 on the most sensational day a Melbourne crowd had ever watched. Within three hours of MacLaren's sending Australia in on a rain-softened pitch, both sides were out, Australia 51 runs ahead. Realizing that mortal wounds could be suffered in the last two hours on the still-sticky wicket, Darling rejigged his batting order. With a cool-headed tail-ender, Trumble, he held out for an hour and a half and thought his 32 one of his best innings. Yet Barnes and Blyth spun five out in the last 20 minutes. Next day on a good wicket held-back batting stars, notably Hill 99, Duff 104, and Armstrong 45 not out, piled up a lead that left England no chance. In winning a Test by 229 after having been sent in, Darling refused to bow to what looked like Fate and responded to quick-changing situations so resourcefully that the captaincy was his for as long as he cared to hold it.

Fate sided with Darling in Adelaide. Strained by 64 overs in the second innings in Melbourne, Barnes' knee gave way in the first hour.

The world's outstanding bowler played no more in the series. Darling and Hill led Australia's six-hour struggle to 315 — the first 300 in the fourth innings by any team to win a Test.

All Darling's stimulating qualities were needed when his well-balanced second team in England ran into a bitterly cold and wet season in 1902. At practice before the first match, a drive by Hill broke off-spin bowler Trumble's right thumb. Five of the 14 went down with flu. More than once some left beds to play. Soaked wickets and grounds caused the omission of Jones from three Tests. As Darling, reading out the names, came near to the end, the fast bowler would call 'Jonah twelfth . . . Haven't you got anybody else for twelfth man?'

Inspired batting by Trumper helped put the side in winning vein. First man to make 100 before lunch in a Test, Victor began the Old Trafford match with an opening stand of 135 in 80 minutes with Reg Duff, on a damp day in which 15 wickets fell. At lunch on the last day England needed only 87 more runs with all wickets standing. MacLaren looked in the Australians' door and said, 'I think we've got you this time, Joe!' Darling: 'We've only got to shift a few of you and the rest will shiver with fright.'

In the closest finish of his Tests abroad, eight more runs were needed when the last Englishman came in, Fred Tate, father of fast-medium bowler Maurice Tate. Asking Trumble to prevent Rhodes scoring off the last three balls of the over, Darling called the fieldsmen in close. That saved any single, so the last man had to face left-hander Jack Saunders. Tate snicked a four but the fourth ball knocked his off stump out, giving Australia victory by three runs. Packing up in the dressing room, wicketkeeper Jim Kelly was walking about hunting for his gloves, accusing mates of hiding them. They were still on his hands. Although not conscious of excitement in the crisis, Darling said he was awakened in the night by a dream of Tate's stump being uprooted.

By scoring 2570 runs, studded with 11 centuries (highest 128), Trumper enriched the game with records that it took a Bradman to challenge or surpass 28 years later. In two ways the oldtime genius's 1902 enchantments and achievements may never be excelled: so many runs and centuries in adverse conditions that doomed most of England's most skilful batsmen to a poor season. Companions knew Victor had one superstition. As he was unbuckling his pads one day he said: 'I knew I wouldn't make runs today with all those parsons around.' Had MacLaren only known this, even such an admirable sportsman might have been tempted to station a cluster of curates by the pavilion gate.

In England's last innings on an Oval wicket responding to spin, a stumping chance failed to deter Gilbert Jessop from springing along the track to pound Saunders and Trumble in the most challenging Test innings ever played on turf, 104 in 75 minutes. I have come across only one instance of Darling's players having felt their Napoleon was persisting with a Moscow-like mistake. He kept Trumble on from the pavilion end, where the Oval outfield is shorter, and Jessop was hitting the off-spinner into the pavilion area. They believed that, had Joe switched Hugh to the city end and Jessop continued to make similar lusty drives, hits that scattered members in the reserve would have come down inside the longer boundary.

That defeat by one wicket was the second loss on the tour. They won 23 of 38 matches, ten by innings margins. *Wisden*'s summing-up: 'In the all-important matter of physical well-being they undoubtedly owed much to the precept and example of their captain . . . He has the rare power of being able to keep a whole team up to something approaching his own standard.'

From the time his players thawed out, Darling believed his team the strongest ever to leave Australia — an honour held until then by Murdochs' 1882 band. The 1902 team was widely recognized as such not only on its own batting, bowling and fielding merits but because it met England at top strength. That could not be said of the opposition crushed by the two most powerful sides since World War I, Armstrong's in 1921 and Bradman's invincible 1948 team. An all-rounder of 23 in 1902, and captain at 41 in 1921, Armstrong told a questioner, 'The 1902 side could play 22 of my chaps and give them a beating.' Under Darling's captaincy Australia won series in two consecutive tours of England, a feat denied Bradman's sides and equalled only by Woodfull's teams in 1930 and 1934.

After two years improving his sheep station without handling a bat, Darling reappeared for South Australia. Alice, by then a mother of six, saw him go to captain Australia in England for the third time, a family man out to give the English the father of a hiding. Disliking the bowler hats that sheltered most Londoners' scalps, the 1905 players wore straw boaters with green-and-gold bands bearing the Australian coat-of-arms.

At 34, Darling was the 1905 side's surest batsman in the Tests, but his tactics suffered because most of his bowlers were not sharing wine's secret of getting better with age. Unfinished games, 19, exceeded wins, sixteen. To deny England quick runs in three Tests, Darling had Armstrong bowling leg-breaks and top-spinners down the leg-side, with up to seven leg-fielders. The Notts crowd hooted and jeered every ball. Armstrong's hours of leg-theory in a drawn

Leeds Test, *Wisden* said, were a confession of weakness, trusting that
sheer impatience would cause batsmen to lose wickets.

These back-slidings from the direct principles espoused by Dave
Gregory were the worst debits in Darling's captaincy account. He
defended them by saying the hooting and jeering surprised him, as
Armstrong copied the leg-theory from Somerset leg-spinner Len
Braund, who had bowled it without English crowds' disapproval.

In 27 years since the first Australian visit the game had become
more sophisticated. Up to this time five in every six Tests had been
finished but the ratio of games left undecided was growing. For the
first time in England players were leaving the field for a tea interval, as
in hotter countries, instead of having tea brought to them on the
ground.

One down, Darling pressed for a win in the fourth Test at all costs.
Apart from four sixes he hit in his 73, Australia's all-or-nothing policy
scarcely got off the ground and England won by an innings.

Having lost all six tosses to Jackson (five Tests and a Marylebone
Cricket Club game), Darling was stripped to the waist at the
Scarborough Festival when his team suggested a wrestle for choice of
innings. Stanley Jackson, less muscular, with the political finesse of a
future knighted Governor of Bengal, hinted that he would depute
George Hirst to act as captain for the purpose. Assessing the
Yorkshire all-rounder's bulk with his eye, Joe concluded that
Australia's chance of batting first would be as good with a coin as a
cross-buttock. Rightly confident that Joe's call would again be wrong,
Jackson did not bother to look at the coin. As both captains were born
on the same day, 21 November 1870, this must be one of the worst
setbacks astrology has suffered.

More than half the 1657 runs the ex-farmer harvested in 34 Tests
against England and South Africa were made opening the innings. As
skipper he mainly batted fourth, fifth or sixth after installing
Trumper and Duff as Australia's first pair. He held 27 catches,
dropped few. Playing 333 innings in 202 first-class games he totalled
10,637 runs at an average of thirty-four. He made 21 centuries. Joe's
highest innings was 210 in 270 minutes as South Australian captain
against Queensland at Brisbane. Though he lost two-thirds of his
tosses, his teams won seven Tests, lost four, drew ten. Of his 18 Tests
as captain against the Englishmen, 15 were in England, the most by
any visiting skipper.

As a father of 15, of whom 12 survived him, Darling ranks second in
virility to Dave Gregory, sire of sixteen. Several of Joe's eight sons
were cricketers in Tasmania where the fourth, Douglas, captained

club and district teams. Joe Darling entered Tasmania's Parliament at 50 when voters of Cambridge County elected him to the Legislative Council as an Independent.

In hospital for the first time in his 75 years, the old warrior, before being wheeled to the theatre, said he hoped Bradman would make a comeback. After surgery for a ruptured gall bladder, he died on 2 January 1946, a day after Bradman's first postwar century (112 for South Australia against the Services XI). As he had given his properties to his sons years before, the probate value of his will, £7000, was a modest residue alongside the £1,700,000 left by his eldest brother John, managing director of Broken Hill Proprietary from 1907 to 1914.

3 The Arthur and Clarrie Show

Arthur Mailey and Clarrie Grimmett were as different as it was possible for two short men to be. Both earned their living by deftness of the right hand — wisecracking Mailey as a cartoonist and journalist, and earnest Grimmett as a signwriter.

Caricaturist Mailey's brown eye took in more than the length of a nose or the set of a chin. A student of character, he sized up opponents off the field before he ever saw them bat in hand. If he judged them to be highly strung or easy-going, vain or modest, he adapted his bowling tactics accordingly. Mailey began his run with a shuffle, then jogged up with five easy steps, weaving from side to side and carrying the ball in his left hand, as if to keep the batsmen guessing what he was up to. At the last moment he took the ball in his right hand and flung his right arm back until it was hidden behind him, while he peeped over his left shoulder at the batsman. His arm came directly over the top, in classic style, and as his fingers ripped across the ball it was difficult to tell from his hand and wrist action whether a leg-break or a wrong'un was coming.

Grimmett stole up with a straight, quick, skippety run of half-a-dozen paces. Whereas Mailey was at full height in delivery, Grimmett bowled with his shoulders hunched. His arm whipped around like a boxer's right swing. He is the nearest to a round-arm bowler seen in big cricket since they ceased pressing trousers out sideways. Because his arm was one-third of the way down towards horizontal he had to drop his wrist to tilt his hand to the angle needed for his wrong 'un, which (like O'Reilly's) turned farther than his leg-break.

That tell-tale roll of the wrist warned observant batsmen which turn to expect. They were thankful for the small mercy. In a less subtle bowler it would have been a great drawback, but Grimmett was too crafty to peg away with clear-cut leg-breaks and boseys. By varying the amount of wrist roll he sent along many in-between balls. Mostly they were overspinners which went straight on, but often there was a doubt in a batsman's mind because he could not be sure the ball would not turn a little one way or the other. In delivering his flipper, which darted from the pitch, he could not silence a snap of the fingers. So that batsmen could not play this one by ear he drilled the fingers of his left hand to snap out a similar sound as his right spun other kinds of balls.

Mailey bowled like a millionaire, Grimmett like a miser. Arthur went all out for curved trickery of flight and biting turn. To produce those effects in Australian conditions he had to put so much snap into his finger action that accuracy was left to take its chance. The legend grew that his full tosses were intentional. Mailey alone knew and, rightly, he wouldn't tell. If practice makes perfect, they were the most finished full-floppers ever bowled.

Twice in Test Matches (at Melbourne, 1925, and the Oval, 1926) Mailey skittled the sagacious Hobbs with full tosses. The fatal ball at Melbourne was the second consecutive full pitch; Hobbs played hardly any kind of stroke at it, as if he were spellbound, and it landed between his feet and the stumps. The explanation of such staggering occurrences was that Mailey could bowl a ball which, when a few yards from the batsman, would dip in from the off as sharply as if it had glanced off some invisible object in the air.

Another time, his twirling fingers dragged the ball down so short that after three or four diminishing bounces it ran along the ground towards Leslie Keating (Victoria). Resorting to boyhood's method of dealing with a creeping grubber, Keating squatted on his haunches and swept his bat along the ground. At the last moment the ball fraudulently hopped over the horizontal bat and bowled him. As the out-generalled batsman departed, Mailey proudly demonstrated to nearby fieldsmen how he placed his fingers on the ball when he wished to deliver such a nonplusser.

Not one of the 73,000 balls bowled by Grimmett in first-class cricket was a double hopper, or anything like it. He put the third dimension of length into googly bowling and never sacrificed control in attempts to get greater spin. He liked least bowling to nimble batsmen who advanced surely to drive the ball before it could turn. To them he pushed most of his deliveries along at a lower trajectory, but he ballooned them high and often enough to embarrass slow-footed players who weren't confident about venturing from the crease. When batsmen dealt it out to Mailey, he continued to float the ball well up, as if to encourage them to gorge themselves and burst. When Victoria made the world record score against New South Wales in 1926, Mailey paid out 362 runs for his four wickets, off 512 balls — heaviest outlay on record in one innings.

Grimmett simply couldn't afford to have such experiences. When quick-footed batsmen attacked him his first aim was to cramp their style, by pushing the ball through at accurate length, and await his chance for revenge. Sometimes he cunningly varied that method if he were hit for four. Pretending that he was losing control under punishment, he would waft the ball along at tempting height. But batsmen who leapt forward devouringly found that the ball would drop short enough and wide enough to be hard to reach; it put them in peril of being stumped or of lofting a catch. Apart from that, Grimmett's basic strategy when he was fighting rearguard actions on Australian pitches was to harp away on a restraining length, constantly varying his flight and pace until he snared the batsmen into playing back his favourite flipper, which skidded through to rap their padded shins in front of the stumps. One-fifth of Grimmett's victims in Tests against England were out leg before wicket, and on Australian turf the proportion rose to more than one-third.

Opinion is divided whether Grimmett, an unparalleled Test wicket-taker of his time, was a greater bowler than Mailey. This is like asking whether a mapping pen is better than a charcoal crayon. To decide, I believe you have first to define what you want in a googly bowler. Slower through the air, Mailey gave batsmen more time to move out to him but the risk of misjudging the ball was higher. In all Tests he got one-sixth of his victims stumped, Grimmett one in eight. On an average in first-class matches Mailey took a wicket for every 46 balls, compared with Grimmett's one in 52 balls.

In Australia I believe Mailey was more dangerous, because his flight was more deceptive in the light atmosphere and he screwed a snappier break from the granite-like turf. Grimmett got more turn on the Adelaide pitch than other Australian grounds. Too wise to wear his fingers to the bone for little gain, he often bowled more straight ones than anything else on the first two days, and relied on wily changes of pace and flight. Mailey's two Test records were put up in his own country — nine wickets in England's second innings at Melbourne, 1921, and 36 wickets in the rubber.

In England Grimmett was the better. In the denser atmosphere he could make the ball dip and duck, and he turned it enough on the less-laundered wickets to bowl some of the greatest batsmen behind their backs, by breaking the ball around their legs. On dead pitches which robbed the keenest breaks of sting and made other slow right-handers ineffective Grimmett's control enabled him to bowl away steadily and wheedle the batsmen out.

Summed up, if you wanted your googly bowler to be a shock-trooper, to be thrown in to capture wickets quickly without much heed to cost, you would vote for Mailey. He was more likely to come to light now and again with an unplayable ball (if there is such a thing) and leave a great and well-set batsman gaping. At 44, six years after he retired from Tests, the pranks he could make the ball perform astonished even such a deep student of bowling as Verity.

If you wanted your slow-googly bowler to undertake a big share of the attack in all weathers and on all wickets your vote would go to Grimmett. Like the quicker O'Reilly he was a dual-purpose bowler: if conditions made the dismissal of the opposition a long task he could peg away with economical perseverance, keeping the batsmen playing hard in the protracted intervals between the fall of wickets.

4 *The Gentleman In Gloves*

A fusion of skill and style distinguished the wicketkeeping of William Albert Stanley Oldfield, who died at 81 in Sydney on 10 August 1977, with some of his feats still unequalled. Matching his bland sportsmanship, a constant quest for perfection rewarded Bertie with the distinction of being the first 'keeper to reach 50 Tests and to play in 54 without missing one through a hand injury.

Oldfield is the only wicketkeeper who dismissed 90 Englishmen in Tests (38) and had 15 wickets in a series in England before Tests were lengthened to five days. He was first to bring off 38 wickets for one bowler, Grimmett, who said he could never have achieved his degree of success without Bertie.

When a German shellburst near Ypres in 1917 buried a squad of stretcher-bearers, Oldfield was dug out unconscious, the only survivor. Well-muscled for a man barely 165 cm (5ft 6in.), he was nicknamed 'Hercy' short for 'pocket Hercules', in the Australian Imperial Forces tour in 1919.

Amid tensions of Test cricket his politeness was reflected in a chapter being headed The Gentleman in Gloves. Batsmen knew better than to assume from his courteous greeting that he would be lenient with a snick or stumble. They had not invented 'walking' before World War II, yet his 130 wickets were obtained with fewer appeals than crowds expect. Sir Jack Hobbs believed Oldfield never appealed unless he believed the umpire would uphold it. Umpire Frank

Chester recalled having been ready to signal Hobbs out leg-before in an Oval Test, but neither leg-spinner Mailey nor Oldfield appealed.

Bertie asked NSW slipfielders hearing a noise as ball passed bat not to appeal until he held the catch aloft.

Hobbs was victim of his widest catch, running to leg slip at Sydney for a glance off Gregory's fast inswinger, and of his most spectacular leg-side stumping, off Ryder, medium-pace, at Melbourne. Yet captain W. M. Woodfull thought his finest wicketkeeping was on the 1926, 1930 and 1934 tours of England, when he was in his thirties.

Kneading emulsion into his gloves and safeguarding his joints with fingerstalls, tape and two sets of inner gloves took Oldfield an hour before each day's play. The courtier of 'keepers based his balance and footwork on orthodox heels-down stance and tried to convert Godfrey Evans from his tilted wait on the balls of his feet. He kept his finger-ends low without touching the grass.

Hobbs thought him the neatest of all 'keepers and team-mates O'Reilly and Ponsford ranked him the best they knew. They nicknamed him 'Cracker'. He has since been excelled in glove speed and safety only by Don Tallon, whom Sir Donald Bradman ranks as the finest of all.

Oldfield's peaceful passing snaps the last Australian link with wicketkeeping as it used to be. Nobody else has stumped 52 Test batsmen. Out-cricket is a changed art since 1947's drastic imbalance of new balls began the eclipse of slow spinners in most countries. Whereas Bertie stumped 40 per cent of his victims, Evans stumped fewer than one-quarter of his Test wickets, Grout one-eighth, Knott, one-thirteenth and Marsh one-twentieth.

Of Oldfield's 130 Test wickets against England, South Africa and West Indies all except 39 were taken up at the stumps, a tribute to his reflexes. Five of his stumpings were off medium-pacers Ryder, Kelleway, McCabe and Hurwood. He stood back only to the fastest bowlers. For 17 years he was one of the first names in selectors' lists.

Oldfield's only absence from a Test through injury was for a skull fracture when at the age of 38 he edged an attempted hook at an offside bouncer from Larwood at Adelaide in the Bodyline series.

Grout 187 and Marsh 160 have passed his Test total but he is the only Australian 'keeper who has exceeded 600 wickets.

English crowds saw more of his polished glovework than by any other Australian 'keeper this century — five visits, including the AIF. Before the third, he married at 35. He was in line for a unique record of the only man to play in every Anglo-Australian series between the two World Wars until errors against G. O. Allen's team at 42 cost him a place in Bradman's 1938 tour team. Problems in detecting

Fleetwood-Smith's left-arm googly and top-spinner undermined his confidence. Though he figured in a number of run-outs as batsman as well as 'keeper, Oldfield was the first gloveman to score 1000 in Tests, total 1427 (average 22). Five centuries in first-class games included 132 at Kimberley, 123 against Warwickshire and 129 for NSW against Victoria.

In World War II the Army used his knowledge of sportsgoods as a major in the Amenities Service. He wrote *The Rattle of the Stumps* at 60, coached schoolboys in Ethiopia at 69 and was awarded the MBE at 76. He died the morning of a lunch date with Harold Larwood.

Herbert Sutcliffe, 81, who batted all day for four of his Test centuries against Australia with Oldfield crouching behind him, wrote from a Yorkshire nursing home to the Australian's widow Ruth: 'Like me, he was a Christian. We will meet in the holy of holies where I am sure Bert will captain the team.'

5 Gilt-Edged

Once every long while cricket produces a player possessing the gift of timing to such a degree that all the long-familiar strokes take on new beauty at his touch. Among batsmen between the wars the one who held this secret in his keeping was Alan Kippax. Perhaps he was helped to find it when, as a fair-haired youth in his mid-teens, he watched Victor Trumper intently, as if trying to get a mental newsreel of his style. Of all the youngsters who admired Trumper, Alan was the one with the natural poise, the grace of movement and the cricketing instincts to reflect much of The Master's batsmanship in his own play.

About the same height, Kippax modelled his stance at the wicket on Trumper's, an ideal pattern for young players. Cover the heads on photographs of each awaiting the bowler and there are few clues to tell one from the other. The similarity extends even to the shirtsleeve folded halfway up the forearm, instead of to the elbow. The feet are some 30 cm apart, weight evenly balanced on both, the left leg hiding the right shin from the bowler's view. The body is inclined no more than necessary for comfortable grip of the bat with the hands together, high on the handle, between the pad-tops. The left shoulder bears outward, just enough to enable the eyes to watch the bowler without nasal obstruction and not enough to reduce the left side's leverage in the stroke.

When Kippax entered first-class cricket in 1918 he was hailed as another Trumper, but he was not that. Though the influence of

Trumper was visible in his polished stroke-play, Kippax composed a batting design of his own, finely shaded, with the colours less vivid here and there. His play sparkled, without reproducing the audacity of the man who did such things as drive the opening ball from a New Zealand fast-medium bowler straight out of the ground. His supple-wristed style was elegant, not so forceful as Bradman's or Macartney's, or so stately as Hammond's.

Kippax's batting had a silky quality not seen in any other player of his time or since. His leg-glancing, forward or back, was so delicate that it had a kind of moonbeam beauty. In square-cutting he stood erect, but when he cut late — the shot which captivated the crowds most — he made a lissom bow over the ball and stroked it away with the bat's face downward, as if to squeeze the ball into the ground.

His advance down the wicket was a glide, with the right foot passing smoothly behind the left. His follow-through with the bat was full and fluent. In driving from the crease, a lift and downthrust of his left foot toward the ball brought his weight effortlessly into the stroke. His favourite drive was between mid-off and cover.

He hooked fast bowling with such unhurried ease that the punishing power of the stroke was revealed only in the way the ball smacked against the fence. Bradman once said that Kippax played the hook better than anyone else he had seen. Sometimes he swayed on to his back foot, found the ball not short enough to hook, and boldly lifted it past the bowler. Once he was too daring with this shot in a Test match and Larwood caught-and-bowled him. Another shot in the Kippax locker — no longer in vogue — was the full-blooded leg hit, played by advancing the left foot and swinging the bat vertically across pitched-up balls just clear of the leg-stump.

Because of maladroit selectorship, this batsman of rare talent was 33 before he represented Australia in England. If that recognition and experience had come to him in his twenties (1921 or 1926) I believe he would have soared to even greater heights. Nothing short of a death-bed confession will clear up the mystery of the failure to send him to England in 1926, the year he turned 29, though two causes which contributed to the blunder are known — interstate rivalry for places in the team, and as strange a piece of witless thinking as anybody ever heard of. The team was chosen in batches (a procedure never repeated). Players from Kippax's State, New South Wales, gained nine of the 16 places, five came from Victoria, two from South Australia. If the selectors' deliberations descended to the level of interstate bargaining, Kippax was not the batsman who should have been squeezed out.

The selection coincided with a curious reaction, chiefly in Victoria, to Kippax's style — a suspicion that his play was too delicately tuned for the hard business of winning matches, that he could not have both speed and safety, grace and guts. Perhaps his mild expression and short-paced walk to the wicket looked irresolute. There were whispers that he was an uncertain starter — Kippax, who in his 22 innings in Sheffield Shield cricket in the four seasons before the selection had been out for under 20 only three times, had outscored every batsman in the land and had easily the highest average of all. The absurdity of such notions was plain when you saw the man bat. His footwork was as foolproof in defence as it was enterprising in attack; his head was always over the ball, which his eyes never left; his bat, straight as a plumb-line, passed close to his pad, leaving no chink in his armour.

M. A. Noble, former Test captain, did not overstate the position when he described the omission of Kippax as 'almost a crime against the cricketing youth of Australia.' There was no consolation for Kippax in the knowledge that he was not the first victim, that Albert Trott, 23 when he was left out of the 1896 team, had gone to Middlesex as a professional and become the greatest all-rounder in England.

I believe the selectors' tardiness in recognizing Kippax's worth caused him to make concessions, to put a rein on his brilliant tendency. If high and fast scoring were not enough to gain him his rightful place, and an appearance of risklessness were necessary, he would provide it. His batting remained as polished as ever but he was more circumspect, especially about going far down the wicket to drive. Now and again he broke the bonds, as when he scored 23 off one over and hit 41 fours in his chanceless 315 not out against Queensland. His 26 innings in first-class matches in the two seasons after his omission yielded nearly 2000 runs, at an average of 85. There was no keeping him on the sidelines after that.

Though Kippax used tall scoring to suit his own purposes, I suspect that, deep down, he had a contempt for averages and record-breaking; he seemed much prouder of having outbatted a string of renowned Test players, when McDonald and Ironmonger caught NSW on a sticky wicket years ago, than of any double centuries. Throughout he remained unselfish, not so occupied with piling up runs for himself that he could not give thought to easing the way for young partners.

In his first season as a regular Test player, against Chapman's English team in 1928-9, his fearless hooking broke the spell which Larwood had cast over Australia's batting. At Melbourne in the third Test, Woodfull and Richardson were out for 15 before Kippax came in, and the third wicket (Hendry 23) fell at 57. Larwood had two of them for six runs. In those days he tested the stuffing of the batsmen by making the ball fly at them, but those who made a fighting response had a sporting chance of hooking without disaster, because the leg field was not packed — a man at mid-on, another near the square-leg umpire, and a third on the fence at fine leg.

Directly after lunch, Kippax hooked Larwood for four fours, three of them in one over. His partner, Ryder, let fly with a similar shot and sliced a six almost behind the wicket, bringing the cost of two overs by Larwood to 23 runs. The pair rallied Australia with a fourth-wicket partnership of 161 before Kippax tried yet another hook off his left ear. The ball shot away to fine leg — one of those boring, low-altitude catches, easy to misjudge — but out on the boundary Jardine's hands closed on it securely. Kippax had scored 100 in 3½ hours. That 100 was worth much more than its face value. Before Kippax began the after-lunch onslaught, Larwood had taken 14 wickets for 256 in 89 overs in Tests that season; from that point on his figures for the remainder of the rubber were 4 for 472, in 170 overs.

Kippax was at the pinnacle of his form that summer. Facing 376 by Victoria in the Christmas match at Melbourne, New South Wales slumped before the bowling of Ironmonger, Hendry, Ebeling and a'Beckett. Soon after Kippax came in, he saw five wickets tumble for four runs, including Bradman and Kelleway. Next day the score was 113 when Kippax (20) was joined by the last man, tall Halford Hooker, later an Australian Broadcasting Commission commentator. The innings had been such a fizzle that the prospect of a last-wicket stand against such able bowlers seemed remote. Though Hooker, as a bowler, could swing the ball about in great style, he had not made a double-figure score for his State.

Yet hour after hour passed as Kippax's lanky partner hung on, showing unsuspected ability to keep a straight bat between the ball and the stumps. With Kippax scoring at the rate of 48 an hour, they batted the day out and carried on into the next. When at last Hooker was caught, their last-wicket partnership had reached 307, the most remarkable of all world batting records. Kippax's share was 240. In all, the NSW captain scored 260 not out (30 fours) by almost 6½ hours of faultless batting.

When he at last got to England in 1930, he was highly successful. Sutcliffe has estimated that it takes an Australian eight weeks to master English conditions. Like Bradman, Kippax was such a fine back player that he had the feel of them in a few days. In his second innings in England, when Essex dismissed the Australians on a lively, two-paced pitch for 157, he topped the score with more than one-third of the runs. In his fourth match, when McDonald's fast bowling burst through the Australians' batting against Lancashire, Kippax hooked the fliers and guided cuts between four slip-fieldsmen. He was going strongly, 40 not out, when the last wicket fell at 115. His first hundred was on a sporty Lord's pitch in an innings in which nobody else passed 35 and Allen's fast bowling took six wickets cheaply.

In his first Test innings in England, Australia collapsed for 144 at Nottingham on a sticky wicket. Amid the ruins Kippax made bad-wicket batting look almost easy, until the downfall of the last man left him high and dry with 64 not out. His skill and determination in getting precious runs when others found the going too difficult prompted his captain, Woodfull, to say: 'When it's tough you can count on Kip.'

In his fighting innings, Kippax's batting remained artistic down to the last stroke. There was no last-ditch look about him. A grim expression would not fit a man of his disposition — serene, amiable, easy-going, a good mixer, fond of music. Though *Who's Who in World Cricket* once listed him as an accomplished soloist, he was a team-man as a public vocalist, as well as in sport, and never missed a beat in that touching bracket of songs, *Rose of Washington Square* and *The Man on the Flying Trapeze*.

Attuned to the pace of English wickets throughout four months of spring and mild summer, the Australians played Sussex in a heat wave at the end of August, 1930, and were caught napping on the fastest wicket of the tour. Seven wickets tumbled for 79, of which Tate took the first six for 18. Kippax, who instantly adjusted his timing to the faster turf, charmed the Brighton crowd with 158 in quick time. In the second innings he ran up 102 not out. Only one other Australian — Bardsley in 1909 — has reached 100 in each innings of a match on his first visit to England.

Kippax's adaptability in all sorts of conditions caused B. J. T. Bosanquet, pioneer Test googly bowler, to call him the greatest living batsman on all wickets. He was the first Australian to score a Test hundred against West Indies' battery of fast bowlers. Encounters with speed bowling provided many of the highlights of his career, but, if anything, he was an even more accomplished player of slows. Grimmett said he would rather bowl to Bradman than to Kippax. One reason for that was that Kippax went forward to meet Grimmett more often, and was harder to trap into playing back to the one that skidded through.

Midway through his 35th year Kippax suffered two fearful blows in the face. In a country match a ball kicked abruptly from a spike which had been left under the matting. It smashed his nose. A month or so later the Aboriginal fast bowler, Gilbert, making the ball fly alarmingly from a green-top wicket at Brisbane, dismissed Wendell Bill and Bradman in his first over. Kippax, who had the answer to such bowling, hooked Gilbert for three or four fours. His hooking was in the classic style, head in line with the ball (like Ranjitsinhji, who had an ear-lobe split when a ball from Jones flicked it).

Another fast bowler, H. M. Thurlow, was on at the other end from Gilbert. Thurlow was speedy enough to gain selection as Australia's fast bowler in the fourth Test against South Africa a few months later, but Gilbert was yards faster at Brisbane that day. The difference in speed was Kippax's downfall. When Thurlow bounced one, the batsman hooked too soon and received the full force of the ball on the right temple. Six stitches were needed to close the gash and Kippax was in hospital three days. The injury kept him out of the game for a while. It left him in no condition to face the Bodyline onslaught. Though he played many beautiful innings after that, and averaged 53 on the 1934 tour of England, he was unable to hook with the same assurance again.

In his 168 first-class games Kippax scored 12,555 runs at an average of 58, with 43 hundreds. In Sheffield Shield cricket he scored 6096 in 61 matches at an average of 70. The figures reveal less of the gilt-edged quality of Alan Kippax's batting than a newspaper's black-and-white reproduction of a great painting does. His batsmanship should have been weighed in carats, not runs.

6 Three Masterpieces

In an era studded with batting triumphs, it was given to one man, Stan McCabe, to play the three greatest innings seen on Test fields in the decade before World War II.

Any one of the three would have been a fitting crown to the finest batsman's career, but it was no accident that all of them were the handicraft of McCabe, not of other master run-makers of the Hobbs-to-Hutton period, such as Bradman, Hammond, Ponsford, Headley, Dempster, Nourse or Merchant.

In fact, none of McCabe's contemporaries attempted such batting — in Test matches, of all places — because nobody else thought it could be done. None had the blend of imagination and skill to feel capable of it; by all the standards of the times none would have dared to hope for enough luck to carry it through. The drama of these exploits by McCabe fascinated the crowds. Their delight at his graceful and venturesome stroke-making was sharpened by the piquant feeling that each moment might be the last, as if they were watching a bolting horse or a runaway train.

First of these breath-catching innings was his lone-hand 187 not out against England in 1932, the boldest innings ever played on the Sydney Cricket Ground, or any other ground. The situation when the 22-year-old McCabe walked in to bat was dispiriting. The Australians had entered the valley of the shadow of Bodyline. Illness had robbed them of their outstanding batsman, Bradman, on the eve of their first encounter with the fast leg-side assault. Only 82 runs were on the board when McCabe, number 5 in the batting order, came in to face Larwood, who was in the middle of a spell in which he took three wickets for seven runs.

McCabe immediately showed his determination not to die a death of shame on a day of dark disgrace, though Jardine, Larwood and Voce were trying to set a noose about his neck. Without a flinch, he stood up to the fearsome bowling; he hooked the short balls as if there were no danger to his ribs or skull, and as if he were unaware of the battalion of catch-awaiting fieldsmen, covered by outer scouts ready for the lofted ball. When the direction of the bowling changed, flowing drives and crisp cuts kept him gliding along. Nobody thought it could last for long, yet when those daring hooks were lifted they continued to fall beyond the fieldsmen's reach. By the day's end he had scored 127 in a little more than three hours, with 17 boundary hits.

Fifty-five minutes on the second day brought the end of Australia's innings. In that time McCabe took command, manoeuvred to keep the strike, and scored 60 while four wickets fell for 10 at the other end. In going for the bowling bald-headed (or almost, for one so young) he was debited with a nominal chance at 170, when he cut Larwood behind point with such stinging power that it would have been captious to blame Voce for not making a catch. At an average rate of 47 an hour, McCabe scored his 187 while his seven partners made fewer than 90. It was like a blood transfusion for a sinking innings. Boundary hits brought him 100 of the runs. Nineteen of the fours were leg strokes, 13 of them hooks which rapped the fence between wide long-on and square leg.

For audacity, skill, effortless power, and courage against the bowling that beset him, no other batsman on the active list could have equalled his performance.

If McCabe's 187 was a transfusion for his side, his 323 in the Nottingham Test, 1938, was a heart-massage innings which revived the patient after hope had been given up. The Englishmen had led off by amassing the overwhelming total of 658 for eight wickets before Hammond declared the innings closed. After Fingleton had gone for 9, Bradman for 51 (after an unsuccessful appeal against the light) and Brown for 48, the Australians' position was desperate.

McCabe, who was vice-captain, had been out of touch for weeks (a few days before the Test he had raised the question whether it would not be better to choose another batsman instead). With about half an hour to go to complete the Saturday's play, he began in the gloaming, yet batted more firmly than his predecessors and scored 19 before stumps were drawn. On Sunday night he had a slight cold but O'Reilly assured him: 'You'll sweat it out by 3 p.m. tomorrow.'

When two more wickets fell in the first quarter-hour on Monday, it seemed as if the innings would peter out before McCabe could work up a single bead of perspiration. Half the side was out, with Australia still more than 500 behind. Farnes was bowling at keen speed, and Wright was making leg-breaks snap from a boot-worn patch. McCabe's way of countering the menace of that patch was to skip forward smartly whenever Wright tried to pitch the ball on it. He played watchfully for more than half an hour until the downfall of Badcock (9) left only the tail-end division of wicketkeeper and three bowlers to come.

That was the signal for McCabe to take the match in his own hands. For the next couple of hours his batting was enchanting. It held every one under its spell, bowlers as well as spectators. From the players' balcony, Bradman called to a few of his team who were inside the pavilion: 'Come and look at this! You've never seen anything like it.' In the Press box, Woodfull was moved to write: 'It is a pity that the whole cricket world could not see this double century scored.'

The 30,000 who were lucky enough to be there watched wonderingly as the vice-captain added 170 while his last four partners scored 38. When he was 123 he gave a sharp chance to square leg, but Edrich did well to get a hand to it and save a four.

The arrival of Fleetwood-Smith as last man was accepted as an infallible sign that the innings was drawing its last breath. Instead, his advent inspired McCabe to unfold the most dazzling half-hour's batting of the match. Hammond spread five fieldsmen around the boundary yet could not prevent fours — McCabe had so many strokes and guided them so surely. The Englishmen fared little better when, near the end of overs, they drew in to encircle him with a net of infielders, trying to block the singles he needed to get the strike at the other end instead of his vulnerable partner. While Fleetwood-Smith rose to the occasion by surviving 18 balls and collecting five runs, Stan scored 72 in the last enthralling 28 minutes — something unheard of in Test cricket, even in the days when Bonnor and Jessop were denting pavilion roofs. McCabe's 232 in 235 minutes (34 fours, one six) is the fastest double century in Test history. His 213 on the second day came up in 200 minutes, his last 127 after lunch in only 80 minutes.

For all the speed of his scoring — he skimmed through his last 100 at the dizzy rate of 109 runs an hour — each stroke was made with the artistry natural to him, each was properly chosen for the ball it had to meet. Despite the urgency of the chase for runs there was not one slogging hit, in fact no show of force, because of the precision of his timing. It was power without violence, dash without slap.

McCabe made his 232 while eight partners were scoring 58 — an achievement without parallel in international cricket. When at last Ames caught him off Sinfield, Australia's arrears had shrunk to 247 and the match had been plucked from England's grasp. He had taken the steam out of the English bowlers and given the Australians fresh heart to face the follow-on justifiably hopeful of keeping England from victory in the 8¾ hours before the time-limit expired.

When McCabe returned to the pavilion, Bradman greeted him with: 'If I could play an innings like that I would be a proud man, Stan.' Surely the highest tribute ever paid a batsman.

Two former English captains, A. E. R. Gilligan and R. E. S. Wyatt, agreed that it was the best Test innings they had seen, and their opinion was shared by a renowned cricketer of an earlier generation, S. F. Barnes, as this dialogue between Neville Cardus and the mighty bowler showed:

Barnes: 'The finest innings I have seen.'
Cardus: 'Think again; you saw Trumper.'
Barnes: 'I can only repeat it is the greatest I ever saw.'
Cardus: 'I'd have liked to see you out there bowling to McCabe.'
Barnes (after a moment's thought): 'I don't think I could have kept him quiet.'

The other striking instance of McCabe's indomitable spirit in adversity — for his deeds were as much a triumph of character as of skill — was his 189 not out at Johannesburg in December, 1935, against the South Africans, who had won their first Test rubber in England earlier that year.

After a fine 231 by A. D. Nourse in South Africa's second innings of 491, the Australians were in a corner. To win, they needed 399 runs in the fourth innings, on a wicket worn by the traffic of three days' play. In Test history no team which had been set the task of getting more than 340 in the fourth innings had ever won, in England, Australia or South Africa. Precedent held out no hope for victory when the Australians began batting after the tea interval on the third afternoon, and, as another day remained for play, the South Africans had ample time to get them out. When the first wicket fell for 17, the Australians were in a tough spot.

The common policy at such times is to attempt a dogged, back-to-the-wall struggle in which the full weight of the task bears incessantly on the batsmen, taxing their nerves until every over is loaded with tension, every run becomes an effort. This psychological pressure and the wearing of the wicket are the two reasons why, dozens of times, 300 in the fourth innings had been beyond the power of Test teams. That was not McCabe's way of meeting the crisis. He never believed that the best defence was defence, anyway. He refused to give the bowlers the advantage of holding the initiative (as Army communiqués put it) because he had the vision to perceive that it made the task more burdensome. That afternoon and next day he carried the fight to the enemy, not in a desperate, headlong sortie, but measuring each blow with cool judgment and delivering it with polished skill.

He sped to his first 100 in 91 minutes, despite the class and variety of the attack by Langton (a great medium-pace bowler), Crisp (fast), Mitchell (googly), Robertson (ultra-slow off-spin) and Bock (medium pace). Several times McCabe had to use his pads to fend off wide-turning balls. Before a sharp leg break got past the patient Fingleton (40) McCabe made 148 of a second-wicket partnership of 177. He scored 100 before lunch on the last day. By then he had been joined by Len Darling, a kindred spirit in putting side before self and in inclination for free stroke-play.

Thunderclouds were banking up from the north-west. Whether the coming downpour would wash the match out or would doom the Australians to finish their struggle on a sticky wicket the batsmen did not know. They pressed on boldly in failing light. Vivid lightning was flashing in the gloom as McCabe, at 166 and 186, cut Crisp's fast bowling above ground and was missed behind point by a fieldsman who had little chance to sight the ball properly. Once Darling edged Langton to the left side of second slip, who groped for the catch without touching the ball. An appeal against the light came at 2.45 p.m., not from the batsmen but from South Africa's captain, H. F. Wade, who said it was dangerous for the fieldsmen. Soon after play had ceased the thunderstorm broke, so soaking the field that the game was abandoned two hours later with Australia 274 for two wickets, McCabe 189 not out and Darling 37 not out.

McCabe's brilliance had so transformed the situation that, instead of struggling to stall off defeat, the Australians were playing like winners, with 125 more runs to get and eight wickets in hand. He batted 3¼ hours for his 189, while 66 were scored at the other end. He hit 29 fours, probably a record for a Test innings under 200. As at Sydney and Nottingham, he won his Johannesburg triumph by tackling a depressing situation in a way that the few other living batsmen possessing enough skill for it would have regarded as too venturesome, even foolhardy. There was something Churchillian in his spirited resistance to his adversaries: he fought them in the crease, and he fought them up the wicket.

McCabe's scores in those three innings were big — so big that they were within the range of only the first flight of the world's batsmen — but size was far from being the only element in their greatness. Other batsmen have made more than a dozen Test scores larger than his highest, but nobody made so many so quickly to rally sides that had been beaten to their knees. As a saver of lost causes he had no rival.

Many a time, bowling which looked troublesome before he came in seemed to lose its terrors after a few overs of his serene stroke-play. Often his dash lightened the burden for others by setting the ball rolling, as when Australia needed 478 to avoid having to follow-on at Manchester in 1934. McCabe scored his second 50 at run-a-minute speed and hit 22 fours in making 137 out of 208 for the second and third wickets.

He made a better fist of batting on rain-affected pitches than most Australians, and some of his match-rescuing feats were on difficult wickets. At Southend in 1938, turf which had not recovered from re-laying in winter had made such a vicious wicket that 40 Australian and Essex wickets fell in two days. The surface of the pitch looked as if, by some confusion in the toolshed, the groundsman had prepared it with a marcel-waving iron instead of a roller. When a bat was laid along it there was room to put the fingers under it in the valleys between the ridges. The Australians lost five wickets for 75 in the second innings and were in a precarious position until McCabe pulled the game around by knocking up 50 in less than an hour.

I think the reason why McCabe dared so much when others had lost heart is that he had no dread of failure. Despite the glare of publicity and the tension of international encounters, the sternest Test match never ceased to be a game of cricket to him. He went in and played in the way he felt the situation required. If he failed he accepted it as just one of those things. He came up smiling again next time. His character is reflected in this and in the sunny nature of his strokes. In McCabe the cricketer you saw McCabe the man — urbane, sociable, unpretentious, straightforward, incapable of anything mean-spirited. Of the players in the Test rubbers immediately before the war he was the best-liked by his own team and by the opponents.

His nickname is 'Napper' — derived from Nap, because of his facial resemblance to Napoleon, even to a mid-forehead tuft denoting where the hairline used to be when he was 19. As he neared 30, the resemblance to the thickset Emperor spread elsewhere, but this chubbiness (weight about 12st. 7 lb., height 5 ft 8 in.) did not lessen the grace of his batting; it simply rounded it out.

Hundreds by McCabe were more infrequent than by other batsmen out of cricket's top drawer. He had not passed 90 in first-class cricket when, at 19, he was chosen for the 1930 Test tour of England, but — as with Denis Compton and Neil Harvey in their teens — anyone who saw McCabe make 20 knew he was watching a player of uncommon gifts. He scored 29 hundreds in first-class matches, an average of one in nine innings, compared with Bradman's one in three, one in five by Ponsford and Woodfull, one in six by Hammond and Kippax and one in seven by Sutcliffe and Hobbs.

McCabe's feet are small (Army doctors found that one was size 5, the other size 6) and he has been subject to trouble underneath the arches for years. Back in 1934 the Board of Control's doctors thought twice about passing him for fear that his feet would not carry him through five months' continuous cricket in England. They began to let him down just before the war, after he had played 24 Tests, the last when he was only 28.

Yet McCabe bowled more in international cricket than any other upper-bracket batsman of his day, except England's champion, Hammond. In Test annals only two other players — Armstrong and Woolley — who scored as many runs as McCabe (2748, average 48), did as much work at the bowling crease. McCabe bowled 3746 balls (medium-pace, with an occasional nippy wrong 'un) in taking 36 English, South African and West Indian wickets, and one-fifth of his overs were maidens. He was an opening bowler in several Tests, but the menace in his bowling was reflected less by that post of honour than by the average cost of his wickets, 43 runs. At second slip and other infield positions he held 42 catches in Tests.

Apart from the calls bowling made on his energy, McCabe could have made more hundreds if he had gone after them, instead of so often undertaking the job of disrupting the opposition's attack. Time and again, in pressing the assault, he got out unexpectedly when well on top of the bowling, in a manner fit to make Bradman and Ponsford rock with laughter. In Tests alone, 13 of his innings exceeded 50 without reaching 100, and he was dismissed eight times between 70 and 93. (When Bradman passed 50 in prewar Tests, bowlers were able to prevent his scoring 100 only seven times, and not once after he got midway through the eighties.) In topping the Australian aggregates in England in 1934, McCabe scored eight hundreds, and needed only 12 runs for another when he sacrificed his innings because his side was hard-pressed for time to win the Nottingham Test.

He was the most adventurous Test batsman in the 20 years after Macartney retired in 1926. Bradman could be venturesome, too, but

Ray Robinson

D. W. Gregory

Joe Darling

Arthur Mailey

(Above, left) Clarrie Grimmett

(Above, right) Chapman caught, and stumped, by Bert Oldfield off Grimmett in the first Test of the 1928-29 series

(Right) Stan McCabe

(Below) Alan Kippax

his disposition was different. When Don chose to cut loose there was usually something calculated in the daring of his whirlwind bursts. Sometimes, when nothing was hanging to the match, Don seemed to set himself to see just how hard and often he could hit without losing control, as if flexing a blade to see how far it would bend without snapping.

Outside Test cricket, Bradman often scored as fast as McCabe, even outpaced him — at Scarborough in 1934 Don made 132 in 90 minutes, four days after his 149 in 104 minutes at Folkestone — but in their century innings in Tests McCabe had the quicker rate, especially against England: 47 runs an hour and 14 boundary hits per 100 runs, compared with Bradman's 37 an hour and 10 boundaries.

McCabe was adventurous by instinct. The sight of the ball leaving the bowler's hand set him thinking of a stroke, not of keeping it out of his stumps. He could not play a cheap shot, even to save his wicket. He was beyond the ordinary measures of scoring, consistency and safety.

He passed 200 only three times, never carried on as far as 250. His big innings were masterpieces, not adapted to mass production, and mostly were produced in response to his side's pressing need. Many of his smaller innings were masterpieces too. When McCabe got out, the melody lingered on, and often it was some time before you noticed what kind of tune the next batsman played.

In all-time averages for Australian scorers of 10,000, only six (Bradman, Ponsford, Woodfull, Brown, Hassett, Kippax) headed McCabe, who made 11,949 runs in 262 innings (20 not out). Judged on results alone he has been one of the world's most successful batsmen in a period when scoring has been higher than ever before, but he was more than that.

McCabe's batting possessed a lyrical impulse which made him different from all others of his generation — a spirit of daring uncommon in his day, compared with times when a batsman's innings did not have to reach 100 or 200 to be regarded as great. In outlook he was a throwback to the Trumper-Macartney-Woolley era. In spirit and charm of stroke-play he was fifth in the noble Sydney dynasty which has not been excelled in the world — a bearer of the torch kindled by Trumper, fanned by Macartney, and kept aglow by Kippax and, while his health lasted, by Jackson.

7 Yabba

The green slope of the Hill at the southern end of Sydney Cricket Ground is intersected by a diagonal streak. The streak is a footworn track, beginning at the asphalt path at the foot of the Hill and leading up the couch-grassed rise to the concrete scoreboard towering in the far corner. The pilgrims who trudge up this track are not the short-sighted, seeking a closer view of the names and figures on the scoreboard, but the thirsty, bound for the bar tucked away under the informative facade. The bar, the track and the green stretch down to the ringside benches close to the white-lattice sightscreen lay in the domain of Yabba.

Australian barrackers are known as masses of people, silently intent, talkatively bored or noisily angry. Yabba was the only one who stepped forward from the ranks of the chorus, so to say, and established himself as an identity. This colloquial wit had a comedian's sense of timing. He had an old soldier's vocabulary, dating back to the South African War, for which he enlisted while on a visit to that country in his early twenties.

On a sleepy afternoon, watching J. W. Hearne break a long scoreless spell with a sudden single, he bellowed: 'Whoa, he's bolted!'

Though nothing was known of his playing experience as schoolboy and youth, he had a knowing appreciation of the game. From his viewpoint, almost in line with the wicket, he could tell when the batsman was not to blame for slow play. Persistent off-theory or leg-

66

theory bowling soon brought him to full cry as spokesman for the resentful crowd. Sarcastically he thundered at one Victorian medium-pace bowler: 'Your length's lousy but you bowl a good width.' Midway through an over in which a bowler consistently pitched the ball well outside the off stump Yabba yelled: 'Wide.'

Again, next ball (louder): 'Wide.'

Next ball (fortissimo): 'DOUBLE wide' (in a tone implying that the bowler had committed an error like a double fault at tennis).

He would not rhapsodize about fast scoring if batsmen were gathering runs by the armful on an easy wicket. 'Can I go in with a walkin' stick?' he would ask.

Yabba was credited with having originated many of the sayings from which tedious repetition has since drained all humour. When two batsmen in long partnership had the fielding side in despair, everybody laughed when he suggested sending for the fire brigade to put them out, or calling for a nurse of shady reputation. He became more widely known in Sydney than many members of Parliament. Cinesound made a newsreel about him. A 14 stone man, about 5 ft 10 in. or 5 ft 11 in. tall, he used to walk through the turnstiles carrying a hamper and a couple of bottles of beer. Lolling or standing on the Hill he would soon be surrounded by a cluster of admirers who made sure his throat never ran dry. His face was fleshy, with more than a hint of a double chin, and his expression was that of a man enjoying himself. He dressed for the part in an open-neck shirt and sometimes a white coat, like a barman who had temporarily deserted his post to steal a peep at the play. On hot days the coat was discarded, exposing his braces. He wore a cloth cap, or a felt hat pushed back.

His voice, coarse and penetrating, had a brassiness which rang through the nondescript yells and mutterings of the mob like Harry James' trumpet above the noises of the band. On Saturdays when there was no first-class match he watched the Glebe club, and was a loyal supporter of *The Cricketers' Arms*, of Warren Bardsley, the left-hand opening batsman, and of Albert Cotter, the fast bowler.

To add to the discomfort of a batsman facing the dreaded Cotter, Yabba would bawl: 'Give him one on the big toe, Tibby!' One afternoon when Cotter was running through North Sydney's batsmen a tail-ender had his middle stump smashed first ball. The crowd laughed unfeelingly. As the shamefaced batsman retreated to the pavilion Yabba consoled him with: 'Don't worry, son; it woulda bowled *me*.'

A harsher note was heard in his voice in an Annandale pub late one winter afternoon in 1940. As he raised a pint from the counter somebody bumped his elbow, spilling the beer on the floor. In righteous wrath, Yabba blasted the clumsy oaf with tavernacular invective, including words which, though some of them appear in the Bible, are forbidden out loud in a public place. For the language, Glebe Court fined him £1 in default 48 hours. Yabba served only one of the 48 hours. He described his liberation in these words: 'It was the longest hour of me life. Also the quietest. When the juice went around that the One and Only was in the clink some of the boys in the village had a zack in the tit-for-tat to get me out.'

By occupation he was a dealer who hawked rabbits. In every street and back lane between Long Nose Point and Iron Cove they knew his two-wheeled cart, with its row of disembowelled rabbits hanging by their tied hind legs, white tails bobbing to the pony's gait. All the cats in Balmain trooped behind his cart; he threw them rabbits' heads. When a customer hailed him Yabba would hitch a rabbit's hindlegs around a hook, expertly peel its skin up to its neck with a flick of the wrist, behead it with a blow of his snickersnee and slap it on to the housewife's plate almost in one action, like a fieldsman picking up and returning a ball. He would drive on, standing up in his striped apron with his vest open to the breeze, calling his wares: 'Rabbie — wild rabbie!' A corruption of his call gave him his nickname, Yabba. Watching one of his cobbers, Alan Bowen, playing football for Balmain, he combined comment and advertisement in one breath: 'You ought to eat my rabbits!'

His voice was not always as bold as brass. One day a batsman was having a sightscreen moved, and umpire George Borwick was holding an arm aloft as a signal to the attendant to keep pushing. The operation took some time. Yabba stared at the umpire's upraised hand and piped up in a schoolboyish falsetto: 'It's no use, umpire; you'll have to wait till playtime like the rest of us.'

The Hill at Sydney has hardly been the same since Yabba died in 1942, at the age of 64, a grandfather. He was a first-generation Australian, born in the inner suburb of Redfern, son of an Englishman and a Sydney woman. Yabba's name was Stephen Harold Gascoigne. His father was a storekeeper who migrated from that centre of learning, Oxford.

8 The Bradman Riddle

The greatest Bradman paradox is that the man who customarily bats surpassingly well should sometimes bat so poorly. These inglorious moments, infrequent among his hours of triumph, have mostly been when rain incited the turf to revolt against the groundsmen's discipline, enabling the quick ball to rear from an awkward length or the spinning ball to cock up as well as screw across.

Because of this, Herbert Sutcliffe, England's opening batsman in 54 Tests, always made a point of adding 'on good wickets' when he described Bradman as the finest batsman of the day. Frank Woolley, Kent's incomparable left-hander, even went to the length of choosing a World XI in his book without giving Bradman a place, because of doubt about his ability on sticky wickets. To me, it would be safer selectorship to put Don in and chance the weather than to run the risk that a team from another planet might engage him and give him the opportunity to beat the World XI's score off his own bat.

More than a dozen times, Bradman has been in Australian sides which English bowlers have trundled out on rain-affected wickets for fewer than 200, or which, in uncompleted innings, seemed unlikely to reach that total. Not all these wickets have been sticky in the exact sense of the word, with the ball snapping up spitefully, like a backfire minus the noise. Some have been puddingy and slow, but all have been damp enough to be difficult for the dry-reared Australians. The matches, the Australians' total, Bradman's part and the highest individual score in the innings have been:

	Match	Total	Bradman	Top Scorer
1928	Brisbane[1]	66	1	Woodfull 30 n.o.
1929	Sydney	128	15	Fairfax 40
1930	Notts[1]	144	8	Kippax 64 n.o.
	Northants	93	22	Bradman 22
	Gloucester	157	42	Ponsford 51
		117	14	McCabe 34
1932	Perth	159	3	McCabe 43
	Melbourne	19 (2w.)	13	—
1933	Sydney	180	1	Rowe 70
		128	71	Bradman 71
1934	Lord's[1]	118	13	Woodfull 43
1936	Brisbane[1]	58	0	Chipperfield 26 n.o.
	Sydney[1]	80	0	O'Reilly 37 n.o.
1938	Middlesex	132	5	Chipperfield 36
	Yorkshire	132	42	Bradman 42

[1]Test Matches.

The figures alone prove nothing except that in these 15 innings, Bradman has passed 15 only four times and has usually been outscored by other members of the team. The element of chance on rain-damaged wickets is so great that, conceivably, the most resourceful of sticky-wicket batsmen might have scored no more. But to brush away these performances by attributing them solely to the luck of the game would be to shrink from facing the issue and to disregard relevant evidence. The point is not that Bradman has usually missed the bus on these drying wickets, but whether he has batted well enough to deserve more runs than he made, or even as many.

The first suggestion I can recall that Don's batting on sticky wickets was not true to label was made by Hunter Hendry (Test all-rounder, 1921–29) after a combined Australian team played D. R. Jardine's English team at Perth, 1932. Bradman (3) was caught by Hammond off Verity on a wicket on which McCabe scored 43.

Yet, in an after-rain period of the Oval Test, 1930, when Don was scoring the fourth 50 of his 232, there had been much more praise for his batting than fault-finding.

Sir Pelham Warner said the wicket was not absolutely difficult; spin turned the ball only slowly, but for a while before lunch the pitch was decidedly unpleasant, and Jackson and Bradman were badly hit by rising balls from Larwood and Hammond. P. G. H. Fender noted that Bradman drew back and tried to cut the nasty balls while Jackson stood up and played them. Bradman was thumped over the heart and on the wrist; Jackson was felled by one blow on the hip and suffered other bruises on the jaw, shoulder, ribs, elbow and wrist. Sir Pelham and Percy Fender assessed the unpleasant period at half an hour. Australia's most readable cricket writer, ex-bowler Arthur Mailey, made it an hour. Maybe he hadn't wound his watch overnight.

At Lord's, 1934, the rash swish which skied a catch for the wicketkeeper was so un-Bradmanlike that — except for the difference in physique — one could almost have wondered whether Test Match rules had somehow been waived to permit the Australians to reinforce their batting by calling in Fleetwood-Smith (who, despite his proficiency in edging the ball over the slips, did not exceed 7 in any innings that season). Even that incorrigible stroke-player probably would have made a shamefaced re-entry to the dressing room after such a shot as Bradman played. Sir Pelham Warner described it as a most unguarded stroke at a critical time. He said he would never forget the look which Woodfull, who was at the bowler's end, gave Bradman as the latter passed him on his way back to the pavilion. Jardine likened the calamitous stroke to 'the old-fashioned cow shot' and added that one would have expected a batsman of Bradman's ability to have taken due warning from an earlier attempt which fell safely. J. B. Hobbs wrote: 'Bradman, one felt, must now realize that it does not pay to hit against the spin on wickets where the ball is turning.'

Of Bradman's blob in the Brisbane Test, 1936, Neville Cardus said the stroke was not fit for public view. About the O in the next Test, at Sydney, Cardus wrote that the ball from Voce was as harmless as ever scuttled a great player; Bradman made an amiable Christmas present to Allen at short leg.

When Bradman was caught by Compton off Nevell for 5, against Middlesex, 1938, ex-captain Woodfull described the wicket as wet but not awkward and added: 'McCabe stood well over the ball. Bradman made the strokes of a beginner.' Cardus declared that Bradman abdicated after a brief innings which told of an acute disinclination to stay there — or anywhere adjacent to the ball; he was missed off a sightless heave before scoring; his innings needed curtains to conceal it.

On an awkward wicket at Sheffield, 1938, Bradman was missed first ball before he scored 42 of Australia's 132. Mailey said Don's discomfiture against W. E. Bowes' bowling amused close-up

Yorkshire fieldsmen; the other batsman, C. L. Badcock, took over the duty of facing Bowes: 'a case of the pupil protecting the master'.

That innings brought a frank comment from A. G. Moyes, a sound judge of cricket who, as a punishing batsman, was chosen in the Australian team in 1914 for a tour of South Africa which was cancelled because of war. Bradman has no more fervent admirer than 'Johnny' Moyes, one of the selectors who brought Don from the country to Sydney in 1926. The two were so close throughout the 1938 tour of England that some of the Australian players jocularly suggested that Bradman sub-edited what Moyes wrote. If sub-editor Bradman was on duty at Sheffield he did not draw his blue pencil through this passage in Moyes' message to Australian newspapers: 'Bowes several times missed the champion's stumps so narrowly that Badcock, turning his back, hid his face in his hands to conceal either laughter or anguish. I have never seen Bradman so obviously bewildered.'

The evidence quoted on the last few pages — probably less than .05 per cent of what has been written about Bradman — is clear as could be, so far as it goes. Yet the summing-up, the reasoning why, is not easy, even for those who know Don enough to have an idea how his mind works. The only thorough-going summing-up I have seen is by C. B. Fry, who knows where each finger and each toe ought to be at any stage of any stroke. But I think Fry's candid analysis gets off the rails at one point.

Fry's finding is that Bradman never took the trouble to make himself into a bad-wicket batsman and preferred to treat such wickets as not worth playing on. Don's slapdash methods pointed to that conclusion, and I know it was the opinion of many of his team-mates, who often discussed it as a curiosity of the game. Yet that judgement may be too bald, too severe. I believe there is more to it than that. I submit, with due deference, that where Fry misdirects the jury is in these sentences:

It would seem that, being sure of his ability to score hugely on true fast wickets in the style he has evolved as his own against the sort of bowling he has to meet — a style that cannot succeed on bad wickets — the Don despises modifications to suit unpleasant conditions. I know how fine a player he would be on difficult wickets if he chose to qualify himself by changes of technique. There is nothing required on treacherous wickets that he could not have incorporated in his game. He could have developed a defence as accurate against the breaking ball as against the straight one. He could have cultivated a fine drive off the front foot. He could have produced himself as a normal, powerful hitter with a 'straight' swing...

No doubt Commander Fry would be ready to demonstrate with an umbrella and an orange in any room where there was no furniture within a three-yard radius and no low-hanging lights to obstruct the follow-through.

The real explanation of this Bradman paradox is, I feel sure, not primarily a matter of technique, but only incidentally. Watching Don on true wickets, you saw that he possessed almost every technical need for success on sticky turf. The laid-down requirements are quick footwork, skilful back-play, getting near the line of the ball and over it (which means being willing to take a few knocks), delayed action while the batsman learns all he can about the ball's misbehaviour before he launches his stroke, ability to get to the pitched-up ball and slam it, and prudence in keeping the bat away from the awkward-length ball if he judges it will not hit the stumps.

Now put Bradman's methods alongside those specifications. I never saw a quicker-moving batsman, or one who could start his stroke later yet finish it on time (often it looked, even then, as if he had time to spare).

The great S. F. Barnes, who had a bowler's-eye-view of most of the first-flight batsmen of the past, said that Bradman, on true wickets, got closer to the ball than anybody in his experience, not excluding Ranjitsinhji.

After studying Don's masterly back-play, Wilfred Rhodes, who bowled against all the 'best ever' batsmen from Grace to Bradman, classed him as the greatest back-foot player he ever saw.

Though he did not use it as often as his back-foot shots, Don owned as fine a drive off the front foot as a great Test batsman could wish to cultivate, as demonstrated in many matches, notably by his powerful, straight hitting in his unforgettable 160 against Middlesex, 1934.

I am at a loss to understand why Fry contended that Bradman needed to develop a defence against the breaking ball, because he proved that he could play on turning wickets. Nobody could wish for better batting on them than Don's innings for New South Wales against England at Sydney, 1932, after overnight rain. Bowes could not make the ball fly but Hammond and Verity turned it widely and dismissed NSW for 128, of which Bradman scored 71 brilliantly. In the Test at Trent Bridge, 1938, the ball was breaking from a pitch so worn that it powdered whenever the ball struck it. Bradman knew all the answers and stayed in the whole day. At Leeds, 1938, his 103 was made on an Edwardian-style wicket on which bowlers were able to turn the ball well and only three other batsmen in the match exceeded 30 in either innings.

On pitches damp or dry, width of break never bothered Don so much as inconsistencies in height.

Those forcing shots to the on, in which he daringly anticipated the course of the ball's bounce, could have been expected to get him into trouble on bad wickets, if he had not shown at other times that he could refrain from attempting them. His methods were never set in one groove. On the harder, faster wickets of his own country he knew when he could hit at the pitch of the ball and get away with it; in England, where that was much more risky, he was more prudent and sometimes discarded it altogether, as easily as if he had never done it in his life.

Technically, the thing most noticeable in Bradman's play on really sticky wickets was not that he did not make the slight modifications necessary to suit the conditions (chiefly by keeping the bat away from length balls that would not hit the stumps — a difficult transformation for one who normally allowed fewer balls to pass than any other batsman). The thing that stood out above all was that he changed his methods too much — turned them so tail-apeak that he was scarcely recognizable as the same batsman.

Normally so sharp-sighted, he played almost as if his vision were blurred by a hangover or fogged by heavy smoking — both out of the question in a non-smoker who did not give strong drink a chance to mock him on the morning after. Those forward lunges, those desperate lashes against the break, those sidlings away from the line of the ball, were all foreign to his usual style. He looked as ill-at-ease as a goldfish tipped from its bowl into a stormy sea. At any moment he seemed likely to be washed up on the rocks.

From behind his Stalin-weight moustache, Joe Darling (who captained the Australians in England in 1899, 1902 and 1905) said that a batsman gifted with such swift co-ordination of eye, brain and foot, and so quick with the bat, should be able to score 50 in a few overs on the worst of wickets before the best of bowlers could get him out.

The reason why Bradman didn't look like doing it was psychological — the working of the mind, not the feet, arms and bat. First, he had a palpable distaste for playing on wickets sticky enough for him to expect the ball to rear. Few batsmen, if any, relish batting in such conditions, but none showed his aversion more plainly.

Bradman's unrivalled skill normally allowed him to do almost as he liked. He was so accustomed to absolute monarchy that a rebellious wicket or a treasonable bumper robbed his batting of authority more than it did humbler batsmen not unacquainted with struggling for runs. He seemed as unhappy as a managing director would be pedalling a bicycle to work after years of having been ceremoniously delivered at the office door by limousine.

Other Australian batsmen of his generation, accustomed to pitches fully protected from rain, have told me they think sticky wickets take the science out of batting. Bradman evidently gave it up as hopeless. Once he lost his admirable mental poise, the co-ordinating link went, his game inevitably fell to pieces, his movements became flurried, his strokes hasty, maladroit.

This is something which Bradman might not care to admit, even to himself, yet it seems to me to be logical, and, as a human limitation, nothing to blush about. I fancy that Anton Dolin, Irina Baronova or any other genius of the ballet would be reduced to stumbling despair if the stage were bucking about like a crazy staircase at Luna Park and the orchestra were side-slipping from tune to tune in one of those infuriating hotch-potches radio announcers call a musical switch.

Bradman had risen to the Australian XI before he ever saw a sticky wicket. In his first Test, at Brisbane, 1928, heavy rain fell in the night before the last day. In the morning he heard the older players talking about a 'sticky' in rueful tones, and he asked: 'What does the ball do on a sticky wicket?' Had his early cricket education been in England, where rain-damaged wickets are a compulsory subject in the course, and had he needed all-weather competence to win his way to the top, few could doubt that it would have been beyond him.

As things are, the fact that Bradman has accomplished so much does not entitle us to demand everything of him. Rather, it was something to be thankful for that some conditions disturbed his sceptred sway and reduced him to tail-enders' gropings. Similarly, there was no reason for Hammond to hang his head because his leg-side play lacked the glory of his stroking to the off.

Heaven preserve the game of cricket from a batsman combining the run capacity of Bradman and Ponsford, the majesty of Hammond, the competency of Hutton, the steadfastness of Woodfull, the composure of Sutcliffe, the assurance of Barnes, the genius of Compton, the power of Miller, the poise of Brown, and the courage of Richardson, even if those qualities were linked with the grace of Kippax and (impossible alliance) the death-or-glory daring of McCabe!

Such cloying perfection would leave us only one course — to pray for a run-out.

9 The Artful Dodger

Good judges often differ about who is the best batsman in the world or the most attractive, but there is no doubt who is the smartest batsman on earth: Sidney George Barnes. In fact, Barnes has been too smart for a lot of people — mostly bowlers and barrackers — and in some ways for himself.

Not for many years, if ever, have Australian cricket-goers been stirred to such noisy annoyance by one of their own countrymen; as critical as any have been his fellow citizens of Sydney, city of sunshine and sinful swimsuits. Their chief complaints have been that Barnes is too cocksure, plays to the gallery too much, yet often scores too slowly. Sometimes it seems as if this Artful Dodger of cricket would rather steal a run like a pickpocket than hit an honest four with a straightforward stroke.

A few years after outshining the other urchins at street cricket on bitumen roadways in the nearby suburb of Stanmore, an unknown wicketkeeper-batsman of eighteen kept his end going on Petersham Oval, four miles west of Sydney, while his team fell to the world's best bowler. In the pavilion after the game the youngster said to the wrecker: 'You bowled rather well today, O'Reilly.' Coming from a whipper-snapper to the man whom England's greatest respected, such patronizing praise was enough to get O'Reilly's Irish up, but the bowler was more interested in the youth's batting than his brashness, and on the spot predicted a Test future for young Barnes. At twenty

Barnes was playing for New South Wales, and at twenty-one he was chosen for the 1938 tour of England after only eight first-class matches, in which he made 664 runs. But the newcomer had proved his confidence in the selection-eve match, when other candidates for the trip were showing signs of feeling the strain: he outscored the best of them with 110, his first hundred in first-class cricket, and 42.

Barnes' rush to fame and fortune was interrupted by a shipboard mishap which put a wrist in plaster for half the tour. He returned to Australia without having made a hundred in a first-class match on the trip. Against Kent and twice in festival matches near the end he was dismissed in the nineties and came off fuming. His room-mate, Badcock (who made four centuries on the tour), said to him consolingly: 'Anyway, Siddy, well played — and you're top score.' Barnes: 'You can afford to get out, Musso. I can't.'

Ambition fired his actions as well as his words. The youth who had been called a rough diamond did his own cutting and shaping. His stocky frame was no longer seen in lumber-jackets and the like but was attired in Savile Row suits; he developed into the Australian team's most fashionable dresser, tartan socks and all. Without swapping his Sydney accent for an Oxford one, he became more careful in his speech, as if he were taking lessons in elocution. The dead-end kids of Stanmore would hardly have recognized their former cobber in the self-possessed man-about-town who married a theological professor's daughter and drove around in a Humber Snipe. Yet he has retained the habit of tilting at those about him, which, in the first place, probably had been his defensive reaction when cricket suddenly yanked him as a youth into unfamiliar circles of life. Some quirk in his nature makes him an incorrigible teaser, whether the targets of his satire are his table companions or 70,000 Melbournians banked up in angry rows. He enjoys saying things to shock people, as when mates goaded him into waving to a photograph of Victor Trumper on the wall and saying: 'Take a back seat!' On the first tee at golf he stage-whispers to his partner (for strangers' benefit): 'None of this counting business — everybody cheats.' When the Marrickville club's coach, Algy Wright, had weightily completed a lesson to schoolboys on the rudiments of cricket and invited questions from the class, it was Barnes who prompted one to ask: 'What's the weight of a bail, Mr Wright?'

Sid Barnes bears a name that another rebellious cricket character had made famous before he was born. Sid the Second would have remade it great in his own right in a few years if he had arisen in a war-free period instead of making his entry in the shadow of Munich. In the last full year before World War II stopped big cricket, Barnes' 1050 runs in 14 innings in eight matches made him the fourth to score 1000 runs in an Australian season when no visiting team increased batting opportunities. Throughout the eight-year gap which war made in Anglo-Australian Test matches Barnes was wrung by the knowledge that he was one of the world's top-shelf batsmen, yet was missing all reward for such eminence. The futility of it all tended to sharpen his self-interest and prod him into more acts of showmanship.

Barnes comes to the wicket with the air of a man who can hardly afford the time before bustling away to more important affairs, such as selling a gross of Jan Vok liqueurs or bargaining about a motor car or an ocean-going tug. On his sturdy legs the tops of the pads flap, giving a strutting importance to his gait. Apparently some business deal or other has kept him occupied up to the last moment before he emerged. At the wicket he takes a quick inventory to make sure he has all he needs. He hoists his pants all around, tests the fitting of his pads, smooths his shirt collar, adjusts his cap by the peak, twitches his feet to verify that his boots are comfortable and takes a fresh grip of his bat. He repeats these actions between balls. He holds the bat upright in front of his curved nose and looks around it at an unlucky bowler, with his face split in a grin like a crack in a boulder.

When this nuggety right-hander of 5 ft 8 in. and 12½ stone settles into his stance you can see he is a self-made batsman, so full of cricket that handicaps in style could not stop him. His body is bowed over the bat, dragged down by his low grip on the handle, throttlingly low. The slope of his bat back behind his right toecap lowers the knuckles of his right hand to knee-level. Preliminary tapping takes the bat farther back. Barnes' chest is as open as his contempt for the bowling; his heels are almost together but the left toe is towards extra cover, slewing him around to bring his right arm and toecap into view. Before the ball is bowled he is ready to step across and hide the wicket from the bowler — a total eclipse. The right foot goes over smartly and the left comes up beside it, like a step in a Scottish dance. While this is going on he gives the bat a wide flourish, circling it towards point and the slips, like a sheriff bailing up a saloonful of desperadoes with one sweep of his shooting-iron. This would be defect enough to make an ordinary batsman vulnerable, yet Barnes' bat is caught wandering as rarely as his attention. Wicketkeepers say he can follow a swinging ball later than any other batsman among Australians, and still get the bat to it with a sudden dig of that low right hand. The worst effect the flourish leaves is that he nicks more balls into his pads than the rest of the Australian XI put together (and at times is given out lbw, as if he has missed).

That side-step of Barnes' brings him behind the ball more

noticeably than any other batsman. This is No. 1 rule for safety, and he observes it so regularly that it becomes almost habitual; he tends to pack up against balls that could be treated more roughly. At times he walls himself up inside his own run factory so that he cannot get out to deliver the goods. One of his specialities has been to get the ball around the corner just as it was about to hit him below the belt; when all other runs dried up he always had one on the hip. He has restricted himself with such safety-first slogans as 'No runs in front of the wicket until 40'.

His jaw is like a set-square — appropriate in a man for tight corners — and is usually tucked down in his shirt collar as he plays. Once, a ball he clumped into the ground injured his nose. It's a wonder that hasn't happened more often. Even in his hooking he tends to fold at the waist over bent knees, making it harder to keep the ball down. In one stern period he rationed himself to three movements: getting behind the ball to block, leg-glide or hook; straddling his legs wide for his unrivalled square-cut; and going down on his right knee to sweep. Though this routine made his play air-tight in one way, it simplified opposing captains' field-placing to curb his scoring, it left him with a back-foot addict's liability to go leg-before-wicket or be caught behind on either side, and it allowed his attackers to bowl their most awkward length. Batsmen, like nations, can make such a fetish of security that, in the process, the things worth securing are sacrificed.

That is why I believe that in some way Barnes outsmarts himself. My opinion of his capabilities is so high that I believe he could have made more runs since the war as a stroke-player, and won popular backing as a candidate for the title of world's best batsman, instead of the austere distinction of looking the hardest Australian to get out. In dour moods, he has been unrecognizable as the Barnes who clouted 40 off an over by the State fast bowler, 'Ginty' Lush, at North Sydney late one afternoon in 1937 (four sixes and four fours with swinging pulls — one six off an outfielder's hands). Twice in 1940 he hooked fast bowlers' first balls for six at Petersham Oval — Ray Lindwall (St George) and Victor Trumper II (Manly).

Barnes' highest score against England, 234 at Sydney, 1946, was one of the most-talked-about innings in Test history and easily the most talked-in. Barnes had the chief speaking part early, to be superseded when Bradman came in, but most of the words were used by the crowd. Barnes had backed himself to make a hundred, despite an approaching thunderstorm. He appealed against the poor light three times in Bedser's opening over, the first time before he faced a ball. Midway through Edrich's first over, Morris had difficulty sighting a faster ball, and the umpires granted a fourth appeal 10 minutes before the storm broke fiercely from the west.

After three hours and two inspections of the saturated pitch, the bedraggled survivors saw Barnes and Morris resume batting with the knowledge that if the wicket became sticky Australia could easily be beaten by an innings, though England had only 255 on the board. One run, then Barnes took a sharp shower as a signal to sprint to the pavilion, out-distancing the other players hurrying off. He passed the gate 20 lengths in front of outfielder Washbrook, with bowler Wright a poor third. By the time Barnes got to the dressing room the shower had eased and the umpires called the players back. Resentment of his alacrity in quitting the scene showed itself in a storm of hooting as he reappeared on the field. Barnes then ran to the wicket. Next source of irritation was the time Barnes took patting the mark each ball made on the soggy pitch. When the crowd barracked him for it he deliberately stepped farther along and gave the turf an extra tap in an unspotted place.

The fall of Morris for five after three-quarters of an hour brought the surprising appearance of Johnson instead of Bradman (who had not fielded earlier that day but had padded up for batting). Bearing instructions to end the day by questioning the fitness of the light before Australia could suffer more losses, Johnson appealed to the umpires twice in one over. Though Barnes, who had scored 21 out of 27, seemed untroubled in the fading light, he took the cue; he added an appeal of his own and ostentatiously walked away, as if that ended the matter. That bluff failed, but the umpires yielded to the fifth appeal in nine minutes and play ceased for the day an hour before the appointed time. (After the season, Barnes said in a broadcast: 'We could have played on, but it was a Test Match and we just had to win. I realized something drastic had to be done or three wickets might be lost. So I appealed after every second ball. I complained of people moving about, the light and, in fact, everything, in an effort to get the appeal upheld...' With this revelation Barnes drew severe criticism on himself. It was characteristic that he should bluntly take responsibility for the whole business without shame.

After 9½ hours at the wicket Barnes passed 200 with a square-cut for his thirteenth four. It was the slowest double century in Anglo-Australian Tests — an unsought record which had been left to W. L. Murdoch for 62 years since he batted a little more than eight hours for 211 for Australia at the Oval in 1884. Barnes gave his first chance in 10 hours when he was dropped at 216. The Barnes-Bradman partnership amassed 405, a world record for the fifth wicket. Amid a late-afternoon massacre of the weary-footed bowlers, Bradman (234 in 6½ hours) went lbw to Yardley.

Barnes was letting the fourth-day crowd see his drive, which he had found somewhere between Monday evening and Tuesday afternoon. For the first time in his life he was satiated by batting, having helped Australia's score rise from 0 to 564 and having played himself in eight times because of interruptions, intervals and overnight stops. 'I can't stick it any longer,' he exclaimed, and was caught off Bedser for 234.

Barnes had stuck it out for 10 hours 42 minutes (not counting comings and goings). Given five minutes more, he would have outlasted Merchant's 10¾ hours for 359 not out for Bombay against Maharashtra in a national championship match at the magnificent Brabourne Stadium in December 1943. Only one man has stayed in longer: Hutton, 13 hours 17 minutes for the Test record of 364 in 1938. If that was the only time they ever saw Barnes, watchers who followed him through his protracted innings took away a picture of his batting methods and his character, brazen yet impressionable, rebellious yet loyal, self-interested yet full of aggressive team spirit, patient in pursuit of his objective, impetuous in getting into trouble and quick-witted in getting out of it.

Barnes has qualified for greatness under the supreme test of batsmanship: he can play all types of bowling on almost any kind of wicket. He and Morris looked the surest of the 1948 Australians in England when the turf aided turn or cut. He does not care what is bowled to him (that is, apart from his favourite long hops). On good wickets there is never any need for him to become preoccupied with safety, permit bowlers to bowl their best at him, and confine himself for hours to short-arm shots.

A century in his first Test at Lord's was the promise Barnes made to his wife, who left their two young children in Scotland when she came down to watch the match with her sister. When Coxon made his trial run, in Yorkshire fashion, Barnes played a vigorous hook at the empty air — as he does every time a bowler's feet or fingers slip and nothing comes along. Barnes liked English wickets, but that day he was too early with the bat in a back shot to leg at Coxon's seventh ball and he was caught at backward short leg for 0. Unabashed by such disgrace, he held the bat up by the wrong end, as if offering the handle to any who thought they could do better. In the second innings he needed luck to keep his promise. At eight, Coxon's appeal for lbw found him with his handkerchief out, wiping his nose with the air of one who had been in this non-combatant attitude when the ball was delivered, unfairly. At 18 he survived a stumping chance on the leg side only because Laker's off-break jumped too sharply from a boot-worn patch. For all his cockiness, Barnes had to wait 4½ hours for his Lord's 100, which included 10 fours and one bow to sarcastic applauders in a dull spell. Barnes celebrated the fortunate fulfilment of his promise by abandoning himself to the joy of lifting drives, like a teetotaller on a bender. Two of them sailed over long-on for sixes which helped to bring him 20 off one of Laker's overs.

When Barnes drives, the ball suffers a stunning blow, as if his bat has been sawn from a red-gum gatepost instead of carved from wide-grained willow. Yet he uses a light bat, about 2 lb. 3 oz. Once, when I asked him about this, he grinned: 'I don't care what my bats weigh as long as they are given to me.'

Often Barnes' last words before leaving the dressing room have been something like this: 'Hey, listen! Who'll lay me fifty bob to five I can't get two hundred?' If he got no takers he would warn the next batsman: 'Better get those pads on quickly, because I won't be long.' Nobody believed that. One bet he lost was that he would score 100 before lunch in the Fifth Test against India, 1948. He led off with 33 in the first three-quarters of an hour but was run out.

The man who boasted he could pick Grimmett's flipper and tauntingly commanded O'Reilly to 'Toss 'em up' was the man who playfully slapped Bedser's broad buttocks with his bat after cutting him for four. His nickname is 'Bagger' — perhaps because he so often has everything in the bag.

Barnes monopolized attention and most of the bowling. Between wickets, he would never take yes for an answer. He did not give up strike stealing even when his partner was Bradman, the master strike-controller, accustomed to unquestioning responses from companions. After Bradman refused to run a single early in an over at Manchester, his sharp cry of 'Right' for one near the over's end found Barnes with his back turned, readjusting his batting gloves. Reproved, Barnes pretended to walk away, and Lancashire fieldsmen heard him say: 'Here, you come and have the lot. I'll starve.' Yet when Morris was run out on Barnes' call in a Sydney Test the hard-boiled caller was so upset that he lost his own wicket soon afterwards.

As a fieldsman at silly-leg, Barnes owes his reputation (and his life) to the gift of sudden movement. He stood so close for O'Reilly that once he flung himself at a batsman's feet to catch a snicked ball rebounding from the pads. Some professed to have seen him take up a position with his left foot on the rolled pitch at Lord's when the Australians played MCC, but I think they were mistaken. Throughout the 1948 tour his boot was usually a yard from the edge, for fast bowling, and occasionally only a foot — with one exception. After the trespassing allegation had fizzled out, the Australians took the field at Bramall Lane to find that the Sheffield groundsman had made a pitch 15 or 16 feet wide, easily half as wide again as wickets elsewhere. At the sight of it, Barnes walked up and ostentatiously planted both feet on it.

When Sen came in to bat for India at Adelaide he pretended to sweep Barnes away with his bat, as if the squatting fieldsman were a wind-blown bundle of paper. After the 1948 Tests, England's captain, Yardley, made the point that consciousness of Barnes' closeness had an unsettling effect on the batsmen, as it affected their concentration, that his fielding there had greatly increased the effectiveness of Lindwall and Miller's fast bowling, but that to suggest it was against the spirit of the game was absurd.

Barnes was almost near enough to count the batsmen's heartbeats as they faced the fast bowling. By rights, they should have been counting his — especially when the bowling changed to Ian Johnson's slow breaks, turning towards the on-side. Despite his unblinking and astonishing interceptions in the air and on the ground at this point-blank range, Barnes has often had no time to get a hand to the ball. Nominal chances have bruised his wrists and chest and stung his knee-cap. When Washbrook hit Lindwall hard to the on at Manchester the ball struck Barnes. It hit him on the right shoulder, but, rather than give a sign that he had been hurt, he stoically refrained from rubbing the spot.

A Lancashire barracker: 'That's the way to shift him.'

Barnes stepped a pace closer.

Next day the shoulder was so sore that he could not lift his arm and could only throw underhand. In the next match Hassett gave him a spell from suicide corner. After a chase to the outfield, Barnes brought the ball in by hand, holding it out beside his hip and menacing to throw it each time the puzzled batsmen looked like starting for the extra run they could easily have taken.

In a Test against India, Barnes had made light of a blow on the back of the shoulder when Phadkar on-drove Johnson. Even when 14 stone Pollard slogged a similar ball into his left ribs in the Manchester Test, Barnes tried to crack hardy. He set out to walk to the bowler's end but staggered across the pitch and collapsed. Four policemen carried him off, purple-faced with agony, and an ambulance took him to Manchester Infirmary. Bearing a bruise like a soup plate, he tried to practise next day, but had to sit on the running-board of a car before he could get back to the pavilion. Yet he went in to bat and hung on for 25 minutes before a quick run caused him to collapse again. On hands and knees, with sunken head, he muttered to fieldsmen who ran to his aid: 'Leave me alone. I can bat. I'm staying here.' Back to hospital they sent him. He was still unfit for the Leeds Test a fortnight later, and after-effects of the injury probably cost him his place in the tentative list for *Wisden's* Five Cricketers of the Year.

Barnes is the quickest fieldsman to render first aid to an injured player. He intercepts groundsmen with buckets of sawdust and takes command of sprinkling it on the footholds. He is the surest at catching stray dogs (to fulfil an earlier jest about blind umpires he tried to present a dog at the Oval to Alex Skelding, who hates dogs).

I have seen Barnes hand his cap to the bowler's umpire and take the ball when, in fact, somebody else was going to bowl. I almost added that he measured out his run, but he hardly gets more than arm's length from the umpire from start to finish of his approach. After this disarming shuffle he tosses up leg-twiddlers, but a quick arm makes the ball nip through; he trapped Hazare and Armanath with successive balls in the New Year Test at Melbourne, 1948.

After umpire Scott caused a fuss by refusing to hold the cap of England's substitute fieldsman, Gibb, the next time Barnes came in to bat he walked straight to Scott, before facing a ball, and handed him his cap. His dark hair is always glossy with brilliantine.

Every time a fieldsman catches a bump-ball from him, Barnes pretends to walk out — a threadbare trick, yet often funny the way he does it. Against the South of England he hooked at the first ball from Trevor Bailey as it flew near his arm. The ball touched his shoulder, but, as soon as he heard players appeal for a catch behind, he walked a few paces away. Then he turned back to the wicket, but found he had been given out.

When his swinging leg-hit landed the ball on the asphalt in front of the little brick pavilion at Scarborough and an umpire signalled four, Barnes faced the scorers with both hands aloft for a six (he was right and the umpire amended his signal). I'd have liked to see Barnes batting with Danny Kaye, while Groucho Marx waited, padded up and puffing a cigar, ready to go in when one ran the other out.

After making 100 for the 1948 Australian XI at Hobart, by spooning up catches just out of reach of the Tasmanians, he too obviously ended his own innings by his own hand. He trod on his stumps, amid uproar. His clowning in the testimonial match for Sir Donald Bradman caused the biggest commotion. His chief trick was to throw aside his bat, produce a toy one from under his pullover and take block with it. The umpire was reluctant to give him guard, but Barnes insisted that the toy bat was legal, as it came within the only dimensions laid down by the Laws of Cricket. After playing one ball from Ian Johnson around the corner, he handed the child's bat to an umpire and carried on with his own to make 89 in a brilliant hour. At the height of the stir about his antics, a stage company wanted to engage Barnes for a fortnight's performance at the Theatre Royal, Brisbane. They couldn't have offered enough. Neither did the tobacco company whose calendar bore photographs of all the Australian team except his.

I never ceased wondering how Barnes could indulge in so many acts of showmanship without impairing in the slightest his efficiency as an all-rounder with only one superior in world cricket, Keith Miller. In fact, reckoning wicketkeeping with batting, bowling and fielding, Barnes, Amarnath and Hampshire's George Brown have been the most complete cricketers modern cricket has known.

Long known as the problem child of Australian cricket, Barnes seems destined to be the centre of odd happenings, as the sparks fly upwards. He vaulted the turnstile at Melbourne because he had given his ticket to a friend who travelled 600 miles to the Test Match. He would stick up for his rights, even to brushing past the notebook of a traffic cop who threatened arrest after Barnes refused to move his car from the grass plot behind the Sydney pavilion. As Petersham captain, he sat on the ground, argued, and induced an umpire at Manly Oval to reverse his disallowance of a catch by the wicketkeeper, Barnes. As NSW captain he jumped the Brisbane fence to protest against mowing of the outfield whose grassiness had checked many of his team's strokes on the preceding day. (The opposing captain, Brown, upheld his point.) His tactics as captain included placing NSW's least sprightly fieldsman, Toshack, a couple of yards from the leg corner of Hutton's bat. Barnes was dumped from the State captaincy after a few matches. He showed his disapproval by lying apart from the others when they rested at the fall of wickets.

First to pop his signature in autograph books with a rubber stamp instead of a flourish of the pen, bushy-browed Barnes was the first man to play for a League club (Burnley) in between Australian seasons. He has done more than any other player to loosen the knots which officialdom increasingly tends to tie around cricketers. After his decision that he could not afford to go to South Africa in 1949–50 for an out-of-pocket allowance of £450 ($900), his wrangle with the NSW authorities about his omission from the Kippax-Oldfield testimonial match brought more publicity for that game than even the last Sydney appearance of Sir Donald Bradman — and helped pack the halls where Barnes showed his cine-camera films of Test cricket for clubs and charities. He made the democratic complaint that the authorities had been guilty of discrimination 'by inviting the retired Sir Donald Bradman to play in the match but ignoring plain Sid Barnes'. In his film commentary, after a sequence of pictures of Brown defending patiently, Barnes said: 'Now I'll brighten cricket for you' — and depicted himself hitting a string of boundaries. When the film showed him writhing on the ground in pain after Pollard's hit injured him, he commented dryly: 'It would have killed any ordinary man.'

For all his buffoonery and bombast, this dealer in quips, quirks, square-cuts and hooks is a man of acumen. He is an opportunist, but an open one, always pleased with himself, always ready to do a good turn — and expect better in return.

Those who know how to take his assertiveness and banter like him. They find him without humbug, grasping yet generous, hard as nails yet quickly sympathetic. He was batting for NSW when a new Queensland opening bowler, A. Price, missed his step and delivered several no-balls. Barnes, at the non-striking end, promptly helped him with advice: 'Ease down a moment — find a length before you go flat out.' When one of his State's team suffered a double bereavement and a broken jaw in one month, Barnes quietly paid money into his bank account to tide him over and began a subscription list with ten guineas.

In all the criticism of Barnes for flagrant showmanship and cross-grained behaviour, the most severe comments come from those who know him from afar, the least from the cricketers who have played with and against him.

10 Poker Face

After Yogi-like meditation over the signature *A L Hassett*, an Indian graphologist came up with conclusions about the character of the writer. Linking of the initials suggested a cautious nature, he found, but a long tail-flourish on the *L* and a powerful finishing loop on the *H* indicated energy. So Hassett would combine caution and energy.

Nothing in the autograph led the expert to mention that with all his other traits Arthur Lindsay Hassett would combine fun — though the way the letters flowed on without pause for full points might have been taken to mean that he did not know when to stop.

Hassett did know when to stop: at the dressing room door as he passed out, bat in hand. His long face would be solemnly set, his long top lip dead straight, his eyes rather downcast beneath the big cap-peak. Opponents could learn no more from his face than the Indian did from his signature. Yet on the other side of the dressing room door team-mates would be gurgling at his parting jest or gesture. Those extremes of private gaiety and public decorum ought to be open to an intriguing explanation, like Africa's Shari crocodile with zebra markings. Yet I think it is simply a sense of duty overpowering a sense of humour.

Hassett playing O'Reilly was a sight worth remembering. In he would walk, his small figure casting little more shadow than his bat. The contest seemed unequal from the start, because O'Reilly, 6 ft 3 in., towered nine inches above him; it would have looked more apt for

Hassett to sell him a newspaper than contend with his bowling. Technically, O'Reilly's knack of making some balls pop higher should have troubled short batsmen most. Yet Hassett gained, and deserved, the reputation of being the best handler of the greatest bowler of the age, defying him with his own special combination of deadbat defence and insolent aggression. Grimmett agreed that Hassett played O'Reilly better than anyone else he saw, and acknowledged his own difficulty in bowling to one so sure in his footwork. Hassett's quick-skipping feet were visible evidence of the speed with which his mind worked to combat the varied pressure of the Master's attack. Often he was hard-pressed by leg-breaks, but when the slower wrong 'un curved along he would detect it and on-drive it with lofty impertinence or plonk it to the leg boundary with a stroke that was a cheeky first cousin to a pull. When a fielder was put deep and square to stop this, Hassett would guide the ball finer. Others found it paid to be silent or civil to 'The Tiger' in the heat of battle, but Hassett would taunt him mischievously. If anything irritated O'Reilly more than being hit it was being edged for runs. One day when his length and flight worried Hassett into scratching several leg-breaks past slip he snapped, as the batsman ran to his end: 'Can't you get even one in the middle of the bat?'

Hassett: 'Don't need to with you, Tige.'

No bat, not even Bradman's, has indulged in such extremes of behaviour as Hassett's. As he awaits the bowler it slopes parallel with his right leg and rests on the line, beside his big toe. Defending, the bat often hangs lifelessly by his shins or is lifted just enough for the bottom to clear the ground as he pushes it forward to lean against the ball. He moves it a few inches for delicate placements. Suddenly the bat comes to life: It flashes up behind his head in backswing for a drive that rocks him up on his front toe in the follow-through; or it clips the ball off his bootlaces toward the leg boundary before the fieldsmen can interfere. On slow grounds it provocatively lofts shots over mid-off and mid-on in a way that alarms faint-hearted supporters. When used for a hook, Hassett's bat seems longer than other men's but it takes no longer to smite the ball; the best hook ever played off Lindwall's bumper was by him for Services in 1945 — clean as the parting in his hair.

Hassett's bat is most in character when it cuts. He lifts it and drops it on the ball, like the fall of an executioner's blade. On the village green of Titipu he would be the one to come in as Ko-Ko and cut all-rounder Pooh-Bah's most authoritative ball through the Mikado's legs into the orchestra. Cutting square, he chops the ball teasingly out of point's reach. Cutting late, he keeps the slips bending. He is the finest and most frequent cutter in postwar cricket, the only Australian with faith enough in the safety of the stroke to use it as soon as he comes in.

The first time Hassett's sense of duty put aside his normal batting methods, Melbourne barrackers passed from incredulous stares to hurt complaints. The crowd knew him as the finest player of a sporting family. At Geelong College he had been captain of cricket and football, 1931 tennis champion of Victorian Public Schools; he had scored a schoolboy record of 2191 runs in 41 innings (six hundreds) in his five years at the college. The crowd liked his enterprising stroke-play and quicksilver footwork, especially his dancing out to drive with a high grip which put taller men to shame. Australia's selectors were slow to recognize his fitness for Test cricket against Allen's English team. Worse, a temporary patch of failure in club matches had caused Victoria's selectors to leave him out of the State side for a couple of matches. (Perhaps I can be forgiven for recalling with satisfaction having taken them to task in big headlines for their lack of vision.) The aforementioned day when he first infuriated the barrackers came after his restoration. But in their indignation about the hours he occupied making about 80, they failed to give the 24-year-old batsman credit for selflessly camping at one end to keep O'Reilly out, thereby saving the match.

Scraping into the oddly-chosen Australian 16 Bradman took to England in 1938, Hassett soon proved himself the best of his country's newer batsmen. None of the five hundreds in his 1589 runs on the tour was as valuable as his 33 on the last day of the low-scoring Leeds Test. On a pitch where 10 English wickets had tumbled for 74 that day, the Australians needed 105 to win. England's hopes soared, rocket-like, when the opening pair fell for nine each and Bradman and McCabe were caught in the mid-teens. Captain and vice-captain could not watch the tense finish. They sat in the room while word was passed through the door from players on the balcony. Merely to stick at the wicket was difficult, much less score. Hassett blinked through the murky light and decided to race a gathering thunderstorm, sink or swim. With pageboy aplomb, he hit up 33 while only eight runs came from other sources. The patter of raindrops bustled his innings to a hurried end, but the storm held off long enough for wicketkeeper Barnett to strike off the winning runs.

In his first match as Test captain in 1949 he was off colour with tonsillitis when he came in at Johannesburg after both openers were out for ducks. With cubic centimetres of penicillin in his bloodstream he nimbly rallied his side with 112.

Rivalling Hassett's reputation for dependability in time of trouble was his name among cricketers for impishness. When a muddy goat's breathing and movement woke McCabe and O'Reilly in their room at Grindleford, in the Derbyshire hills, the guilt for smuggling it in was never sheeted home, but Hassett's sending a suit to the cleaners next morning was accepted as circumstantial evidence.

As captain of the AIF team in Palestine and Egypt and of the Services' XI in England and India, Hassett left loyal friends and grinning acquaintances in many lands. He joked about himself, lamenting the need for a bucket to eke out his height on interesting occasions.

There is something incongruous in the sight of husky bowlers going on and off at the behest of the smallest man on the ground, and fieldsmen trotting about at his direction. Without looking around, he would signal an outfielder behind him to a different spot with an inconspicuous motion, as if brushing dust from his sharply-creased trousers. An exception was a match at Lahore, where an all-rounder took a few wickets, became indisposed in the heat and retired from the field. After missing him in the hottest part of the day his team-mates saw him reappear late in the afternoon. Hassett ceremoniously waved him to the right, then a little to the left, then motioned him backward — until the fielder found he had been waved back out the gate.

Before Bradman re-entered cricket after the war and Miller came to the fore, Ponsford was one of several good judges who ranked Hassett Australia's best batsman, just ahead of Barnes. Others fancied Barnes or bracketed the pair, with Brown close up.

The little Victorian with an appetite for oysters and half-volleys was the tenth Australian to pass 40 centuries in first-class cricket and the eighth to score seven hundreds on a tour of Britain. He and Macartney are the only two who twice made three consecutive hundreds on tour. In South Africa in 1950 he took his career total past 12,400 for 227 innings in first-class cricket. Admiring his stroke-play, South Africa's captain, Nourse, said: 'I imagine that if Hassett desired to concentrate on making centuries they would simply flow from his bat.'

Hassett's sense of duty impelled him in several Test Matches after the war to stick faithfully to the course laid down for the team, though it meant giving up his natural style of play and brought him a blasting from barrackers and critics. At those times he forfeited the crowd's goodwill, earned by other innings. In his first Test in Australia, 1946, he came in when two wickets had gone for 46, to see Bradman edging the ball disquietingly and spared at 28 by disallowance of a slip catch off Voce. Hassett consecrated himself to the task of holding one end safe and husbanding the strength of his partner, who was not fully fit and sometimes limped. He played this supporting role so thoroughly in a record Australian third-wicket partnership of 276 that Duckworth described him as the rock on which Australia's innings of 645 was built. But Hassett screwed himself down so tightly that he was unable to undo the screws and let himself out.

'Have a go, Lindsay!' the sun-grilled Brisbane barrackers chorused. One with less patience and patriotism bawled: 'Have a go, you mug!' When the scoreboard mistakenly credited a single by the vice-captain to his partner the crowd argued among themselves as if it was a meeting of the Foreign Ministers. At lunch on the second day Hassett ate his cold beef and salad with the knowledge that after 5½ hours' batting he still needed two runs for 100. He laboured 6½ hours for 128 before Yardley caught him smartly at mid-on.

Most significant was the way this enchained Hassett played the slowish googly bowling of Wright, who made the going harder for him with jumping top-spinners and wrong 'uns, thereby exposing him to the risk of being chest-before-wicket. Hassett remained in captivity in most of his Test innings against the Kent spin bowler, yet played him with more freedom in other innings when, as captain of Victoria, responsibility for batting strategy rested on his shoulders. In the Adelaide Test, Fate again timed his entry for Australia's most trying moment. Two were out for 15 (Mervyn Harvey 12, Bradman 0) in reply to England's 460. The captain's failure to score led a few critics to suggest that he was unwise to go in only 20 minutes before the day's end, but I thought such criticism was not justified. With the wicket bathed in sunshine, the light was excellent, the pitch was easy and better conditions could not be imagined. In the feverish atmosphere after Bradman's downfall Hassett came in to weather England's keyed-up attack in the last 10 minutes of the Saturday.

As he set off on the long chase on the third day I was sorry to see responsibility for getting Australia out of trouble descend on him again, because of the danger that if he were called on too often for shut-teeth methods his Test batting would become prematurely bowed with care. Cardus took a long look, then wrote: 'Yardley appealed for leg before when Hassett had somehow made 22 in 80 minutes. Hassett clearly was legally not out, but he deserved to be; the sight of a cricketer of his gifts continuing to deny his eye and technique in a Test Match was enough to make any umpire go mad and, like the judge in Chesterton's story, administer justice instead of law.'

The crowd did not spare him. A barracker shouted to umpire Borwick: 'Give him out!' Another commanded his batting partner, Morris: 'Run him out!' Even when he unwound to swing a no-ball from Bedser over the leg fence for six the chief spokesman for the Mound crowd was not mollified and soon croaked hoarsely: 'Have a go, Hassett!'

He stayed there 3¾ hours for 78. The contrast between that loyal vigil and his batting in other matches caused ex-captain Woodfull, never a frivolous performer himself, to suggest that Hassett was ranking Test cricket unnecessarily high. In between, he whipped up 200 at 50 runs an hour for Victoria against Queensland. He scored at the same lively rate in his 190 (22 fours and a six) against the NSW attack, headed by Lindwall, Toshack and Pettiford — a fighting innings while no other Victorian reached 45.

In his highest Test innings, 198 not out against India in 1948, his stroke-play charmed the Adelaide crowd. Yet after England's downfall for 165 in the Nottingham Test, 1948, he again dutifully disciplined his bat to fall in with Bradman's passive strategy on that curious second day. The Englishmen's imposition of run-saving field-placing and bowling was accepted so resignedly that the crowd protestingly clapped every defensive push and cheered when a ball went past Bradman for one bye. In that innings Hassett batted almost six hours for 137 and stayed around until Australia was more than 300 ahead. He enjoyed himself more on the last afternoon of the match, pointing out to his partner dark clouds sweeping toward Trent Bridge, and using six times an over strokes he had guardedly released six times an hour in the first innings.

His average of 74 in Britain in 1948 has been surpassed by only two Australians, Bradman and Ponsford. One of the seven hundreds in his 1563 runs on the tour was 110 against Surrey in an innings when Barnes scored 176, Morris 65 and Bradman 146. Surrey fieldsmen ranked Hassett's as the smoothest innings of the match. His batting is run by a jewelled movement, and nobody makes the art look so easy as Hassett when, in top form, he scores a run a minute without sign of hurry.

Always a neat figure in the field, Hassett has been one of the surest in the game; he was Australia's finest fieldsman in the 1946–7 Tests. Close to the ground, he runs down the ball with scurrying feet.

He is apt to give a running batsman a scare by unexpectedly throwing to the end he isn't looking at. Yet when Lindwall knocked Compton's bat to the ground at the Oval, and Denis fumbled for it instead of responding to his partner's call for a run, Hassett withheld his throw from the gully until Compton was safely on his way. That chivalrous pause underlined that Hassett lacked the killer instinct which, some say, is necessary for reaching the top. When a ball from Lindwall at Port Elizabeth struck Ray Connell (Eastern Province) behind the ear and cannoned to the wicket, dislodging a bail, the batsman was legally out, but no appeal was uttered; from the covers Hassett gave a cue to Johnson to move quietly from first slip and replace the bail.

Hassett was nearly 35 before I saw him drop a catch. Then he spilled two in one afternoon of a Test at Manchester — high hooks to long leg by Washbrook off Lindwall. Next the little culprit took the helmet of a policeman patrolling the boundary and held it upside-down in front of him to show what he needed.

When Hardstaff, close to the first hundred against the 1948 Australians, stole a single in the nineties from a pat near the pitch, wicketkeeper Tallon tore off his glove and tried to throw him out at the bowler's end. Almost simultaneously Hassett darted in, whipped up the glove and returned it right over the bails to Lindwall, who had run to the keeper's end.

His humour as a batsman was inaudible to the crowd and mostly invisible. An exception: if an off-theory ball pitched safely distant from the stumps on a length too good for punishment he would remain in his original stance, not a muscle of his poker face moving, as if still waiting for the bowler to deliver the ball. That poker face has been an asset to him as skipper. In one of the nine matches in which he took over the captaincy in Britain in 1948, Hampshire, led by urbane Desmond Eagar, gained a lead of 78 by bundling the Australians out for 117. They felt the odds were against them when they reached the ground for the last day on a pitch saturated by rain the preceding afternoon. A battle of wits began immediately. Eagar told Hassett he thought the ground would be fit for play on time. Instead of stalling for time with a disagreement, which would have revealed that the Australians were worried, Hassett replied instantly: 'That'll do me,' without bothering to inspect the turf. Eagar wisely did not have the wicket rolled, so as to avoid squeezing the water to the surface and hastening drying. Hassett's air of confidence led Eagar to believe that, against such redoubtable opponents, it would be more important for Hampshire to increase its lead to 180 or 200, before declaring the innings closed, than to hit out and get them in quickly while the wicket was most difficult.

By the time five Hampshire wickets had gone for 45, making their lead 123, the situation looked so ominous to Hassett that he thought the Australians' only hope was to keep Hampshire batting until the pitch improved. The problem was to achieve this without letting Eagar suspect the ruse and counter it by closing the innings. Miller and the left-handed Johnston played their part cleverly by bowling many balls short enough to be off the length which would have been most awkward on the moist turf. Hassett gradually edged his infielders away to positions where they could save runs instead of quickening the fall of wickets. When a four to long-on gave him a pretext for banishing Johnston's second slip to the outfield Hampshire players thought it strange; only fear of taking the all-conquering Australians too cheaply prevented them from seeing through Hassett's stratagem. Two and a quarter hours of the pre-lunch session had passed before his men had to bat on the drying pitch. After lunch it had hardened enough for Brown, Ian Johnson and Hassett to win the match by a misleading margin.

With similar ruses on another rain-damaged wicket at Durban in 1950, Hassett and his bowlers gained breathing space for the Australians when they should have gone down for the first time since the war. Though their first innings of 75 left them 236 behind South Africa they schemed and battled through to win with five wickets to spare.

Hassett has never been one to lie awake at night ruminating on past tactics and scheming new. He treats cricket as a game, not a military campaign. He has brought a calm and penetrating mind to each match's problems and met them with a practical and observant cricketer's commonsense. His fostering of left-handed Johnston as an around-the-wicket spin bowler was the most far-reaching single piece of captaincy on the 1948 tour. In the most important of all requirements of captaincy — bringing the best out of his players — he has earned full marks. He has the uncommon capacity to remain one of the boys yet lead his team with unstarched dignity.

In making decisions based on his own intuition Hassett has never been deterred by misgivings about the consequences if the luck of the game spoils his plans. On wickets he estimated would help bowlers he sent opponents in more often than any other captain in Australian first-class cricket since World War II. Slowness of the Board of Control to award him captaincy of Australia was not because the venerable members feared anything unorthodox in his captaincy but because they failed to measure the value of his frank and puckish personality. Despite his success as skipper of the Services, only one of the 13 board members voted for him as leader of the Australians 1946 tour of New Zealand. Next season, when Bradman reappeared as captain, Hassett became vice-captain only because a thumb injury put

W. A. Brown out of action. No team could have a greater deputy-skipper than the Australians in England in 1948. With Bradman (never much of a mixer) absorbed by the duties and interests of an active businessman-captain, Hassett never spared himself in keeping the side ticking over as a companionable party.

Yet in the Board of Control's telegraphic ballot to appoint Australia's captain for the 1949–50 tour of South Africa, I believe it took the last telegram to elect him and save the Board from an act of disgusting ingratitude. That counts for little beside the fact that, wherever cricket has taken him about the world, Lindsay Hassett has left people feeling a little warmer toward Australians than before.

11 Guided Missiles

Ray Lindwall's fast bowling changed the look of international cricket and the expression on a thousand batsmen's faces. When this loose-flannelled genius of the crease entered the Test arena he was the only speedman in sight. No other country had one. Lindwall's example was as a spark to tinder. He had the distinction of restoring a neglected art to its place in the forefront of Test cricket's excitements. Before his career ended, four countries had bowlers too quick for batsmen's peace of mind.

In a spacecraft age we have grown used to speed, which is more than could be said of batsmen who faced Lindwall. None could ever say, paraphrasing *My Fair Lady*, that they had grown accustomed to his pace. Lindwall had more paces than they could keep up with. Between the extremes of a fearsome bouncer and a late outswinger, he tried to keep batsmen guessing all the while. Hundreds guessed wrongly, if they had time to guess at all.

For a half-dozen years before Trueman trod a Test field Lindwall reigned as the world's No. 1 fast bowler, a matchwinner through a period of Australian dominance in international cricket. In those years before he passed his zenith he played in 36 Test Matches, helped win 26 and was on the losing side only three times. Batsmen have since seen, if that is the word, the ball hurtle faster from the hands of Tyson, Hall and Lillee — fractionally yet frighteningly faster — but their awesome presence did not confer on their teams such

(Above) Sid Barnes with Don Bradman during the 1938 England tour. Out of action with a wrist injury, Barnes became an expert amateur film-maker

(Above) Don Bradman

(Below) Lindsay Hassett

(Below) Ray Lindwall

Keith Miller

Bert Sutcliffe, New Zealand's greatest batsman

Martin Donnelly

Frank Worrell

redoubtability as the sides which had Lindwall from 1946 to 1952. With Miller sharing the new ball and Bradman making hundreds in six of those Tests, it was like a conjunction of Mars, Jupiter and Saturn.

As one who saw Lindwall take his first English Test wicket (Sir Leonard Hutton in 1946) his last (Roy Swetman in 1959) and most of those against six countries in between, watching him deliver thousands of balls etched his exemplary approach on my memory. The mind's eye sees a sandy-haired player of Swedish-Irish extraction almost 180 cm (5 ft 11 in.) tall. His step is short, making the least possible call on muscle and sinew until all-out effort is needed. The batsman sees him swivel his arms, mark time with high-raised knees and flex his hamstrings by dragging each boot-heel up behind him — loosening exercises begun by jogging in the dressing room. Sweater to umpire, and he turns at the windward end to pace out a 16 metre (18 yard) run-up. He licks his first two fingers before placing them on the glossy ball.

Anxiously, the striker watches him move from two walking steps into the 13 running strides which form a model of accelerating approach. On the twelfth stride a high-leading left arm sets the line for a side-on delivery, with his back arched. Body momentum tows his arm over and a flick of the wrist propels the ball on its destructive way. The sight of that rhythmic approach made Sir Pelham Warner exclaim: 'Poetry!' Lindwall's artistry might make it look almost effortless but his own lungs, limbs, groin and back told him differently. As Leslie Barlow showed a Test film, I sat beside Ray, watching him bowl an eight-ball over on the screen. As he saw himself running up, he muttered, rather surprised, 'I don't look tired!'

Though influenced as a schoolboy by having seen Larwood bowl, Lindwall gathered speed more gradually and took one stride fewer. Instead of grounding his right boot parallel with the crease he pointed its plate-guarded toecap ahead. The plate scraped furrows across the line. His follow-through carried him aside quickly, so he seldom caused complaints about roughening the pitch. In his book, *Flying Stumps*, he tells how he tried to act on well-meant advice that he should bring his right arm over at a higher angle than his habitual one, about 30 degrees from perpendicular. It made a side-on body position uncomfortable so, after consulting the oracular O'Reilly, he stuck to his natural method. Whereas Miller's high-handed bouncer frequently sailed overhead, batsmen felt Lindwall's bumper was boring at their throats. Hutton, who ranked him first among bowlers he faced, found him hardest of all to sight, because the backdrop behind his hand was often the umpire, rising from a stoop.

An inauspicious day for batsmen was 3 October 1921, birthday of Raymond Russell Lindwall at Mascot, between Botany Bay and Sydney Harbour. From Marist Brothers' College, Kogarah, Ray went on to the Brothers' High School, Darlinghurst. There he became captain of cricket and football and was champion athlete. He would play in a boys' team on Saturday morning, then pedal his bicycle breathlessly to play in a man's match after lunch — all in a renowned sporting district, St George. A few weeks after he turned 20, New South Wales sent him to Brisbane for his first interstate match but a week later Japan's entry into the war ended first-class cricket in Australia.

At 24 Lindwall emerged from Army service in New Guinea and the Pacific Islands. Atebrin tablets gradually cleared up after-effects of tropical fevers but throughout his career he was plagued by dermatitis in a place subject to chafing. His twelfth first-class match was a Test at Wellington, NZ, in 1946. At Christchurch a bruised left-hander, Jack Smith, suggested photographing a batsman in a crash helmet and sending it on to the next city as a hint on how to play Lindwall. To further his unfolding career Ray quit his job in a Sydney engineer's office because he could not get time off to play and practise. When he said, 'Fast bowling is the toughest job in sport — tougher even than Rugby League', Lindwall was speaking as an 80 kg (12 st. 8 lb.) fullback who had won State selection before giving up football to conserve his physical assets for cricket. He enjoyed golf but before each summer ran roads like a training boxer and exercised like a gymnast. Chickenpox interrupted the new fast bowler's onslaughts on England's first postwar tour of Australia but on Adelaide Oval he electrified 31,000 watchers by taking three wickets in four balls. Lindwall mowed down 7 for 63 in the first innings of the next Test in Sydney. In between, he sent a bail flying 43½ metres when he bowled Geoffery Noblet (South Australia). In taking 7 for 38 in India's second innings in Adelaide in 1948 he dealt out four ducks.

After the 1947 change sanctioning delivery with the back foot lifted, provided part of it was behind the line, a film showed that his right foot's drag across the crease carried him, sometimes, nearly a metre (3 ft) past the stumps before the ball left his hand. (Others were to go further.) A Sydney umpire Cyril Wigzell no-balled him for drag five times in three overs of an interstate match. Before a battery of cameras at Worcester in 1948, Ray's take-off 45 cm (18 inches) behind the crease was passed by the umpires, though English batsmen felt the mark-back should have been doubled. Delivering the last ball before tea on greasy turf in his first Test in England Lindwall pulled a muscle in the right groin. It left him permanently susceptible to strains in this ticklish region. By the third Test he was fully fit and bowled his swiftest overs in Britain in a dramatic clash with Compton and Edrich at Manchester.

Through postwar Britain, Lindwall left a trail of shaken nerves and shattered stumps. The effect on dressing room atmosphere can be judged from Yorkshire off-spinner Ellis Robinson's pantomime. Purporting to be the next man in, Ellis would begin pouring a drink of ale. 'Who's bowling, Ray Lindwall?' he would ask anxiously, his trembling hand rattling the bottle against the glass. 'What? Colin McCool ... ah!' and the rattling ceased as a steady hand finished the pouring.

But the rattling of stumps continued. Lindwall's most deadly spell was 5 wickets for 8 runs in 49 balls after lunch in the Oval Test. By taking 27 wickets in the five Tests he shared a then record for a fast bowler in a series in England. Praising Bradman for his captaincy, Ray said, 'Not once did Don keep me on for an extra over when I should have been given a rest'.

To prepare for Ray in 1949, some South African batsmen called in baseball pitchers at practice. More groin trouble and rising weight mostly saved their having to face him at his fastest. Running up at Port Elizabeth, Lindwall twice stopped when he saw Eastern Province opening batsman Ray Connell standing forward from his crease. 'Anything wrong?' he asked. Connell: 'I always stand in front of the crease to fast bowling.' Lindwall: 'Not to me you don't!' Soon a forehead-high bumper knocked Connell unconscious over his stumps. Walking to his captain, Ray spoke to Hassett, who signalled to slip-fielder Johnson to replace the bails. When Connell recovered he resumed his innings later in the day.

Still chary of imposing full-stretch strain on his groin, Lindwall 29, was alongside the non-striker, Dr George Thoms, in a pause in play at Melbourne. Thoms happened to say, 'It is only a few years since I was sitting in the stand, watching you hurl them down at full speed.' An incautious remark, worth adding to the list of famous last words! Three balls later Thoms' stumps were scattered by a ball he scarcely saw. The departing Victorian's philosophic comment: 'As I walked away, it was no use yelling back that I hadn't meant it that way.'

An umpire cautioned Miller for too many short-pitched balls in a Brisbane Test against the West Indies but two other umpires took no action in Sydney when West Indians said they counted 25 bouncers in 40 balls by Lindwall to Everton Weekes. In six overs 10 got up to shoulder-high or head-high, while an extra fielder reinforced the standard Australian quota of three leg-fieldsmen for fast bowling.

Lindwall always contended that, as Weekes continued trying to hook the fliers — against his captain's admonitions — he was justified in repeating them. O'Reilly believed the umpires should have intervened, although most of the offending balls flew over the middle and off stumps; the anti-intimidation law at that time specified balls 'at a batsman standing clear of his wicket'.

That match in 1952 and the Manchester instance in 1948 were the only times I saw Lindwall, in Tests, bounce three consecutive balls head-high to a batsman, but after surviving a fiery onslaught on a Sydney grasstop, Hassett, captaining Victoria, asked the umpire what was his definition of intimidation! After ducking, England's opener Hutton sometimes smiled — a smile like a man who has just escaped from under a moving train. Once Lindwall heard him mutter, 'Remember laad, one day we'll have a fasst bowler ... '

Twice bumpers struck batsmen full in the face: Gordon Woolmer, who attempted a hook while batting for The Rest of NSW in 1947, and opening batsman Jack Robertson, who tried to duck in Middlesex's second innings in 1948. Neither took any further part in the match. Ray told me afterwards, 'The sight of their injuries, bruised and swollen, upset me so much I could hardly sleep. On a later visit to England, Robertson asked me to broadcast with him and told listeners I was one of his greatest friends. I'm not sure Jack's wife has forgiven me, though.' The ball that gashed Compton between the eyes at Manchester glanced up from an attempted hook. No inventory was kept of bruised torsos. The dreaded speedman did not seem to mind being nicknamed 'Killer' saying, 'There's no sitting duck like a scared duck.'

Lindwall's £1300 fee for six months with Nelson in 1952 set a new high level for the Lancashire League. There he added an indipper to his armoury. On his second tour of Britain sponsors of a smaller ball invited the great bowler to Lord's to try it. By making it swing excessively either way, to pick off whichever stump he nominated, he caused the project to be dropped.

After Lindwall's first appearance before television cameras, a woman lip-reader wrote asking him to moderate his language on the field. She had seen him, so she said, make remarks after an umpire rejected his lbw appeal. In apologizing, Ray added a rider that such vocabulary was unbecoming to a gentlewoman! After he yorked Reg Simpson, first ball, in a Brisbane Test a writer asked how long Simpson batted. The scorer: 'One minute.' When Ray heard of that, his dry comment was 'Slowest ball I ever bowled!'

His response to calls on his stamina deepened admiration for his fitness and team spirit. In a desperate attempt to prevent England regaining the Ashes at the Oval in 1953 he bowled 13 overs before lunch on the last day, 11 of them on the trot.

Tyson and Statham ousted him from the centre of the stage in 1954. The contrast in speed was heightened because Lindwall was affected by hepatitis which kept him below his best during three years of enforced teetotalism.

No fast bowler had lasted long enough in Test cricket to reach 100 wickets until he proved it could be done, at the age of 33 in his twenty-sixth Test. Lindwall's breaking the 100-wicket barrier was soon followed by fast bowlers of five countries: Miller, Johnston, Davidson and McKenzie of Australia, Statham, Trueman and Snow of England, Adcock and Pollock of South Africa, Hall of the West Indies and Motz of New Zealand. Proliferation, if you like. Twenty months after his hundredth victim, Lindwall's fifty-second Test brought his two hundredth wicket — a total which had been attained by only two men, Grimmett, a slow bowler with a six-step approach (216 wickets in 37 Tests) and Bedser, England's medium-pace giant who lumbered up nine strides to confound 236 batsmen in 51 Tests.

A Leeds Test brought a fine tribute to his fair play. A head-high leg-side full toss from Ian Johnson to May was swung downward behind square, where a sprawling Lindwall rolled over with the ball and held it up, claiming a catch. May naturally waited until the appeal was upheld. When his partner, Washbrook, came off at the day's end he asked Peter, 'Were you out?' May: 'I couldn't tell whether it carried to him but, knowing Lindwall ...'

Because newspaper articles about the tour appeared under his name before the side returned home, the Australian Board docked £50 from his good-conduct bonus. A plea that the infringement was a syndication error beyond his control failed to absolve him, though it probably averted a heavier penalty like the £100 imposed on Miller.

Cricket and his family life intertwined. Visiting Brisbane to play in a match Ray met a budding blonde model, Peggy Robinson, at a Slazenger party for golfer Bobby Locke. Their son, born in Manchester while the father was Nelson's professional, showed promise as a left-handed medium-pacer but pressure of law studies diverted him from cricket. A daughter, Carolyn, arrived in Brisbane while Ray was playing against the West Indies in Jamaica.

After his third tour of England, in 1956, his seven Indian wickets for 43 helped bring a win at Madras. Lindwall was 35 when he captained his country in a Test at Bombay. Weakened by injuries and illness, it was a scratch side but you'd never have thought so, seeing the way they responded to his inspiringly aggressive captaincy in the heat. The Brabourne Stadium wicket was too good to permit a finish. Ray recalls:

> The thing I remember most is being a captain without bowlers. Injuries kept Johnson, Miller and Archer out. Stomach trouble affected Davidson. Crawford strained a hip, Wilson pulled a muscle and a fever made Benaud too ill to bowl for part of the game. We had McDonald fielding as a substitute when he caught Ramchand for over 100. Burke and Harvey made centuries, enabling me to close with seven down and a good lead. Over 1000 runs were scored in the game but bowlers could not average five wickets a day.

The name Lindwall was missing from the Australian XI for two years. Determined not to accept eclipse, he pedalled a stationary training cycle on his lawn for half an hour each morning for three months. To correct a deviation from proper side-on delivery, he rigged up a pulley to help exercises restore his left arm to the desired elevation.

As a veteran of 37 with experience in 55 Tests, he was selected to play under a fourth captain, nine years his junior — Richie Benaud in his first season as skipper. A likely source of embarrassment, you might think, but sportsmanship and team spirit enabled them to accept the situation with reciprocal grace. In a group discussing a day's play in Adelaide, Benaud said, 'I couldn't do anything with Peter May.' Lindwall: 'You were instrumental in getting him out.' Richie, astonished: '*I* was instrumental .. ?' Ray: 'Yes, you made him over-confident.'

With his first ball of a Melbourne Test, Lindwall had Bailey caught by Davidson — at fourth slip, mind you. When he bowled Bailey for 0 in England's second innings he turned to wave to the woman guests' enclosure, where Peggy waved back; she had waited four days to see him lift the Australian Test record past leg-spinner Grimmett's total 216.

Though he continued pace bowling until four months past 38, still respected if no longer dreaded, this did not dilute his career striking-rate past 60 balls a wicket. Lindwall's last four tests in Pakistan and India lifted his total to 228 wickets, taken with 13,666 balls in 61 Tests. Among the 228 were 145 in the first six of the batting order, 67 of them opening batsmen. He bowled 103 men in Test Matches and skittled 14 Englishmen for 0. His expense rate was 38 runs per 100 balls. His 789 wickets in 224 first-class games are the most by any

Australian fast bowler for his country and State. I calculate that Ray ran more than 668 kilometres to bowling creases and walked a similar distance between balls. An all-rounder, he topped 1,500 runs in Tests and held 26 catches. His Melbourne 100 off English bowling in 1946 came in 113 minutes, aided by three chances. In Barbados he climbed out of a vinegar-and-water bath (a precaution against stiffness) to raise a ton in 145 minutes. Lindwall's control of the ball at speed has yet to be equalled. To the end he usually completed an eight-ball over inside four minutes — a credit to himself and a reflection on others.

A fall in a single-wicket match at 44 severely damaged his right knee. An operation next day averted the risk of permanent injury. He partnered his wife as a florist in Fortitude Valley, Brisbane. For such a warrior on the cricket field, a life amid sheaves, posies and blooms may seem rather incongruous until we remember how often he cut down the flower of England's batting.

12 The Master Miller

To young eyes, quickest to perceive the things that make cricket, Keith Miller is as an Olympian god among mortals. He brings boys' dreams to life. He is the cricketer they would all like to be, the one who can hit more gloriously and bowl faster than anybody on earth. When Neville Cardus called him a young eagle among crows and daws, Miller was not a champion playing out of his class; sharing the field with him were the elect of the world's two greatest cricketing countries, Bradman, Hammond and bearers of other famous names, Compton and other men of personality.

Since World War II Miller has made his mark on pavilion roofs across half the earth. He was not clear of his teens when the war began; before long it hid from view a youth from Melbourne High School who at 17 had scored 181 against Tasmania in his first innings in first-class cricket and, just twenty, overcame the difficulties of Grimmett's bowling in making 108 against South Australia in his fourth match in the Sheffield Shield competition.

As a Flying-Officer of twenty-five he gave up piloting Mosquitoes in 1945 to become the mainstay of the Australian Services' batting. As such, he seldom lifted the ball in the Victory Tests, but towards the end of the season he began coping with coping-stones and other upstair targets around English cricket fields. In his 185 for the Dominions he drove England's bowlers to seven spots among the

104

buildings enclosing Lord's ground.

The Times' own R. B. Vincent, discriminating and droll, began to wonder whether Lord's was a big enough ground for such terrific hitting. The first and farthest six crashed into the top-tier seats between the towers of the pavilion. Next morning one with less carry struck the southern tower, above the broadcasters' eyrie. They were among the highest blows Lord's pavilion had felt this century though they left intact the all-time record by an earlier exile from Victoria, Albert Trott, who in 1899 drove a ball over the hallowed edifice. Miller lifted his overnight total by 124 before lunch on the last day of the match. Only such an innings as his 185 could have won the game.

Even at tense moments in Test Matches he is as ready for a bit of fun as for a good ball or a sharp catch. When a bowler goes through an experimental run-up and delivery without the ball he promptly hooks an imaginary long-hop to the fence. The crowds share his enjoyment of cricket and he enjoys their presence. In a Test at Lord's he was in line to be third victim of a hat-trick; as the next ball struck his leg the crowd excitedly shouted: 'How's that?' Miller shook his head sorrowfully to the mass appealers, as if it grieved him to disappoint them. Onlookers are amused by his mimicry of the umpire signalling a wide against him, his drop-kicking the ball to the wicketkeeper after a running catch, his boyish exuberance in the scrambling horseplay for souvenir stumps at the end. No stage villain looks more melodramatic than Miller the bowler, staring at an umpire who refuses one of his whirling appeals. Once he toppled over backwards and appealed sitting on the pitch. When a bowler stops Miller's hard drive and menaces to throw him out, the tall batsman does not scamper back to the crease but holds up a stern hand, forbidding all tomfoolery.

Superb technique has enabled Miller to look for runs where others look for trouble. He blends with Melbourne forthrightness the allurements of style typical of Sydney, with a dash of Kent and Gloucestershire to bring out the full flavour. Watch him stride into the field, toes straight ahead but eyes looking about, following the fieldsmen's throwing to become accustomed to quick focusing in the outdoor light. At the wicket he takes in the positions of the backing-away fielders as he spins his bat upright with his left hand and stops it revolving with his right. Taking 'two legs' block, he marks the spot between middle and leg stumps by drawing a V back from the crease with two geometric strokes of his right toe. He adjusts his shirt-neck and smooths his long brown hair back with his left hand as he settles in his stance, the most easy and natural stance of all. In this he combines everything to produce dominating reach. His legs are straight but not taut, his body leans just enough for him to hold the bat comfortably. Comfortably and commandingly because Miller's hands clasp the handle high — as unwelcome a sight as bowlers and fieldsmen can see.

Miller's forward play is unrivalled in splendour. He is the grandest player of cricket's grandest stroke, the drive. Left shoulder and elbow lead his body in unison with the thrust of his left foot towards the ball. As a thermometer responds to the sun's warmth, the height of his backswing varies in accordance with his estimate of the ball's quality. If he judges it to be coming within range of his matchless drive his swing is as full as a six-footer can keep in control throughout its menacing arc; his hands extend back to neck-height and cocked wrists point the bat skyward. At the moment of impact straight arms transmit the energy of true-lined shoulders to whipping wrists. Usually the ball is close to his front pad before the bat smashes through and onwards in the direction the shot has taken. To put the kernel of his style in one sentence he wields the straightest bat with the greatest power. When Miller springs a stride or two forward both feet grip the pitch for the drive as firmly as when he advances only the front leg, and the purchase they obtain forces his knees inward.

His bowling has been chock-full of life and personality, and full of shocks for batsmen — some of them nasty shocks. He gathers momentum in a much shorter run than other fast bowlers, shorter than Wright takes for a slow-medium googly. Nine loose-jointed strides are usually enough, sometimes fewer. He is the only Test-class bowler with such a flexible approach, and the only one I have seen drop the ball as he ran, scoop it up and deliver it without a trace of the interruption. Once he bowled in odd boots, one size nine and a borrowed ten, because the stress of fast bowling had broken his own. After his short run Miller generates pace with such a convulsive body effort that it is a wonder his back and sides have not troubled him more often. His delivery is high-handed (in more senses than one), especially for his indipper. Not satisfied with late swerve either way, break-backs and a wide range of pace-changes, he rings in a leg-break or a round-armer now and again. Batsmen find it hard to understand Miller's bowling. Some of it is well over their heads.

We came to expect one like that whenever he was hit for four. That indignity stung the same combative streak in him as a bowler that a crisis did as a batsman (I preferred to see him hit the roof when he was batting). Tossing back his mane like a mettlesome colt with dilated nostrils, he would stride back, giving a hurrying clap to the fieldsman and thrusting out his hand to command a quick return, in eagerness to get at the batsman again. Rushing up, he would fling down a bumper that made the batsman duck penitently; or occasionally it would be an exaggerated full toss instead. For the most frequent bouncer in post-war cricket he seldom hit a batsman — the ball usually bounced too high — but such moments transformed him from hero to villain, and he has been hooted at Nottingham, Madras, Perth, Adelaide, Brisbane and other points east and west. How much of his apparent anger was simulated only those close at hand could tell. As he ran up Miller did not always look at the batsman, and once started to bowl without noticing that the umpire's arm barred his path because the striker was not ready. When he almost collided with it he changed in a flash from his bowling action to shake the umpire's outstretched hand. His personality abolishes the boundary and brings the crowd into the game with him.

13 A Pair of Southpaws

Youngest of the three sons of a farmer at Ngaruawahia, Martin Paterson Donnelly used to toddle around the Waikato province of New Zealand with his oldest cricketing brother, Harry. Martin knew all about runs before he went to school to learn about the other three Rs at Eltham and at New Plymouth High School.

In his last year at high school, the first Donnelly saw of English cricketers was the terrifying sight of Hopper Read rushing up to bowl for Errol Holmes's team against Taranaki. The waiting batsman could see the soles of Read's boots, all sprigs. Martin survived the onrush of the human harrow but was stranded when he swished at a slow ball that Jim Sims turned the wrong way. Between innings Joe Hardstaff gave the 18-year-old country boy this tip: 'If you have difficulty in picking the wrong 'un play down the wicket as far as you can with a dead bat so that the ball, if nicked, won't carry as far as slip. Do that and hang around and you'll soon find it.' Donnelly did that, and his 49 in the second innings saved Taranaki and staked his claim for the tour of England a year later.

When selection time came he was in poor form but the selectors must have been judges of quality, because they gave places to Donnelly, 19, and sturdy, right-handed Mervyn Wallace, 20. The two under-21 members of the team headed the batting, Wallace with 1641 runs and Donnelly with 1414.

Donnelly is the youngest New Zealander to have played in a Test

Match at Lord's. At 19 years 252 days he made his Test debut in the same match as Hutton, just 21, and the same year as Compton, 19 (seven months younger), and Washbrook, 22. Like Hutton, he began with 0. He tried to sweep the first ball from James Parks and was lbw when it drifted back. It might have been 0 and 0. When Verity bowled in the second innings with two short-leg fieldsmen Donnelly seemed almost mesmerized. A ball rolled from his bat but, instead of starting for his first run in Test cricket, he stood while his partner sprinted up the pitch calling: 'Run! Run! Run!'

Once that was over Donnelly was cool as the summit of Mount Cook. Coolness was needed, because only three wickets stood between New Zealand and defeat. One of them belonged to Jack Kerr, usually an opening batsman, whose chin had been gashed earlier in the game but who came in with two hours to go to save the match. To make sure he did not retreat from the first international fast bowler he had faced on a Test wicket, Donnelly stepped across to the off as Alf Gover delivered the ball. It worked, because the ball was seldom far enough up to find him out and his movement put him in position to hook. Donnelly watched all the bowlers closely for clues to their intentions. As Gover came up with his long run, all knees and elbows, Donnelly detected the shoulder movement that warned of a coming bouncer. It flew near his ears (the smallest in Test cricket) but the left-hander had already taken up position and he hooked hard. The ball grazed Hardstaff's curly hair at short leg before he could duck and reached the boundary before cold sweat came out on him.

The last over came with Kerr (38) and Donnelly (21) still there. With the match saved, the youngster exuberantly flashed a square-cut at the last ball and snicked it into Ames's gloves.

A few matches later Brian Sellers closed Yorkshire's innings at Leeds on the last morning with a lead of 348, leaving four hours for his effective bowlers — Bowes, Smailes, Verity, Robinson, Yardley and Turner — to dismiss NZ. The first six batsmen out went their careful ways for a total of 58 but Donnelly did not allow Yorkshire's strategy to put him off playing each ball as he saw it coming. After hitting 16 fours in 97 he noticed Bowes bring his arm down quicker, so stepped inside his crease looking for a short, rising ball to hook. Instead, it bounded through to hit the stumps. Donnelly had never made a hundred in a first-class match, so his captain, M. L. Page, exclaimed 'You silly young beggar . . .' and said he had a good mind to administer a painful form of torture with the six stumps, sharp end first.

For all that, Donnelly seemed to have saved the match, as only seven wickets were down at 6.30 p.m. But Sellers, chock-full of enterprise, claimed a country captain's right to an extra half-hour. To hasten the arrival of 200 runs and get a new ball Sellers bowled four balls past pained wicketkeeper Wood to the boundary for 16 byes. Given the new ball, Bowes and Smailes soon got two wickets but the last pair, wicketkeeper Eric Tindill and bowler Jack Cowie, were still there when the clock struck seven.

Clambering from a tank in Italy when the war ended, Donnelly flew to Britain, read history at Oxford for his Bachelor of Arts degree, scored six centuries for the University in his first season and became captain in his second. By playing rugger for England against Ireland (at centre-three-quarter instead of his usual position, stand-off half) he joined the few who have attained international rank in two sports.

As the only New Zealander (with a West Indian, a South African and eight Australians) in the Dominions XI which beat England in 1945 he played an innings of 133 which is remembered with Keith Miller's epic 185, a few weeks after the first atomic bomb was dropped on Japan. Next year he came to Lord's to make the pavilion ring in praise of his 142 for Oxford against Cambridge at almost 50 runs an hour. Next year even greater acclamation was earned by his even faster 162 not out for Gentlemen against Players, with its wind-up of 50 in 40 minutes. In his last Test at Lord's, in 1949, he set a record for NZ with a chanceless 206 (26 fours), fighting 3½ hours for the first 100, then exacting the last 106 from England's bowlers in an hour less. With those centuries for his University, the amateurs and his country he equalled the three-sided record of a larger left-hander, Percy Chapman, for Cambridge, the Gentlemen and England.

Because their Board of Control found it more profitable to invite teams from more distant lands, Australian crowds hardly set eyes on Donnelly. But after Courtauld's sent him to Australia he was invited by R. G. Menzies (whose appreciation of cricket is deeper than any hue in his I Zingari tie) to play for the Prime Minister's XI against the West Indies. On that morning in 1951 he charmed Canberra's lucky few thousand at tree-girt Manuka Oval and made them understand why England ranked Martin Donnelly as the finest left-hander of the day.

From Donnelly the baton in New Zealand's southpaw relay passed into the safe hands of Bert Sutcliffe, though sticklers for conventional batting regarded those hands as rather unsafe. This was not because of anything wrong with his strokes except his eagerness to play them. When Sutcliffe strode in to open the innings and began to hook in the first over, orthodox believers felt that he would soon be sent back to his pa (Maori for pavilion). Instead, he has stayed in to make and break more records than any other postwar batsman.

His team-mates have never shared custom-chained strangers' lack of faith but have always been surprised when he gets out. Batting with him, they have seen his freedom from characteristics which usually add fascination and risk to left-handers' play. Next to his enterprising outlook and footwork perhaps his most valuable attribute is that he is a left-hander batting like a right-hander, more difficult for bowlers than if he were a right-hander of equal skill. In all forward or back strokes requiring a straight bat Sutcliffe's blade goes up and down the line of the ball. The southpaw slash past point or through the covers is not evident, because he goes over with feet and body like a right-hander. Unlike Donnelly, whose starting position was more unconventional than his stroke-play, Sutcliffe has almost a classic side-on stance, leaning no more than is necessary to take a fairly high grip of the bat, which rests easily behind the left toecap of his rubber-soled boots.

His bearing strikes a note as happy as his fingers do from the piano at a sing-song or his guitar in train or dressing room as he accompanies himself in songs to suit all company. His disposition is cheerful and he is full of confidence without being unduly assertive. His whole attitude bespeaks his intention to get on with the game, not by biff-bang assault but by stroking the ball firmly. Despite the speed of his scoring this dapper batsman never looks as if he is forcing the pace.

Sutcliffe first handled a bat when he was too young to remember. 'Dad tells me he put a bat in my hand when I was three years old,' he said. This farseeing parent greatly admired that noble pillar of Yorkshire batting, Herbert Sutcliffe, but a premonition of the confusion that might result from two great cricketers having identical names caused the father to compromise and call his son plain Bert. Except for similarity in name and appetite for runs, Bert bears little resemblance to the brown-eyed, dark-haired English right-hander.

Bert comes from Dunedin in Otago province, about the last port of call before Antarctica. He was 13 when he made his first hundred at Takapuna Grammar School, 19 when he scored a thousand runs in a season for Parnell Seniors. After two years at Teachers' Training College he went to war. As Sergeant Sutcliffe he put up the highest score, 163, in the battle of El Alamein between an Empire side and a United Kingdom team — a sideline to the main contest in which Field Marshal Montgomery, in his own words, hit Rommel for six out of Egypt. Within two years of the war's end Sutcliffe made himself the first New Zealander to score two separate hundreds against a visiting MCC team, 197 and 128 for Otago at his first sight of Bedser, Voce, Pollard, Wright, Yardley and Edrich. The first innings was marred by two slip chances but at 96 he lifted Pollard over the fence for six.

When New Zealand toured Britain in 1949 he shattered the accepted doctrine about how innings ought to be opened. Early, he was caught a number of times when he did not connect properly with hooks but, like Harvey, he never lowered his colours. In height, 5 ft 8 in., weight, an athletic 10 st. 4 lb., southpaw stance and outlook he is like the Australian, and postwar cricket has been lucky to have two batsmen of such genius flourishing simultaneously. After playing against both, England's Freddie Brown ranked the New Zealander top left-hander. That, in my estimation, was tantamount to awarding him second place to Len Hutton among the world's batsmen. Sutcliffe hits more sixes than Harvey and for his size I doubt whether there has ever been a batsman who could land the ball over the fence so often.

The first morning Sutcliffe opened an innings in England, in Bradford's football weather, an early change brought on Ellis Robinson's off-spinners instead of Coxon's pace. Seeing a couple of balls pitch short Sutcliffe stepped back into position so smartly for hooks that, instead of being content with fours, he had time to swing them for six into the overcoats behind deep square leg. At practice his 6 ft 2 in. skipper, W. A. Hadlee, trained the bowling on Sutcliffe's leg-stump, which was exposed too often in the first six weeks until he adjusted his movement into the wicket.

He soon made himself an expert fieldsman at leg slip, a position most players regard as the most difficult in the field. In 29 matches he held 31 catches and many of them were taken there.

Like most people in Africa, India and the West Indies, few New Zealanders ever saw Bradman bat. Sutcliffe was disappointed at missing the sight by a couple of days when the NZ team passed through Sydney in 1949 and had to be content with meeting Sir Donald in mufti. Donnelly, so often Sutcliffe's partner in success, believes that had the Otago left-hander been an Englishman or Australian and enjoyed their greater opportunities he would have outstripped all rivals and have been almost another Bradman. How little patriotism has exaggerated here is shown by Bert's figures and Sir Donald's after the same number of innings:

	Innings	Not Out	Runs	Centuries
Bradman (1927–34)	166	15	9728	35
Sutcliffe (1944–54)	166	10	9540	29

A significant difference was that Bradman was not quite 26 when he played his 166th innings, whereas Sutcliffe was 31. As the first New Zealander to make two thousand on a tour of England, the left-hander amassed more in a season (2627) than any other visiting player except

Bradman (2960 in 1930). Sutcliffe's seven centuries on tour are a New
Zealand record and include the highest score for a Maori-lander
abroad, 243 against Essex. With 100 not out in the second innings
against Essex he made himself, at 25, the youngest cricketer to have
scored two separate centuries in a match four times. The only
batsmen who have done this more often, Hammond (seven times),
Hobbs (six) and Fry (five) played hundreds more innings. Hammond
made his fourth set of twin centuries at 30, Fry at 33, Herbert
Sutcliffe at 34, Hardinge at 35, Jessop at 37, Bradman at 39 and Perrin,
Hobbs, Hendren and Fishlock in the forties.

Sutcliffe holds the world's highest score by a left-hander in first-
class cricket, 385 for Otago against Canterbury at Christchurch in
1952, with three sixes and 46 fours. For 51 years the record had been
the 365 not out by Clem Hill for South Australia against New South
Wales at the age of 23. Like Hill, Sutcliffe made his triple-century at
the rate of 40 runs an hour. None of the other ten Otago players
reached 30. Sutcliffe and Don Taylor (later of Warwickshire) are the
only batsmen who have put up two double-century opening
partnerships in one match, 220 and 286 for Auckland against
Canterbury in 1948–49.

On his passing acquaintance with Australian wickets in 1954 he
was an instant and striking success. The New Zealanders played three
matches and Sutcliffe scored a century in each — 142 against Western
Australia, 149 against South Australia, 117 against Victoria. In
Melbourne they are still talking of the centuries by Sutcliffe and his
sturdy right-hand companion John Reid, with their refreshing
outlook on the art of batting. Only once before had a man made
hundreds in his first three matches in Australia — England's Jardine,
who had a rather different concept of how to use a bat. The New
Zealanders were then on their way home from South Africa, where
Sutcliffe topped their batting with 1155 at an average of 46. Louis
Duffus recorded that of 29 sixes by the team, 22 were hit by Sutcliffe
(14) and Reid (8). The pair scored four of the side's five centuries,
made more than one-third of the total runs and, apart from wicketkeeper Frank Mooney, held most catches (Sutcliffe 15, Reid 11). Reid
is the first cricketer to have scored a thousand runs and taken fifty
wickets in a South African season.

On this tour the youngest of New Zealand's five left-handers, John
Beck, 19, missed a Test century by the unluckiest margin, 99 run out,
and Lawrie Miller, 30, touched the lowest point in his cosmopolitan
career by making ducks in four consecutive Test innings in mid-
season. You'd have thought the New Zealanders would have avoided
Miller's bat like a leper's handshake but plump schoolteacher-batsman

Murray Chapple borrowed it to open the innings against Western Province. 'I want to see if it really works,' he said. Experimenter Chapple scored 33 runs before Clive van Ryneveld found a hole in it to trap him lbw.

After falling cheaply to Tayfield twice in the first Test, Sutcliffe dropped from No. 1 to No. 4 in the batting order. He stepped up from vice-captaincy to captain NZ for the last four matches after a ball broke a bone in one of Rabone's feet.

Only one bowler has been able to take the initiative away from Sutcliffe and make him give ground, even flinch. He is Neil Adcock, the South African fast bowler who is 6 ft 3 in. and towers over Sutcliffe like a lamp-post over a water-bubbler. The physical contrast does not overawe Sutcliffe — not even Bedser could do that. The first time Sutcliffe met the Transvaal terror several balls beat him but he courageously hooked bumpers off his collarbone. But after painful experiences on two lively Test wickets the New Zealander unashamedly admits that Adcock has troubled him more than any other bowler, including England and West Indies' best. Once Skipper Rabone, though knocked down himself, tried to shield the left-hander by sticking at the dangerous end, like another Woodfull, and bravely refusing singles.

Adcock and Sutcliffe were the central figures in the most sensational drama since Bodyline rocked the cricket world 21 years earlier. The chief difference was that the batsmen under fire from Adcock's bouncers were not tied to the stake by Jardine's ring of leg-fieldsmen.

The scene of the drama is Ellis Park, where half-mast flags mourn the death of 151 people in the Christmas Eve train disaster between Wellington and Auckland. At this Johannesburg ground a few years earlier Arthur Morris made his first 0 in big cricket and Australians facing the Springbok fast bowler Cuan McCarthy on a greentop were within an ace of losing their first three wickets without a run.

The pitch's hard surface has a thicker topcoat of grass on Boxing Day, 1953. It is the kind of wicket that adds yards to a bowler's speed, feet to his bounce and inches to his smile of exultation. The South Africans estimate it to be faster — though not by much — than the Sydney wicket on which Lindwall and Miller shot them out for 173. Meeting such a bowler on such turf for the first time in their lives throws New Zealanders into confusion. Quick-flying balls from Adcock bruise several batsmen. One is bowled off his ribs, two collapse beside the wicket and another, Miller, goes to hospital coughing up blood after a blow on the chest.

When Sutcliffe comes in after New Zealand's first two wickets have gone for nine there is no sign that his thoughts may be straying to his wife and toddlers Gary and Christine back in Dunedin. As usual his fair, curly head is capless. Immediately a ball from Adcock rears toward him he tries to flick it away. It strikes the side of his ducking head with a crack heard all around Ellis Park like a gunshot. Sutcliffe sinks to the turf, one hand pressed to his burst left ear. The other still clings to his bat.

In horrified silence the crowd of 22,000 watch first-aid attendants bring out a stretcher to remove him. Many fear that the blow has killed him. After five minutes Sutcliffe rises on staggering feet, waves aside the stretcher-bearers and is helped from the field by his captain. The ambulance takes him to hospital where he faints while the injury is being treated. An X-ray is taken and by the time he returns to Ellis Park in the afternoon six NZ wickets have gone for 82. Wicketkeeper Mooney hangs on, doggedly keeping the ball out for more than two hours and rubbing his bruises between overs. Though Adcock is resting after his deadly effort the New Zealanders hardly look like reaching the 122 needed to avoid having to follow on their innings.

The crowd shouts a hero's welcome as Sutcliffe reappears through the tunnel from the players' rooms deep in the stand. A pad of cotton-wool is strapped over his ear. To the fieldsmen he looks dazed. The first thing he does is clout a medium-paced ball for six. The ball's fall over the leg boundary sets the tempo for the most thrilling onslaught on Test bowling since McCabe took his hook and cover-drive into retirement.

Movement loosens Sutcliffe's ear-pad, so at 25 first-aid attendants go out to bandage his head. Looking like a warrior in a battle scene in the gallery of the Palace of Versailles, he saves the follow-on with three wickets to go.

New Zealand's need for runs becomes so urgent that Sutcliffe cannot be content to try for fours. The field's thick carpet of kikuyu takes the pace out of ground-strokes. So, if he can measure the ball quickly enough for a full-blooded stroke Sutcliffe goes the limit and smacks it over the wire fence. No slogging at everything, though. Sutcliffe the six-hitter remains Sutcliffe the batsman, his bandaged brow over the ball and a straight bat ready for anything demanding it.

That morning the team had left pace bowler R. W. Blair, 22, in his hotel room overcome by the tragic news that his fiancee, Nerissa Ann Love, 19, was killed in the railway disaster. They were to have married a few weeks after Blair, a linotype operator, returned to Wellington in March, 1954. So when the ninth wicket falls at 154 it looks like the end of the innings and the players begin to move toward the tunnel. But, with his team in a desperate plight, grief-stricken Bob Blair has come to Ellis Park to help if he can.

Amid a hush, he unexpectedly appears on the field. Walking to meet him, Sutcliffe puts a comforting arm around his bereaved mate's shoulders. As they go to the pitch together the crowd breaks the silence with prolonged applause.

The innings rushes to an end packed with excitement. Sutcliffe lifts his fourth, fifth and sixth sixes off Tayfield in one over. Thousands stand to roar appreciation of each stroke. Blair swings the off-spinner for another six to bring the cost of the over to 25. It is his only scoring stroke. The score leaps by 33 in ten minutes before Waite stumps Blair off Tayfield at 187.

Sutcliffe remains unconquered. Of New Zealand's 105 runs since his reappearance he has made 80, snatched from the torrent of disaster, with seven sixes and four fours. Johannesburg writer Vivian Granger's tribute: 'The greatest 80 ever made in Test cricket.'

Nobody doubts that. Until Sutcliffe played it, such an innings did not exist outside schoolboys' dreams.

14 First of his Race

The sun was declining toward the blue sea west of the reef-encircled island of Barbados, little changed from the days when Bridgetown's anchorage was filled with the tall masts of ships come to load the sugar and the cotton.

For its size, only 166 square miles — little larger than the Isle of Wight — Barbados produces a surprising quantity of the world's best rum, ginger and cricketers. About a mile along the coast from Bridgetown some of the cricketers were hard pressed on Kensington Oval by their great rivals who had flown in from Trinidad, at the southern end of the West Indies.

Shadows were lengthening as quickly as Barbadian faces as the third batsman fell with the score still 342 short of Trinidad's declared innings. A strongly-built man, John Goddard, strode in, his legs bulky with the pads, and set himself in a left-hand stance with the manner of one who would take shifting.

At the other end a slim dark youth of 19, a year out of school, seemed barely interested in the proceedings. Instead of moving aside when his partner drove a ball he languidly parted his feet just in time to let it through. His name, Frank Worrell, was already becoming known all around the slopes of Mount Hillaby. It was his sixth match for Barbados since he was chosen in the island's team as a 17-year-old left-arm bowler from Combermere Secondary School and was sent in as the tail-ender.

When he thought a run too risky he said: 'Naw!' In fact, to hear the Irish accents of Worrell and Goddard, a visitor could have imagined himself in Ballintogher instead of Barbados. The pair prevented further loss in the last ten minutes of the day. Morning brought another glorious day and Trinidad's bowlers returned to the task refreshed. A couple of hours later the freshness had worn off. With it went the hope that the lunch interval would break the batsmen's concentration.

Goddard's batting was forthright. No fine shades of meaning softened its bluntness. He drove half-volleys with noisy muscularity. His hooking of short balls was as full-bodied as the beverage he marketed in the Gold Braid bottles. Twice in his long innings he broke bats. Three times he nearly broke a fieldsman's fingers with shots too hard to be fairly called chances. Trinidad's bowlers found his defence proof against their best, in fact overproof. If a ball nearly got through, his bat came down on it like a falling bough.

When the strike changed, young Worrell looked as flexible as a palm frond. Swaying into position, he gave himself so much time to deal with each ball that his strokes had almost the guise of laziness, deceiving all except the fieldsmen who had to intercept his shots in the 5½ acre field. It is the same size as Lord's but white planks mark the boundary, as at the Oval.

On the easy wicket the fastest bowlers seemed to suit his strokes best — tall Lance Pierre, 6ft 2½in., and husky Prior Jones, 5ft 11½in., who looks like Paul Robeson without Lindy Lou. Cutting, driving, hooking and glancing, Worrell extended his punishment to all the bowling — Sealy's lively medium-pace swingers, burly Pouchet's left-hand spin and Stollmeyer's leg-breaks. Worrell's only error — a return chance to Stollmeyer at 104 — was caused by a well-flighted ball, not an exuberant shot in celebration of his 100.

Trinidad captain G. E. Gomez put every player on to bowl except wicketkeeper A. G. Ganteaume. When Tang Choon, the little Chinese, spun along his leg-breaks he was the twentieth bowler used in the match, something most men never see in a lifetime. Goddard passed his 100 and Worrell reached 200 ten minutes before time for drawing stumps. He acknowledged the applause by lifting his blue cap, with its crest of Britannia riding the waves. Excited barrackers ran on to the ground to congratulate the young Barbadian and prevented any more play that evening. The invasion relieved their feelings after standing all day, as most spectators have to do at Kensington Oval, though some sit on the grassy mound at the southern end, on either side of a wall 75 feet long which serves as a sightscreen.

On the fourth morning of the match — the pair's third day at the wicket — chattering masses streamed from Bridgetown along the road to the oval by buses, by cars, by hundreds of bicycles and on foot, disentangled with leisurely good humour by policemen in curved straw hats who could have stepped straight from the stage of *H.M.S. Pinafore.* Worrell's total mounted toward the record score for a Trinidad batsman in Barbados, Stollmeyer's 210 earlier in the match. Excitement rose faster. A man dropped dead from the sightscreen wall.

When Worrell topped Stollmeyer's 210 a Barbadian ran forward from the crowd holding a white object. At the wicket he presented it to his young compatriot. It was a large chicken, whether from his own henhouse or another's nobody knew or cared. As Worrell had to bat on, the donor held the chicken until he could take delivery later and make pelow with it — a tasty dish of chopped-up chicken with rice, almost rivalling the famous calaboo and crab.

Cheers swelled to a tumultuous roar as Worrell hit his twenty-fourth boundary and reached 300, youngest batsman ever to score a triple-century in a first-class match. His rate of scoring had gradually accelerated, the first 100 in 211 minutes, the second in 158 and the third in 135 minutes. Worrell was 308, Goddard 218 and the fourth-wicket partnership had reached 502 in 404 minutes when T. N. Peirce declared the Barbados innings closed with a lead of 160. Delirious barrackers carried the pair off shoulder-high. Their partnership beat the West Indian record for any wicket, 487 unfinished by George Headley, aged 22, and bow-legged Clarence Passailaigue for Jamaica's sixth wicket against Lord Tennyson's English team in 1932. The only higher West Indian score than Worrell's was the 344 not out by Headley, who astonished England's bowlers by showing that he could play the ball even later than Bradman.

The track worn by the teenagers Derek Sealey, Stollmeyer, Gomez, Barrow and Worrell has never become overgrown. At 17 years eight months Garfield Sobers, a slight left-handed Barbadian, took four English wickets in his first Test innings, at Kingston, Jamaica, in 1954. At 18, Jamaica's A. P. H. Scott bowled leg-breaks in a Test against India on the same ground. Bruce Pairaudeau, of British Guiana, who scored 115 against India in his first Test, and Trinidad's Ken Trestrail, of the 1950 team in England, both entered first-class cricket at 16.

Worrell's trail has led upward with very few dips. His total of runs must rival the pounds his mother, living in Brooklyn, New York, is reputed to have won in an Irish Sweep. Between breaking records for Radcliffe in the Central Lancashire League, he studied optical work at Manchester University. For the first Commonwealth XI in India his

223 not out at Cawnpore was top score of the rubber. For the second team he made himself the first ever to score 1,900 runs on a tour of India and Ceylon. His 285 is the highest innings Ceylon has seen.

In England in 1950 this sepia stroke-maker piled triumph on triumph. Worrell, Weekes and Walcott were respectfully named the W Formation. Twenty centuries came from their freely-swung bats and Weekes alone scored five double-centuries in his 2310 runs. In six Test innings Worrell made 539 runs, 31 more than Sir Donald Bradman in nine innings two years earlier. The pinnacle was reached in the Test at Nottingham. There, Worrell's 261 exceeded the highest individual scores made by England and Australia's greatest batsmen at Trent Bridge ground (until Compton's 278 against Pakistan in 1954). When Weekes came in to join Worrell he said: 'Frankie, my knee's not too good, so no short ones.' Together they hit 52 fours, besides Worrell's two sixes, in pillaging the bowling for 283 at a rate about 80 an hour.

Englishmen spoke of Worrell as the best batsman in the world, excepting Hutton on turning wickets. Bedser said Worrell and Weekes had no peers. Their successes were won by batting as colourful as an aurora but dazzling to English eyes accustomed to more restraint in leading Test batsmen. While relishing the brilliant spectacle, many Englishmen felt that this kind of batting could not possibly go on for long without disaster. Worrell and Weekes showed that it could, for men with the eye, the footwork and the confidence to act as if a good wicket was a place especially made for completely mastering bowlers, instead of the give-and-take of an even duel between ball and bat. Outdoing in certainty the efforts of many who prided themselves on safe methods, they exploded two theories that had grown on the game like moss. One was that, when a batsman was scoring fast, his partner's first duty was to hold the other end steady, not go for the bowling too. During a W Formation partnership hard-pressed bowlers were given no breather when the strike changed but had nowhere to turn, were allowed no peace at either end. The sleeping-partner theory which they disproved has been certified dead but it won't lie down.

The other mossy theory is that defensive batting against bowlers allowed to do their best is safer than judiciously carrying the fight to them to put them off their game. To the expostulation, 'But you can't do it in a Test Match!' Worrell and Weekes replied by going out and doing it. Like the Bradman whom England first knew and Compton and Miller in the mid-1940s, they could not force a lasting revision of the conservative conception of what constituted a risk in batting. But their play did much to give their country's cricket its greatest lift, because that team of Goddard's took back £35,000 to the Indies. The sounds since made by some cricket legislators suggest that they know that crowds will still pay to see cricket worth watching.

In Australia Worrell was tickled by the inconsistency of people who in one breath praised the West Indians' outlook on batting yet in the next clucked disapproval whenever a batsman lost his wicket to an attacking stroke, as must happen now and again. He would duck his crinkly-curly head with a chuckle or his even teeth would gleam white in a face the hue of fruit-and-nut chocolate as he laughed his high, mocking cackle. After one Test he hung a small noose and a razorblade inside the door of his team's room in the Sydney pavilion. Asked why, he drawled: 'With ahl the talk about our players committin' suicide at vital stages of a match, Ah've provided for anyone who wants to do the job properly.'

They are a wide-awake pair of personalities, Frankie and Shorty, though Worrell's heavy-lidded eyes close easily for a doze in the dressing room. Forty winks are as good as a hundred runs to him. Putting on his pads, he stretches himself on a bench. Barbadians reckon he could sleep on a block of ice. If he is still slumbering when the wicket falls mates rouse him, he splashes water on his eyes and walks out at sauntering pace to get accustomed to the light. He never asks the departing batsman what a bowler is doing. 'He prefers to find out for himself,' says Goddard, adding: 'He thinks he might get the wrong information.' However Worrell may doze in the room, he is never in a daze on the field, batting, bowling or catching. Others may catch him napping but not bowlers.

The 6ft Barbadian pulls on coffee-coloured gloves whose loose tops, held by elastic bands, look rather like bloomers around lean wrists that swing a bat with seemingly no more effort than he uses to play a calypso accompaniment or 'Galway Bay' on the piano. He looks well groomed in his cream flannels, though less dandified now that he is without his fashionable bow tie, American-cut suit, panama hat with gay pugaree, and smart shoes (which he hates cleaning and often buys a new pair to save the trouble). His expression is that of a man pleased with life and himself. After marking block with a precise toe he rubs his boots on the pitch, like a boxer's shoes in resin, then inclines into a relaxed stance. Below his gloves two inches or more of the handle show and the bottom of the bat rests in line with his right little toe, instead of behind the toecap, as with Weekes and Walcott. Worrell lifts the other toe jauntily for a moment but lowers it before the bowler delivers. After swaying his body back to add power to his square-cut he sometimes leapfrogs over his bat in starting to run.

When Worrell first came up against Australia's Lindwall, Miller and

Johnston it was in a Test Match at Brisbane, yet he whistled as he waited for them to attack him. The only whistling ever heard before when these three pace bowlers were in action was the sound the ball made as it flew past batsmen's ears. It was the first time he had seen high-speed bowling and the first bumper Lindwall bounced past his shoulder sent a visible shock through him. Worrell's response to most of the fliers bumped in his direction afterward was to try to score off them in his own original ways. These included stepping back for an uppercut over the slips' heads. It rarely connected and in one attempt the ball glanced off his glove for a catch by wicketkeeper Langley, who set a new Australian record with 21 wickets in the rubber.

Worrell's timing never became fully synchronized with the pace of Australian wickets, which did not play up to their reputations. After the Brisbane turf's unexpected slowness he was told at Melbourne: 'This is a really fast wicket.' He played forward through a ball from Ring as he would have on a fast wicket in the Indies, but was too early and spooned a catch to mid-on. After this second blow to his confidence he repeatedly checked the follow-through that used to be as full and true as Miller's and his bat sometimes came across the ball's course — two things it had not done before his seasons on the slow, turning wickets of Lancashire. As he played this check-shot the face of the blade shut like a half-closed door. It deflected the ball into his wicket four times in 10 Test innings, besides narrowing his driving to the segment between the bowler and mid-wicket, leaving coverpoint almost a bystander. Only occasionally was he recognizable as the beautiful straight driver whose shots bisected both corners of the pitch.

A fatalistic trait had revealed itself earlier in Worrell's remark after hours of practice under India's burning sun. He drawled: 'Why ahl this practice, man? It's ahl written in d'book whether Ah make a hundred or nothin'.' His fatalism was plumbed to the depths in Australia when an unlucky stretch culminated in Geoffrey Noblet dismissing him for 0 and 0 in Adelaide.

If Australia did not see Worrell in all his glory the Melbourne crowd admired his pluck as he made the first Test century for his team. Worrell came to the wicket before the match was half an hour old. Australia's fast bowlers were swinging the ball late and sometimes it pranced in the manner often seen on the Melbourne wicket on the first morning. With one that rose abruptly from a length Miller hit Worrell where the thumb joins the hand. Three more blows by Lindwall, Johnston and Ring's top-spinner made his right hand so painful that as he passed the forties he wincingly withdrew it from his bat while playing most balls. He survived two slip chances off attempted drives and by the time he reached the eighties he was steering the bat with the top hand only — something like a tennis left-hander's backhand. Yet in Lindwall's fourth over with a new ball he on-drove the fast bowler to the boundary with a one-handed pendulum swing, something any batsman using both hands would be pleased to do. His single-handed defensive prod edged the next ball into his stumps, ending at 108 a game innings that recalled Tennyson's epic stand against Australia's fast bowlers in 1921.

From the ground Worrell was driven to hospital, where an X-ray of his swollen right hand showed that he had been lucky enough to escape a fracture. As a persistent thigh injury hampered Weekes during the last four Test Matches and back trouble kept Walcott out of two of them, the mighty W Formation was reduced to a mere w formation (in fact, one inhospitable critic called them the Wobbly W's). They said they had never met such difficult bowling and never had to fight so hard for runs. In their total of 42 innings in first-class matches they fell directly to Australia's three-sided pace attack 19 times. Yet without another run West Indies would have beaten Australia, three Tests to two, but for fatal errors in the field — five dropped catches in the close Brisbane Test and agitated fumbling of a winning situation in the last hour at Melbourne.

Clyde Walcott, 6ft 1½in., has a punch like his world heavyweight namesake, Jersey Joe. In his deep voice, the olive-skinned giant modestly disclaims any right to be put on the same plane as Worrell and Weekes. In style, Walcott cannot be compared to either because of bent knees, a lowish grip for a tall man, a flourish in the back-lift and a habit of stepping a foot behind the blockhole, regardless of the kind of ball. Yet he is the greatest back-foot driver in the game, up on his toes exerting leverage as if the bat weighs like lead, his body curved like a tree in the wind as his 14 stone smashes the ball away, anywhere from past the bowler to wide of cover. His sixes smash chairs. Walcott knows only one answer to a bumper — a heaving hook. Taking in a new bat at Sydney, he left the paper band around it like a forgetful cigar-smoker. He had hardly begun denting its virgin blade when he was caught off his glove trying to hook a Miller bumper over the fence. On the occasions when Clyde Walcott rises indomitably over rough going his massive grandeur lifts him to a level which either of the more skilful members of the W Formation would be proud to attain.

Bowlers of other countries find it hard to credit that Everton Weekes had 16 innings in Australia without a century, in the light of his wonderful batting everywhere else he has played. First batsman in the world to score five Test centuries in a row, he has passed Headley as West Indies' heaviest scorer and holds the records for most runs in a rubber at home (716 in eight innings) and abroad (779 in seven innings in India). The fact is that the fibres of the main muscles in his right thigh were torn so severely that for most of the tour of Australia he could hardly walk upstairs. Yet West Indies felt they could not spare him, and yards of sticking plaster were used to patch him up. That curtailed this great batsman's footwork when he needed its full cat-like range to succeed on Australian turf with his low-grip style favouring square strokes across the ball's flight. The premature furrows in the bandy Barbadian's forehead probably grew deeper, though he never lost the sense of humour he had shown when a shipboard interviewer, striving to identify the team, asked: 'You are a batsman, Mr Weekes?' The double-century expert's non-committal answer: 'Believed to be.'

Weekes's addiction to hooking bumpers, even those high overhead, led Lindwall into the much-debated incident which helped to hasten revision of Law 46. The fast bowler flung along a dozen high-rising bumpers in six overs. Incidentally, he had four on-side fieldsmen, which I regard as the limit before bouncing becomes Bodyline. One was deep to catch a hook, another at short mid-on and two infielders crouched close.

Weekes stepped across and lashed at every one he received but his hook was a shade late each time. The sight and sound of Stollmeyer twice walking down and advising Weekes against attempting strokes at bumpers induced Lindwall to persist with them. The temptation to take advantage of the conflict between the batsman's habit and his captain's orders was too much for the fast bowler. He let fly a third consecutive bumper. Weekes, indecisive, finished by raising his bat to guard his head. The rearing ball hit his fingers and the handle in front of his face and glanced through to be caught by the wicketkeeper. Instead of the applause Australian crowds give a bowler at the end of a wicket-taking over, there was dead silence. O'Reilly contended that the umpires should have cautioned his old protege, Lindwall, for intimidation. With due deference to an opinion from such a quarter, I think the fast bowler kept within the law. Six bumpers in 16 balls were certainly 'persistent and systematic bowling of fast, short-pitched balls' but as nearly all pitched on the middle and off stumps, or outside, they were not 'directed at a batsman standing clear of his wicket,' so the umpires had no right to intervene under Law 46's unrealistic Note 4 on unfair play (since revised).

The justification of legality may be adequate, but no bowling which causes ill-feeling reflects credit on the side resorting to it. The West Indians made no public objections but private conversations showed it would be a gross error to mistake their restraint for condonation of that day's tactics.

When some other country finds fast bowlers capable of it, an innocent generation of Australian batsmen may suffer for the excess under Bradman's captaincy at Sydney, 1947, and Manchester, 1948, and under Hassett's at Sydney, 1952.

Isolated instances tend to be remembered as characteristic. In the islands in 1954 England's Fred Trueman bowled as if he believed the Australians had bounced the West Indians out of the rubber. Reports suggested that he set a pattern of bumper bowling and that the 6ft 2in. Barbadian, Frank King, taller, leaner and faster, was not averse to responding in kind. After gashing Laker's right eyebrow in the Trinidad Test, King included among his bumpers at Sabina Park, Jamaica, a burst of three in four balls and loosened Bailey's jaw on its hinges. With a new ball in West Indies' second innings Trueman, by all accounts, let fly ten bumpers in three six-ball overs — a terrorizing frequency which made the most intense Lindwall-Miller barrage seem restrained, if not abstemious. The first three were consecutive balls to Worrell, who took one on his back while some of the crowd hooted the bowler. Next over two more Trueman bumpers drove Worrell on to his back foot and one hit his glove. As Trueman pitched the next ball short, Worrell, expecting it to jump, lowered his bat and began to bend out of its way. Instead, the ball skidded through, hit the shoulder of the bat and finished in Graveney's hands for a slip catch. In the next nine balls Trueman let fly four bumpers at Walcott, who hooked at the lot with mixed, but not disastrous, results. Former Essex captain Charles Bray, of London's *Daily Herald*, said far too many bumpers were bowled by both sides. They would not have been permitted in England and he hoped the West Indies Board of Control would encourage and support its umpires to stop their use to such an extent. On the facts reported, if the umpires did not caution either fast bowler the explanation would seem to have been that suggested by E. W. Swanton in his book, *West Indian Adventure:* '... It seems too much to ask umpires to take the extreme step of forbidding the bowler to bowl again in the innings on their interpretation of the words "persistent and systematic". No bowler has been suspended in this way and it seems that some further clarification of the Law may be worth consideration.' West Indies Board of Control president Sir Errol dos Santos said at a reception to the English team: 'I regret that these days cricket resembles more a battle than friendly rivalry. I hope the authorities will take steps immediately to ban bumpers before some terrible accident occurs.'

On his way to Australia for the 1954–55 Tests, Hutton said he did not regard four fast short-pitched bouncers in an over as cricket.

Before the Australians were due in the West Indies in 1955 the W Formation had rebuilt their imposing edifice. In six hours of back-foot mastery at Queen's Park, Trinidad, Weekes scored his first Test double-century against England, 206, to be brilliantly caught by Bailey just when he looked like topping his 207 against India on the same jute matting wicket a year earlier. Worrell's 167 was the first Test century the Trinidad crowd had seen from him and once again he dragged a ball on to his wicket. Without reproducing the magnificence of their 283 at Nottingham the pair put on 338, a new record partnership for Tests between West Indies and England.

Coins glinted in the afternoon sun as the packed crowd tossed them into a sheet and three cricket bags carried around by members for a collection to recognize the record. It yielded £250 and the third member of the W Formation was admitted to a share when he weighed in with 124. It was the second time in two years that the three Ws had hoisted centuries in the same innings, as Worrell made 237, Weekes 109 and Walcott 118 against India at Kingston.

For Frank Worrell the Trinidad Test of 1954 brought a prouder moment to remember. The regular skipper, Stollmeyer, was injured and Worrell, a little more than ten years after he had been rewarded with a chicken, took over, first of his race to captain the West Indies.

15 The Man Behind the Centenary Test

Batsmen going to England usually hope to have boyhood daydreams fulfilled by scoring 100 in their first game. Sydney player Hugh Massie began the feat 95 years ago. Bill Woodfull opened it up in 1926 and Sir Donald Bradman repeated it on each of his four trips.

We hear much less about a rarer feat than an introductory 100, an Australian bowler taking a wicket with his first ball on English soil. It was achieved by Victorian fast-medium bowler Hans Ebeling, now adding to cricket history as the man who thought up the Centenary Test for Melbourne for 12 to 17 March 1977, 100 years after the first of all Test Matches.

Ebeling's career with Melbourne Cricket Club began when he was a 17-year-old Caulfield Grammar boy under Warwick Armstrong's captaincy. Forty years later he was a vice-president when a brainwave came to propose a Centenary Test. He put it to fellow Melbourne Cricket Club committeemen that they prompt the Victorian Cricket Association to approach the Australian Cricket Board.

People tended to be sceptical. It all seemed rather grandiose. They doubted that enough funds could be found to make it workable.

It would have taken more than that to discourage an ex-bowler who had striven for Bradman, Ponsford, Woodfull, Hammond and Leyland's wickets on the turf of the 1930s.

Ebeling found supporters, too, notably Victorian Cricket Association president W. J. Dowling. The board sent feelers to

England's Test and County Cricket Board. When a listed tour of South Africa for this year was replaced by a visit to India and Sri Lanka the Englishmen agreed to come on to Australia to play a warm-up game in Perth before the Centenary Test.

It happens that 1977 is a year of Victorian Cricket Association chairman Bob Parish's term as Board chairman. With Victoria's other Board delegates, Ray Steele (treasurer) and Len Maddocks and Victorian Cricket Association secretary David Richards, Hans has been co-opted, with Sir John Holland representing the State Government.

Hans' parallel idea of inviting remaining players of England v Australia Tests is followed up with extra enthusiasm because of the personal mateship involved. TAA fly the Australian veterans to Melbourne. Melbourne Hilton puts them all up. Qantas fly England's oldtimers here and back.

But back to Ebeling's first wicket feat. After fast bowler Tim Wall bowled the opening over of the 1934 tour captain Woodfull brought Ebeling on against the wind at Worcester.

A ripping indipper scattered Harold Gibbons' timberyard. Posters appeared on London streets: AUSSIE BOWLER'S WICKET FIRST BALL.

Ebeling was the nearest Australia got in the 1930s to Max Walker. A strongly built six-footer (1.8 metres), he ran up about the same distance and bowled the most intrusive indipper around. No tanglefoot skip in his follow-through, though.

Opening batsmen trying to allow for his inswing were bothered by a straight one he rang in to flick from the bat's outer edge to wicketkeeper or slips. To add to their problems Hans would deliver from the edge of the return crease to accentuate his indipper.

In county games the strapping Victorian picked off several of England's Test players — captain Bob Wyatt for 7, Charles Barnett for 1, Maurice Leyland for 43 and 27. He got Somerset opener Frank Lee (later a leading umpire) for one and at Lord's skittled Middlesex batsman Joe Hume for 0 in each innings. Hans' best innings figures were 5 for 38 against Derbyshire at Chesterfield.

Bill O'Reilly recalls: 'England's retired master batsman Jack Hobbs kept saying throughout the tour he could not understand why a team like ours did not have Ebeling in the Test side'.

Senior umpire Frank Chester had told Woodfull it was no use Ebeling asking for leg-before-wicket as he had no hope of getting one. The rule then required the ball to pitch in line with the stumps. Once a ball landed outside the off stump a batsman could pad up without a shot, unlike today.

I do not know how much the leading umpire's hint influenced Australia's captain. It contained an element of theorizing. More than half Hans' wickets on tour were out bowled.

Ebeling had to wait for his chance until final Test at the Oval, where he shared the new ball with Wall. He was rewarded by England's prize wicket when Walter Hammond, 15, tried to cut him and nicked a catch to wicketkeeper Bert Oldfield. Hans hit the stumps to get Gubby Allen 19 and Hedley Verity 19. His 3 wickets helped clinch the series.

Chosen in 1935 to tour South Africa, Ebeling had to withdraw for business reasons, a managership in a big oil company. Instead of opening the bowling with Ernie McCormick abroad he led Victoria at home.

Ebeling's next encounter with Wally Hammond came when the great Englishman was having a successful tour with Gubby Allen's Test side in 1936–37. Hammond made 107 in Perth, 104 and 136 against South Australia, 91 against New South Wales, and 231 not out in the Sydney Test.

For Victoria in February Hans tackled him with an attack headed by three pacemen, McCormick, Laurie Nash and himself.

With an indipper delivered from near the corner of the return crease, he deceived Hammond on 14 into shouldering arms from a ball that bowled him. Victoria's pacemen dismissed the Englishmen for 187 and there were mutterings about bumpers by Nash, the great South Melbourne footballer.

Because Australia's selection policy was seemingly to look for a younger opening bowler than 32, Ebeling's career for Victoria ended early in the 1937–38 season, though he was still getting good figures.

He bowled 9497 whole-hearted balls for his State in taking 109 wickets, in addition to his tour of England and Test trial matches.

Under his aggressive captaincy Victoria won the Sheffield Shield three years out of four. One of the opposing captains was Sir Donald Bradman (South Australia) in 1935–36.

Perhaps now, England has forgiven Ebeling for having got Wally Hammond out cheaply a couple of times!

16 Old Irongloves

In a long-suffering race — wicketkeepers — Rodney Marsh is the one whose activities have most in common with a railway-siding buffer and a box-kite. At the receiving end of Australia's high-speed battery, the solid West Australian has the tough physique and resilient spirit to stand up to bruising pressures without giving ground.

Since Jeff Thomson joined Dennis Lillee in using a new ball as a projectile, Marsh has the most stressful job of any international 'keeper I have seen. The range he has to cover is the widest. His leaps for bouncers are the highest, bordering on ethereal. His sprints up to the stumps to receive fieldsmen's returns are the longest. On the fastest wickets the bowlers' velocity has driven him up to 27 paces behind the sticks — further than Godfrey Evans stood for Frank Tyson in Australia.

Errant balls streaking down the leg-side make normal footwork inadequate. Before you can say Jeff Thomson, Rod launches himself at them with a horizontal heave. Nature has considerably cushioned his hips for landings.

Amid a busy sequence of matches in Australia last season Marsh's pummelled hands had to be rested from his State's match against MCC. Sometimes he tucked them under his armpits, much like a caned schoolboy trying to ease smarting palms. Watching Rod wind tape around each finger and pack his gloves with foam rubber, Greg Chappell asked, 'What's the date of your bout with Tony Mundine,

Bacchus?' This nickname is no hangover from days when Marsh was plump enough to have personified the Roman god of wine. When an interstate train stopped at a Victorian country station players saw the name MARSH in large letters. As the train moved they read its full name BACCHUS MARSH.

Born on 4 November 1947, Rodney William Marsh is five years younger than his tall brother Graham, whose golf earnings around the world dwarf the modest rewards international cricket yields. So that he could keep wicket for the WA University XI Rod entered an arts course. While a third-year student he scored 0 and 104 on his debut for WA against West Indies at 20, standing on the left-hand side of the bat. He is a right-hander in everything else.

To shed lard-like layers from a 15½ stone figure 5 ft 8½ in. tall, Marsh said, 'I gave up my favourite drink, beer, each winter, cut out potatoes and bread and trimmed lunch to three pieces of fruit.' Greater love hath no man than that he lay down his knife (and fork) to ascend in his chosen sport.

Choice of Marsh, 23, as Test 'keeper, replacing popular Brian Taber, 30, caused groans in Sydney, gasps in Brisbane (home city of John Maclean, 24) and glee in Perth. I assumed that selectors Sir Donald Bradman, Neil Harvey and Sam Loxton felt there was so little between leading 'keepers that they chose the one with most batting potential. Australia's youngest-ever 'keeper had kept in only 13 first-class games. Test-debut nervousness was heightened by his having felt almost a stranger in the team room. 'Except for Garth McKenzie, I hardly knew a soul,' he said, 'though I'd played against some of them once or twice.'

Rod held four catches in his first Test but three chances of sorts escaped from his podgy paws. Through John Snow's golf chum Guy Wolstenholme word came that the English XI had nicknamed Marsh 'Irongloves'. Guy and Peter Thomson ribbed Graham about his younger brother, for whom most critics could not find a good word. Rod's self-criticism was almost as harsh; feeling unworthy of the green cap, he left it in his locker and finished the Brisbane Test bareheaded.

'I felt worse for being shown up by Alan Knott, keeping like a dream,' he recalls. Knott was credited with the finest season ever by a visiting wicketkeeper — a star who made the semi-streamlined West Australian seem like a bit player. But a big heart and an unquenchable sense of humour brought Rod through without his nerve cracking. Recovery of confidence was symbolized by the green cap reappearing to shade his brown eyes.

Before he turned 25 Marsh rose to be a topliner. Lillee gratefully acknowledged his agile support. While England's batsmen could not pick Massie's either-way swing, Rod knew which way each ball would veer. His 23 wickets in five Tests in 1972 set a record for a series in England.

He had been 92 in a Melbourne Test when the innings was declared before he could make himself the first 'keeper to score 100 for Australia. One of Rod's philosophic comments: 'I might have got out at 99.'

In a hopeless situation at Old Trafford on his first visit the outplayed Australians were losing dismally. Marsh lifted their spirits with a valiant 91; four sixes sailed into the crowd in a few overs. Since that buccaneering onslaught the sight of Rod taking guard tends to give bowlers feelings like those of ancient mariners seeing a ship run the Jolly Roger to the masthead.

Two of his seven centuries were in Tests — 132 against New Zealand and 118 against Pakistan. His thunderous 236 for WA against the Pakistanis is the highest score by an Australian wicketkeeper in 93 years since Murdoch's 321 for NSW.

Stuart Surridge ranks Marsh 'the greatest 'keeper to pace bowling the world has seen'. As Surrey skipper, Surridge saw Don Tallon taking Lindwall and Miller. I have come across nothing to rival such a roundly-criticized cricketer's rapid rise to dynamic influence in a Test side. In discernment of potential it ranks as a selection masterpiece.

Untidily effective, Marsh has more important things to do than tuck his shirt in. By day's end his flannels often bear green and brown stains. His conversation has down-to-earth touches, too. Originally a high school teacher, he became a Swan Brewery market development executive.

No 'keeper had reached 50 wickets in an Australian summer until his 64 in 14 matches last season. Asked about his best catch, he reflected: 'Getting one glove to a far-out leg-side chance from Bevan Congdon off Tangles Walker in the 1974 Auckland Test.' It was Marsh's 100th wicket in 25 Tests. Only Wally Grout reached that figure in fewer Tests (24). Knott's 100th came in his 30th Test. Deryck Murray has 87 in 29 Tests for West Indies, Ken Wadsworth 85 in 30 for New Zealand and Farokh Engineer 82 in 42 Tests for India.

Marsh is at the heart, as well as the hub, of the out-cricket that has lifted Australia from the depths of 1971 to the heights of 1975. He means so much to the Australian XI that if he missed a Test through injury or illness, dismay would be felt across 3000 miles from Perth to Surfers Paradise.

17 A Mind of His Own

Players differ from each other much as trees do, elm from oak, bluegum from stringybark. Cricket's equivalent of arborists need no scoreboard to identify one international batsman from another. Build, gait, bearing and mannerisms are distinctive. To me, Greg Chappell is the game's poplar, upright in growth with little spread.

In his walk to the wicket, the erectness of his tall figure conveys confidence. His straight back has no ramrod stiffness. His steps look short for a man of his height: 185 cm (6 ft 1 in.).

What gives Greg Chappell's batting its slender elegance? Crowds relish his way of leaning into strokes like a poplar in wind. Drives rattle the base of the sightscreen or skim by mid-on and mid-wicket. He finishes strokes standing taller than most others of his time. Except when balls tend to prop, he plays fluently right through them; long-armed follow-through adds to the eye-appeal. Frequently the bat finishes pointing to the sky — a pointed hint to his average. His kind of average knows how to take a hint. It has a python-like capacity for digesting heavy meals. Greg's 380 runs in two courses which NZ chefs served at Wellington when he was 25 are the tallest total by anybody in one Test Match. No other Australian has twice made a hundred in each innings of a Test.

Martin and Jeanne Chappell's second son Gregory Stephen was born on 7 August 1948. Martin told me, 'Even as a kid Greg had the shot he whips away off his left hip instead of turning the ball as others do.' His build was in the Chappell mould, fairly solid, until at 15 he began shooting up past 6 ft while at Prince Alfred College. His spare frame took ten more years to reach 76 kg (12 st.).

Ian was touring South Africa when the Adelaide Oval scoreboard used his nameplate for Greg's first match for SA at 18. The youth's 53 and 62 not out gave him 115 for one dismissal.

Chappell first trod on a Sydney wicket after removal of tons of a midfield hump had lowered it by 45 cm (18 in.). While the pitch was convalescent after major surgery batsmen's scores were low, too. No visitor could get near 100 on it. Coming in fifth as SA sagged against Test bowlers Corling, Gleeson and Philpott, Greg topped the score, 68 not out. Impressed by his talent and temperament, I sought him out to discover more about a potential Test player and wish him well on his way to add lustre to the family name. A week later Greg scored 104 at Brisbane, his first State century in his seventh game at 18.

A second Chappell nameplate was painted when Greg, 19, and Ian appeared in the SA XI in 1967. Ability in crises continued to show up. Garth McKenzie had four wickets for 18 before Greg made 154 without a chance against WA. A batsman with new sideburns down his cheeks was learning the password to gain admittance to the upper circle of Test batsmen.

On the way, two seasons with Somerset advanced his game. Scoring 2500 runs on county tracks tightened his defence against balls deviating off the seam. As the John Player League's bottom club, Somerset looked least likely to have the first centurymaker in these 40-overs-a-side games. League leaders Surrey had one Somerset wicket for five when Chappell walked in to rip 100 off 35 overs in 88 minutes. Off 38 overs he lashed 128 not out.

In SA's second innings against NSW in the next season, Greg was not feeling well. As he went in with two out for 39 his parting remark was: 'There'll be a few shots played.' Fifteen of those shots pounded the pickets as Chappell ran away with 100 in 92 minutes.

With a recently dislocated thumb strapped, Greg Chappell made 129 and 156 not out against Queensland in Brisbane five months after turning 21, the youngest postwar player with a century in each innings in Australia. After examination disclosed an enlarged spleen and glandular fever I felt Sir Donald Bradman thought it better not to subject him to a heavy tour of India and South Africa. Instead, Greg exceeded 500 runs in seven games for another Australian team in NZ.

In SA's second innings against the Englishmen in 1970 Greg smote 102 off 100 balls in 118 minutes. Given a place at Perth in the second Test, he saw John Snow and Peter Lever get five out for 107 before he joined Ian Redpath in a double-century stand. One of the largest prime-viewing-hour audiences watched Chappell approaching 100. Suddenly the WACA ground was replaced on the screen by 7 o'clock news. The switch away from Chappell on 98 provoked the fattest bagful of protesting letters of the year. A century in his first Test innings at 22 prompted him to say, 'Maybe I'll be Greg Chappell from now on, not Ian's young brother or Victor Richardson's grandson.'

When Snow's bouncer felled Terry Jenner at Sydney, the ball rebounded from his skull to coverpoint. His hair matted with congealed blood, Jenner heard room-mate Greg say, 'There was a single in it,' in a tone regretting a lost opportunity.

As winners at Old Trafford in 1972, England shaped for another victory at Lord's by grabbing Australia's first two wickets for seven. Through six chanceless hours Greg kept out 301 balls, ever conscious of his side's dependence on his intact wicket, yet picking the right balls to hit 14 fours in 131. English praise was headed by Trevor Bailey calling his 131 the outstanding innings of the series. It was one of the best innings in any batsman's career.

In the final Test at the Oval, Arnold and Snow shot the openers out for 34 yet Greg tackled them with assurance. By contrast with Lord's, some 14 shots rapped the boundaries in three hours on his way to 100 in 190 minutes. He hit 17 fours in 113, again chanceless, of a 201 stand with Ian, the first instance of brothers making hundreds in the same Test.

Watching the first live telecast of a Test via satellite, Australians saw Greg play forward to a ball that rose abruptly to his throat. He dropped his bat and walked yards away. (To my questions later he replied, 'It didn't make me feel sick but it was hard to breathe for a while.') Batting on such a track was like Russian roulette. Scoreless overs made televiewers anxiously wonder whether the struggling Australians could get another run. To break the shackles, Chappell quick-stepped forward to lift Underwood over vacant mid-off to the fence.

His dry wit was enjoyed by the Australian Cricket Society's Newcastle branch. As guest speaker he began by recalling that, after a similar club night, one man told him it was the worst after-dinner speech he had ever heard. Told of this, the club president said soothingly, 'Don't worry, Greg — he's not worth bothering about. He just goes around saying what everyone else says.'

First Australian to score 1 000 in the West Indies, Chappell totalled 1 110 in 17 innings in 10 games.

Greg was nearing 25 when Channel 0 director Ronald Archer and other go-ahead Queenslanders lured him to Brisbane with an offer said to be worth at least $15,000 a year. Chappell made State captaincy an essential, and wicketkeeper John Maclean, a friend from their NZ tour, made way for him.

No man totalled 1000 in a season for Queensland until his 1178 in nine games, 1013 of them in eight Sheffield Shield matches. Only Greg and Barry Richards (1145 in 1970–1) had totted up 1000 in a Shield season in 18 years since Norman O'Neill added his name to a prewar pair, Ponsford and Bradman.

A cricketer's hours in public view are less than one-third of his day. Pressures in the other two-thirds can be greater than tense stretches on the field. In the most demanding of Greg's first eight years in first-class cricket, 1973–4, he underwent patchy health, floods fouling their Kenmore home, his wife losing her baby — it says much for his ability to apply his mind to the job in hand that he created a world Test record.

In a fraternal run-fiesta at Wellington, the Chappells became the only brothers with a hundred each in both innings of a Test. Ian 145 and 121, Greg 247 not out and 133. Their 646 topped even Ponsford's and Bradman's tallest united effort, 625 at the Oval in 1934.

Greg's 247 spurted from his bat at 40 runs an hour, imperious hours spangled with a six and 30 fours. His first 100 came off 160 balls, 47 balls fewer than Ian's 100. Passing Ken Barrington's 1763 Down Under in 1963, Greg set a record for an Australian with 1880 in 17 matches in both countries. He shared with Bradman the record of a century in each innings of four matches.

Throat and lung troubles required treatment throughout the 1974–5 series against England, yet as the straightest player in either side he scored most runs in the season, 1484, and made most catches in the Tests, 14. Ian would not call on him to bowl and Greg left early after each day's play to rest. Surgery to his tonsils threw him out of normal training. During a bad trot, his seven Test innings in England totalled 106, about as many runs as people expect of him in one day before the tea interval.

Coming in as prospective third victim in a hat-trick is scarcely a moment to begin a rapid century. Glamorgan left-hander Malcolm Nash sent back Alan Turner and Ian Chappell with two balls before Greg entered at Swansea. Yet Chappell made 100 off 77 balls. The 100 leapt on to the board in 66 minutes, seven minutes quicker than Bradman's fastest in England.

Autographs had led to Greg meeting an office equipment supplier's daughter in a Sydney suburb, Bexley. Judy Donaldson's sister Elizabeth wrote to Adelaide for signatures. Next time SA played in Sydney, tickets were given to the Donaldsons. Imagine the effect when Greg found Judy to be an exquisite green-eyed beauty. At 23 he travelled to Bexley to wed Judy, 21, in 1971.

After tours of England and West Indies, he was batting for Queensland in Sydney when he could not see her in the stand and learned that his wife was in hospital, having lost their first baby. She had not wanted him to know until the match was over. World Cup matches took him to England again three weeks before the birth of their first son. Stephen was three months old before his father saw him.

The slender pillar of Australia's batting plays most balls with broad-bladed style into the sector between mid-wicket and extra cover. His straight bat lulls his stumps into a sense of security. Adept at placing, he is Australia's finest cutter since Hassett. For shots across the line Greg awaits suitable balls ... well mostly. In his sweep he stays fairly upright, less likely to be caught than players going down on the back knee. Unlike Ian, he is no frequent hooker. Only a few of the swiftest bowlers have been too quick to let footwork put him in position for a safe hit by square leg. I thought him incapable of anything clumsy or ungraceful until, to escape decapitation by a steep Holding bouncer in Perth, he fell over backwards. Even then, it looked as if his spine were as flexible as whalebone.

Greg is a bowler's dream of a fieldsman. The hands at the ends of his long arms are so sure and his confidence in them so complete that the ball usually seems to fasten to them. His upward reach brings down everything except perhaps a homewarding angel. Batsmen think the way he picks up ankle-low slip chances is devilish. Seven catches against England in a Perth Test made him first to bring off so many in one Test.

Self-discipline yields when sportive impulse prompts Greg to try a backhand sweep, a crossed-wristed shot that smacks off balls down the gully. His eyes gleamed when he first saw Mushtaq Mohammad play this insolent shot at Northampton. It brings a laugh from everyone except the cheapened bowler and the startled slips. Chappell told me:

It's a shot for special occasions only. You wait for the right ball on the offside and you help it further. It scares sodomy out of the slips. I played it more in the West Indies where it really tickled and it got me out a couple of times. In Melbourne left-hander Ray Bright was bowling to a six-man off field to make scoring difficult when I tried it. Keith Stackpole caught the rising ball and I was given out. Bowlers probably hope I'll keep playing it.

When the national selectors named Greg Test captain at 27 he had played in 34 Tests in four countries. Nine hundreds were among his 2507 Test runs and he had caught 46 batsmen in addition to having taken 24 wickets as a medium-pace seamer who bowls better than a batsman should. As vice-captain in England he directed the Australians in five out of 14 games; his brother twice let him run the side in the field while Ian himself fielded. He had led Queensland to 11 wins in 21 games.

Greg lost his first toss to Lloyd six months after the 190 cm (6 ft 3 in) Guyanese led West Indies through India and Pakistan with success. Lloyd had won acclaim for his matchwinning part in the Prudential World Cup final, putting Australia down by 17 runs.

The ultimate in boyhood daydreams was fulfilled by the outstanding part Greg played in his first-up win as captain. Only two Australians before him had reached 100 the first time they batted as Test skippers, Noble in 1903 and Hassett in 1949. As partner watching him play Gibbs and googly left-hander Inshan Ali when Australia needed 219 on a worn Brisbane track, his brother saw him cope with their turn for two and a half hours. With frequent singles in his 74 not out Ian gave him two-thirds of the strike. Greg's respect for awkward turning balls was matched by power and placing of his strokes in his chanceless 109 not out off 172 balls. A panel voted him Man of the Match, first incoming Test captain to score a century in each innings.

Incoming batsmen invariably found him crowding them with close fieldsmen in the Benaud-Chappell manner. The sight of bold shots crossing untenanted outfields did not bustle him into switching infielders back from catching positions. Preferring to let batsmen try to hit over the top, he was rewarded with some prized wickets.

A 1902 penny, a two-up relic given Greg by Ray McRae of Seppelt's Vineyard, fell wrongly for his opponent in the last five tosses, whether Lloyd called tails or heads. In Adelaide Clive rumbled, 'Oh no, you're not using that ugly thing again!' Greg is the only Australian toss-winner who has won four Tests by sending opponents in. Two were in succession against the West Indies. No one else has sent opponents in six times.

The first time Greg captained Australia in Adelaide was a 40-overs game a few days after his team had been thrashed by an innings in the Perth Test. Without Thomson, Australia dismissed the World Cup conquerors for 224 in 37.6 overs in Adelaide then made 225 for five wickets off 31.5 overs. The effect of the reverse on the one-day champions became plainer when Australia avenged the Perth hiding by winning the next Test in Melbourne.

England's captain Tony Greig knew what to look for in sizing up a future opponent. He said:

> There comes a time when every captain has to prove to his players
> that he is a good leader. Greg Chappell did so in Melbourne by
> decision and example, though it couldn't have been easy after
> humiliating defeat in Perth. His 182 not out in Sydney was the
> finest crisis innings I have seen by a captain. For a side in trouble,
> with possible defeat ahead, he responded with confidence and
> dedication ...

For all their similarities Greg's dynamism is less positive than Ian's. He said: 'I think I'll be a bit tougher but I can't see myself cracking the whip.' Having a mind of his own showed up in several variations mattering enough to influence prospects. After a couple of Tests, Greg began amending field-settings that had served Australia well. 'West Indians are not like Englishmen standing there trying to exist,' he said. 'They are playing shots at our best balls. Rather than wait in slips for catches to come, we will have to use more strategy.' Among variations we saw a deepish point as well as gully to counter Fredericks' back-foot square-drive and adjustment of leg-outfielders brought three Test-swaying catches in Sydney.

To move Ian from first slip would have seemed sacrilegious until Greg swapped places. For Queensland, he found it easier to size up positions. Greg runs from slip to make suggestions to his bowlers more than any predecessor. We soon had evidences of readiness to scrap regular tactics.

After Gilmour's blazing 95 in Adelaide the West Indians began batting five minutes before lunch. Instead of Lillee with the breeze Chappell gave the ball to Gary to bowl into it, though he was limping. Greg chose the left-hander because his shorter run gave a possibility of starting another over. Gilmour's fifth-ball trapping of Fredericks crowned the move. In the second innings, rather than bat on to increase Australia's lead beyond 489, he declared with seven out because he wanted to get half an hour's bowling before lunch. Initiative was again rewarded when Lillee got Fredericks in his third over.

Confidence in his own judgement reached a peak when Greg reshaped the pace attack which had been the dominant element in Australia's climb to the top through 1972 to 1976. For 23 Tests before and after Lillee overcame back injury Ian always gave Dennis first use of the new ball, downwind. After pleurisy kept Lillee out of the Sydney Test, Greg bowled Gilmour and Thomson for ten overs in

Adelaide before calling on him. In the final Melbourne Test Thomson handled the ball first each time and in the second innings Lillee was first change into the breeze for the eighth over. It was rather like a Prime Minister being ushered into a secondary seat. Lillee missed a fresh ball's extra life but it did not show up in the averages. Compared with Thomson's 29 wickets in six Tests Lillee's 27 in five Tests fell to a quicker striking-rate, 39 balls to 42.

The captain was one of eight Test players who pedalled bicycles to the Melbourne ground past long queues on the day 85,596 watched a Test open. The ride was arranged by Lillee in his new job as promotions manager for Eurocars. Those wondering whether the captain should have taken part have little concept of the rally-around mateship that gives the Australians' team spirit such reality.

Chappell's third consecutive 1000-a-season in Australia yielded 1547 runs in 15 matches. Only Bradman, Harvey and South African left-hander Trevor Goddard have made more. Greg's Queenslanders carried off the 1976 Gillette cup. His closing gesture was to smite 28 off an over from Mallett.

He incurred well-founded criticism for not having told Marsh and Cosier to go for a win when the wicketkeeper and all-rounder's failure to attempt 56 in the last 15 overs let the Adelaide crowd and television viewers down. Benaud winced. The let-off allowed Pakistan to square the rubber when Imran Khan carved off 12 wickets in Sydney.

In the Melbourne Centenary Test umpire Tom Brooks gave Derek Randall out at 161. From the bowler's end it looked as if a snick carried to Marsh's gloves. When Derek, departing, did not hear Rod's call that it was no catch Greg called him back. The win by 45 was Chappell's eighth victory in 12 Tests.

Greg was the 1977 side's only scorer of 1000 runs. His 112 at Old Trafford, third of his five centuries, was his fourteenth in 48 Tests. After he played Derek Underwood on, the side looked like a dismasted yacht, as it often seemed while England won three consecutive Tests. It allowed them to apply more pressure to him.

Chappell's image with cricket followers suffered when they heard he had been bound to secrecy when he signed a tough contract to play World Series Cricket for a private promoter, Kerry Packer, who launched it as a lever to prise sole television rights from an unwilling Australian Cricket Board. Insiders were aware that Greg weighed his decision so long that he was the last Australian to join.

He was dismayed when news of the contracts came out in May instead of after the tour. 'WSC was foreign to all I had known about cricket,' he said. 'I understand how people were shocked, because that's how I felt at first. For people to whom cricket was almost a religion we were heretics.' Two factors swayed him. One was the standover attitude arising from the Board's monopoly. The other was that Packer's contracts came at a moment when he was finding it difficult to justify the time he was giving to cricket without being rewarded with security.

He wrote to Sir Donald Bradman and Board chairman Bob Parish on behalf of the players to explain why they joined WSC, to put their case before the Board decided how to react. No reply came. When Parish arrived for International Cricket Council discussions he stayed in the team's hotel, the Waldorf. When their paths crossed in the foyer nothing was said. Finally Greg went to Parish and said he would like to talk with him. Parish told him: 'I don't think we have anything to talk about.'

Travelling with the Australians it was curious to observe cross-currents of propaganda fired at cricket-goers uneasy about the future of their game. Inescapably, when 12 Packer signees were in a coach discussing prospects they would drop this subject if joined by others not involved. I noticed a tendency for similar groupings at meals. My impression was that repeated media references created more hubbub outside and around the team than a division within the side. Nevertheless, I felt Craig Serjeant was unlucky to miss three Tests.

Some odd statements I read looked even stranger in the light of the first-hand assessment by Geoffrey Boycott: 'I guess they may have been conscious of the Packer business but it didn't seem to affect the spirit in the field. I can say without a shadow of doubt that I have never played against an Australian side that tried harder. Throughout the game when the Australians were bowling and fielding all the players were encouraging each other and egging each other on, particularly Chappell and vice-captain Marsh. They could not have done more to keep the spirit going.

On return from the tour Chappell reiterated his belief that World Series would have benefits for cricket, in addition to having brought bigger rewards for players.

The ruthless reality of commercialism took only two years to land Packer a hand-over of his TV prize. As well, the Board gave him promotional rights for 10 years, estimated to yield vastly more than his $4 million outlay.

On $40 000 a year with two more years to go, Greg was the world's highest-paid cricketer when he resumed as Queensland captain.

He had summoned up extraordinary resolution to begin the achievements that made him the outstanding Australian batsman in WSC's last year. To relieve constant jarring of a strained right forearm in a Perth Supertest he frequently had to play shots one-handed. He defied the World XI attack for 5¾ hours in making 174. As acting captain at VFL Park he was 246 not out when he closed the innings at six for 538. Waving aside a question why he declared one run short of his record score, he said the position of the game was all that mattered.

When palsy caused by an ear virus paralyzed his right eyelid he was ruled unfit until a flicker allowed him to tour the West Indies. Primarily a front-foot player, he had not noticed that the battery headed by Roberts and Holding had driven him onto the back foot in Australia. Extra bowling by Lillee after practice did not uncover the cause of a lean sequence. Finally he realized that he had fallen into a compromise shuffle, neither forward nor back. Detection of the flaw and his eyelid's recovery enabled Greg to score 90 at Bridgetown in the second Supertest, 150 at Port of Spain, 113 at Georgetown and finish with 104 and 85 in Antigua.

Because of the blistering firepower faced, that cluster stands out as the greatest sequence of his career. One of the last to wear a helmet, he felt he had regained his surest touch and concentration. His 1416 in 14 Supertests, average 54, more than doubled the total of the nearest Australian (Ian, 693).

He re-entered traditional Tests with 74 and 124 against the West Indies at Brisbane and wound up a twin-series with 114 and 40 not out against England at Melbourne. He attributed Australia's reversal of the 1977 losses in England to the experience his side had gained. Mike Brearley gave much of the credit to Greg when he said England had no complaint about the Australians' behaviour.

Pakistan's superior spinners won the Karachi Test before two draws. After seven hours lost by rain at Faisalabad a refusal to play on the rest day caused Chappell to say his side would bat on for practice. His part in a record total, 617, was 235 not out (23 fours). It took over the record between the countries from Ian's 196 at Adelaide. Greg batted 7 hours 23 minutes, his longest Test innings.

Part II

Memorable Feats and Matches

18 Hal Hooker's
Great Stand

A rare balance of good-natured personality and persistence enabled tail-ender Halford Hooker to carry through his share of cricket's least likely record, a triple century for the last wicket. When Hooker died in 1982 his 307 stand with New South Wales captain Alan Kippax (260 not out) in Melbourne had not been approached in any country for 54 years.

Until that unheralded deviation into batting the only notice attracted by John Edward Halford Hooker as a cricketer had been as a fast-medium bowler. Hal was born on 6 March 1898 at Summer Hill. From Mosman Primary and Fort Street High School he had emerged as an accurate bowler who did much to lift Mosman club into first grade. The lean right-hander's delivery made the most of his height, 6ft 2in., and his controlled swing either way was exceptionally late.

His first-class debut was in Melbourne at 26. He took 63 wickets in 18 matches, two of which were against touring Englishmen. His striking-rate was 80 balls a wicket. In his third game thousands of vacant seats mocked the NSW team on Christmas morning 1928. Fall of the ninth wicket at 113 brought in Hooker, who said: 'I thought it would be worthwhile keeping it for Kippax, to get a few to regain confidence and end a trot he had suffered.'

Despite that trot, Kippax 20, had been chosen for the third Test against Percy Chapman's Englishmen on the same ground a week later but Victorians were criticizing his selection. As Hooker took centre talkative wicketkeeper Jack Ellis said: 'Have a go, Hal, the bowling's easy.' Ellis talked so incessantly, as if to break his concentration, that Hooker turned and said: 'My word, you talk to yourself a lot, Jack.' But when Hooker was still there after several overs, Ellis encouraged him by saying: 'Stick there, Hal.'

'When I had the strike for the last over, captain Jack Ryder put on an opening batsman, Fred Baring — the slowest off-spinner I ever saw — to tempt me into a stupid shot. "Kip" signalled to me to be careful, reinforcing my resolve not to risk a change of style.'

The tail-ender survived all that a'Beckett, Ebeling, Ironmonger and Hendry could fire before lunch but nobody thought NSW had a chance. Hal said: 'The partisan crowd had booed "Kip" at the toss because he had held his place in two Tests. But by six o'clock they were supporting us.'

During the day Victorian cricket-lovers tuned in their crystal sets and as the news of the defiant NSW partnership came through the earphones many left their Christmas dinners to flock to the ground. Some were said to have used threepences and sixpences from Christmas puddings to pay their way in.

As the NSW score improved, the pressure and the fielding became more intent. 'As the scores came closer, Ryder had fieldsmen packed closer around me,' Hooker said. ' "Kip" came along to say that as two of them had boots on the wicket I would be entitled to ask the umpire to have them moved back.

'I said to him: "What surprises me most is that the bowlers are so straight that they can get the ball through without touching the infielders!"

'For my club, Mosman, I usually went in No. 10 or No. 11 but I had absorbed enough from watching such great batsmen as Hobbs and Hutton to avoid giving a chance until we had topped Victoria's 376. Our aim was to give "Kip" most of the strike but once he found I was set he no longer forfeited singles if they left me to play most of an over.

'From lunch to tea on a hot day I went from 18 to 22. The scorer told me that through the innings I averaged five balls out of eight. I had never been so close for long to such a magnificent batsman in top flight. His back-cut, a lost art today, often passed between first and second slip. At tea Alan looked at the board and said: "We're going pretty well. We'll get these. We need only 193." I said: "Do that sum again, we only need 93."

'Alan finished the day on 222 and we were nine short overnight. The trouble was to put the bowling out of mind and get to sleep. Next morning I asked him: "How did you sleep?"

'Completely relaxed, "Kip" said: "I always sleep well".

'Next morning "Kip" faced veteran left-arm spinner Bert Ironmonger who had impressed the great Walter Hammond with the way he could swing the ball from off to leg-stump then turn it across.

'When he cut two and four I walked up to him and said: "Don't take such risks, please."

'"Kip" replied: "Listen, son, it's the size of a football."

'My heart jumped again when he stepped inside a lifting inswinger from Hans Ebeling and hooked it for four.'

When a classic cut off Ironmonger put NSW in front a loud laugh came from in the pavilion where St Kilda captain Bert Cohen collected a bet.

'Bert had said early in the match he thought Kippax, Jackson and Bradman made NSW's batting too strong for Victoria. Friends laughed him down. One scoffed: "You can have 500 to one." Cohen: "I'll have a bob's worth of that." He collected 25 pounds.'

Hooker was regarded as the best Australian bowler never to tour England. Bill O'Reilly said that, with his change of pace, he would have been a great success there.

If Bradman had accepted Accrington's £1500 offer after his first tour of England, 1930, a job would have been arranged for Hooker so that the club could have him bowling as an amateur.

But back to **that** innings ...

'We were 44 ahead when Ryder caught me at slip off fast-medium Ted a'Beckett for 62,' Hooker said.

'Though I was in good nick, using different muscles, I had never batted so long, five hours four minutes, and I was sore for a couple of days.'

Hooker did not mention it, but I heard Victorians criticized Ryder for not bringing on leg-spinner Bill Rayson before Hal became set and for having limited him to seven overs.

Hooker was not chosen in NSW's next two matches so it was in only his fourth game when he landed another record with his specialist art, in Melbourne.

With his last three balls in Victoria's first innings he skittled Ebeling and Gamble and took a return catch from Ironmonger. His first ball in Victoria's follow-on bowled Austen to give him four wickets in four balls. The onset of the 1929–30 depression caused Hooker's job as a manufacturers' agent in the canvas trade to fold up, so Kippax put him in to run a branch sports shop in Newcastle.

In 1933 Sir Charles Moses had him broadcasting rugby league, soccer and cricket Tests for the ABC, dividing his time with 2KO Newcastle. Between then and 1952, Hooker went around Australia several times, broadcasting with Alan McGilvray and other greats.

In addition to 58 wickets in 15 Sheffield Shield games, eight wickets against touring English and West Indian teams made his career total 66 wickets for 2001 in 19 matches.

Hal's unfailing good humour, showing out in light-hearted actions on the field, was an asset to team spirit. In days before air travel and portable radios players relished breaks from card playing and reading. Hal was a ringleader in such novelties as encouraging Hugh Chilvers to blow tunes on a midget mouth-organ faster than Archie Jackson could tap dance to quicken his footwork.

In a leg-pulling remark, Hal said to umpire Wal French: 'That bat of Bill Ponsford's looks very wide. Has anyone ever measured it?' French got calipers to check whether the widest part exceeded 4½ inches.

Ponsford objected indignantly: 'It's made by a reputable maker and that's good enough for me.'

After captain Bill Woodfull persuaded Ponsford to allow measurement, groundsman Bill Stewart produced a spokes shave.

Ponsford: 'They're not going to use that tool on my bat.' To the umpire: 'How much do you say it is?'

French: 'Calipers showed a slight thickness at the busiest part. A few scrapes with a piece of broken glass made it comply with the law.'

19 Voodoo at Woolloongabba

In the language of the Aborigines who roamed south-eastern Queensland, Woolloongabba means scented wattles. The wattle trees disappeared as Brisbane's cricket ground took shape at the spot. Now, the pathway from the gates toward the grandstand lies in the dappled shade of poincianas, scarlet-flowered tropical trees named after a governor of the French West Indies.

Without a backing of crested palms and dense jungle, the poincianas could not provide an adequate setting for the events we were to witness. They could not transform this piece of Australia to resemble the island outpost of voodooism, Haiti, fringing the Caribbean Sea east of Jamaica.

We had been warned, but not in terms that would have prepared us for a sight so strange (that would have required a message beaten out by tom-toms, with perhaps a smell of burnt offering). We had heard that, in enabling West Indies to win the 1950 Test cricket rubber in England, two bowlers had taken 50 out of 70 wickets without rolling their sleeves up. Overjoyed calypso singers with guitars had marched around the field chanting:

> Praise to the bowling, super-fine,
> Of Ramadhin and Valentine!

Denis Compton had told us that all he could see as Ramadhin bowled to him was a blur of black hand, white sleeve and red ball. The camera

149

bore that out; in photographs where everything else was clear, Ramadhin's hand was blurred. Still we were sceptical that a ball delivered so quickly could grip and turn on hard-baked Australian wickets as it had done on Britain's softer soil. Besides, Ramadhin and Valentine had played only a couple of first-class matches before selection and had only just turned 20 as the English season opened. Everybody familiar with cricket history knew that spin bowlers took years to develop and did not reach the front rank until an age when, in any other sport, they would be on their last legs.

The conquerors of England came to Australia to decide, in effect, the cricket championship of the world. On this November morning they entered the field in West Indian file and surrounded their first intended victims, Australian vice-captain Arthur Morris and his opening partner, Ken Archer. In weather hot enough for a Turkish bath on ladies' night, numbers of bare-shoulder frocks were worn in the outer ground and grandstand, but — after an ordering-out in an earlier match — not one was visible on the inner side of the barbed wire Members' Reserve; figures there were mostly more matronly, anyway. Ramadhin also gave the crowd of 22,000 a glimpse of his brown forearms by fielding in the opening overs with sleeves rolled to the elbow. As three other fieldsmen kept their sleeves down, this added to the general air of mystery and confusion.

In reply to West Indies' innings of 216, Australia's first pair made 30 investigatory runs before Valentine crossed their path and, with his fifth ball, had Archer caught. Here was the first hint of the uncanny — John Goddard's supernatural catching of a low ball yards from him. As he rose, half his volatile team rushed to brush grass clippings from his flannels with congratulatory slaps.

Under cover of the excitement, Ramadhin got his sleeves down without anybody noticing, just in time to bowl to the Vulture Street end — the most sinister bowling end in the world. Before the day was out, Ramadhin and Valentine looked like becoming as widely known in Australia as such famous combinations as O'Reilly and Grimmett, Burke and Wills or Dugan and Mears (Australia's notorious pair of jail-breakers). In their own way, they were as hard to subdue as the last-named pair in a more desperate sphere of life's struggle.

Except for their chocolate hue and sleeves buttoned at the wrist, the two bowlers have little in common. Ramadhin licks his fingers and bowls right-hand over the wicket; Valentine rubs his left hand in the dust and bowls round the wicket.

Sonny Ramadhin, only 5 ft 4 in., wears a Chaplin-style moustache and a smile like a toothpaste advertisement in a Bombay newspaper. To one grandfather, who went from India to work on a cocoa estate, he owes his small bones, glistening wavy hair and, no doubt, an infusion of the mysticism of the East with the witch-doctor type of magic he inherits from the other side of the family. Whisked from a South Trinidad oilfield into his country's team at 19, Ramadhin knows no first-name except Sonny.

Alfred Lewis Valentine is 6 ft tall and every inch a Negro, with crinkly hair and full lips. Before taking the field this lean Jamaican has rubbed his dark face and hands with an eau-de-Cologne lotion to prevent sunburn. As he bowls in the sunshine, some hidden power is suggested by flashes from his spectacles, from a gold chain bracelet on his right wrist and from his teeth, bared in an expectant grimace.

Valentine comes around the wicket with four long, bent-kneed strides, like Groucho Marx getting into a lift before the door closes. On the way to the crease Valentine passes the ball from his bangle hand into his business hand, jamming it between the first two fingers. He coils the wrist inward and straightens it with a flick that imparts more leg-spin to the ball than any left-hander since Victoria's renowned Ironmonger between the wars. As the ball leaves, his forefinger pokes after it — pointing the bone at the batsman.

Ramadhin forks his first two fingers, small, lean and damp, over the ball's seam. He flits across the crease with six lively paces. The ball shoots at the batsman from a one-two-three flutter of black and white, because he flaps his right and left sleeves over before his right hand delivers in its next circle. As this hand comes up behind his head, something mysterious happens too quickly for the eye to take in — a half-hint that his elbow bows and straightens. That is Ramadhin's secret, an essential part of his voodoo rite. The bewitched ball darts from the pitch, mostly whipping back from the off. Occasionally Ramadhin releases a slower ball which looks as if it will be a full toss but dips late in its flight. Sometimes this slower ball is the sly leg-break which batsmen have trouble in detecting from his hand, or it may be a retarded version of his off-break. Lynx-eyed opponents take a slightly higher ball as a sign that a leg-break is coming.

Australia's top batsmen, proven masters of Englishmen's bowling, rational and civilized, were spellbound when they first came up against the Caribbean conjurations of Ramadhin and Valentine. The inky illusionists humbled the finest batsmen in a manner not see on a good wicket since the Bodyline ordeal nearly 20 years before. The last man, Bill Johnston, was in before Ian Johnson put Australia ahead amid howls of excitement.

Though Valentine's left-hand turn and quicker straight balls took five wickets in the first innings to his partner's one, Ramadhin's original flight and spin beat the bat more and upset the batsmen most.

Ramadhin reminded me of a kerbside salesman holding the people's attention while his accomplice picked their pockets. Not all the resource of Morris and Hassett, men of calm purpose, or the dash of Harvey, daringly brilliant, could break the spell, though it was partly lifted by the death-or-glory hitting of Miller and Lindwall and the spirited strokes of Hole who, at 20, was too old to believe in fairies yet not old enough for cares and superstitions.

Among those outside the teams who underestimated the potency of the voodoo was Sir Donald Bradman. On the last morning, when the Australians needed only 128 runs and had eight wickets to get them, Sir Donald laughed aside a friend's suggestion that they were still in peril. In little more than half an hour three of the best wickets went for 31, half the side was out and the game had swung against Australia. Gripped by the Australians' struggle for survival, the thousands were so silent you could have heard a bail drop. We did. It was Harvey's, dislodged by a swerving yorker from Ramadhin.

After an hour's unchanged bowling, the captain took a new ball, long overdue, but, fearful of interrupting Ramadhin and Valentine and relaxing the pressure, he did not call on his new-ball bowlers. Instead, the shiny, red ball was rubbed against the pitch before the same pair carried on. We presumed that this was done to roughen its surface for their finger grip but, looking at the match in perspective, I have since wondered whether the West Indians were rubbing the ball, Aladdin-like, to summon up some genie. If so, Hole, Lindwall and Ring were not conscious of his presence, and Australia scraped home. Ramadhin and Valentine bowled 647 consecutive balls in the last innings (after 392 in the first innings before a rest) and they equally shared 12 of the 16 Australian wickets taken by bowlers.

After dismissing Hassett cheaply at their first three meetings Ramadhin joked to the Australian captain before the second Test: 'So long, rabbit. Ah'll catch up with you in Sydney.' But the hard Sydney and Melbourne turf was unkind to Ramadhin. With Harvey and Miller, Hassett took advantage of that to exorcize the bowler's occult powers. The outcome brought a one-word comment from *Sun* columnist Jim Macdougall: 'Ramadhidn't'. Under presure from quick-footed stroke-play, the midget bowler lost length and heart. He was only 21, and in his short career had no experience of contending with rough treatment. In Melbourne, as the West Indians' chance for a second victory slipped from their agitated grasp, Ramadhin left the field ten minutes before the finish, a woebegone little figure unrecognizable as the witch-doctor of Woolloongabba. His trouble was diagnosed as depression and muscular fatigue and he was ordered several days' rest in bed. When the five Tests ended, Ramadhin had bowled 1859 balls for 14 costly wickets. Of tougher fibre, Valentine had bowled 1737 balls for 24 wickets. No other West Indian bowled half as many balls.

In the next two seasons back in the islands Alf Valentine spun his way on to become easily the youngest player ever to take 100 wickets in Test Matches. He was then 23 years 304 days — six years younger than Johnston had been when he reached 100 for Australia. Valentine accomplished the feat in his nineteenth Test. He is the only bowler to reach 100 wickets in quicker than four years.

It was all done with two fingers, and he had to miss West Indies' last two Tests of 1954 because of finger trouble. Val had the consolation that it freed him to concentrate on his marriage to a Jamaican nurse.

Meanwhile, batsmen were not finished with Ramadhin, though they might have imagined so when he lost his zip and, for the first time since his sensational advent, West Indies dropped him from the last Test against India in Jamaica in 1953.

Ramadhin does not sweat and long stretches of bowling make his fingers sore. In the first Test against England in 1954 his chief spinning finger — third on the right hand — blistered and burst. Despite that, English batsmen thought runs as hard to find in the pair's bowling as ever, though their spin turned the ball less on their own wickets than in Britain four years earlier. In one day at Bridgetown, Barbados, 101 overs for 111 runs told their own story of accuracy undisturbed. For the first time, Ramadhin outshone Valentine as wicket-taker and 24 victims in five Tests lifted his total to within twelve of 100. Once again the calypso singers could chorus with gusto:

> *Ram is a magic bowler.*
> *He say he climb rope all up in India.*
> *Christiani is known as Mandrake,*
> *And Worrell he dressed up like fruit-cake ...*
> *What did de crowd say?*

> *We want Ramadhin on de ball,*
> *We want Ramadhin on de ball,*
> *We want Ramadhin on de ball;*
> *Keep him on de ball —*
> *And a lot of runs on de board.*

The calypso takes the Australians' minds back to that November day in Brisbane. They survived that scare, yet, till the end of their days, they will lower their voices when they speak of the voodoo at Woolloongabba.

20 Catches Win Matches

For some, the road to fame runs straight, however narrow, long and steep. For Hugh Tayfield it is full of crooked miles.

His approach to the bowling crease is not a simple, direct matter but involves a digressive ritual. First, Tayfield walks toward the stumps and sights over them toward the batting end. Whether this is to gauge the batsman's vulnerability to leg-before-wicket, or to verify that all three stumps are still there awaiting his attention, is hard to say.

To leave nothing to chance, as he hands his folded green cap to the umpire he rubs his thumb on its Springbok badge for luck. Next, he kicks the ground with his toe once or twice to notify the demons who live under cricket pitches that he is about to need their assistance.

These preliminaries attended to, he puts his heels together as if he has half a mind to salute the batsman. But he quickly shows his intentions are far from deferential. In four paces he is at the crease, his right arm upright as a flagpole as his fingers spin the ball on its way. In his follow-through stride he hunches forward, like one expecting to see falling bails or ready to pounce on a return catch.

The Australians gave Hugh Joseph Tayfield the nickname 'Toey' on the tour of South Africa in 1949–50. While batting, too, he gives the pitch behind him a stab with his toe before the bowler delivers. As he bowled for South Africa against Yorkshire in 1951, this habit was aped by the playful left-hander, Johnny Wardle, who tapped the ground simultaneously with his toe. The by-play delighted the

Sheffield crowd, who guffawed heartily. A few balls later Tayfield had his imitator caught for 0 and as Wardle departed he called to him: 'Sort that one out!'

This handsome 6ft car salesman found a length and a fiancee at his first port of call in Australia. The length served him wherever he bowled. The girl, Barbara Metcalf, a Perth mannequin, married him in Durban in 1954 after a courtship by letter, telegram, long-distance telephone and closer persuasion. Before his good-humoured brown eyes ever sighted Australia, Tayfield already held the South Africa record for most Australian wickets in a Test innings — seven for 23, with 69 balls on a rain-spoilt Kingsmead wicket a week or so before he turned 22.

Cricket sadly needed Tayfield's success and the development by South Africa's captain, Jack Cheetham, of the brilliant fielding combination which made it possible. The South Africans, who had just lost all their best-known cricketers by retirement or disciplinary action, arrived in an atmosphere of anticlimax engendered by Australian victories having become monotonous — only two defeats in 31 Tests since the war. Even those who saw the team practise fielding as no other touring side had done hardly guessed that Cheetham would be able to carry through his plan to make his team of unknowns a match for the conquerors of every Test country on the map. With Cheetham injured, the outlook was as depressing as the weather in Melbourne when heavy rain interrupted play. Acting-captains D. J. McGlew and D. T. Ring inspected the pitch. Having been covered, the wicket was ready for South Africa to continue batting but the surrounding area looked too sodden for the Victorian fieldsmen and would soon have made the ball greasy for the bowlers. McGlew suggested resuming play, fully expecting that Ring would disagree and that the decision would pass to the umpires. Looking around at the few thousand overcoated cricket-lovers who had chanced the weather to see the match, Ring suddenly exclaimed: 'Yes. Let's play. The game is dying fast enough without our giving it a dose of cyanide.'

Tayfield was playing his third match. He had begun with five wickets in his first innings against Western Australia and would have had five South Australians had Jack Wilson's bails been less stubborn. In the second innings against Victoria after the ground dried, his seven wickets included the first hat-trick on the Melbourne ground since Hans Ebeling routed Queensland in 1929. It was a split hat-trick. Off the last ball of his nineteenth over Keith caught Fitchett in the leg-trap. Off the first ball of the his next over, Endean gave a sign of his catching wizardry by hauling down one of Ring's 14 stone drives on the boundary. With the next ball Tayfield skittled Ian McDonald, wicketkeeping brother of the Victorian opening batsman.

To be sent in to bat on a strange wicket after losing the toss, as happened to the South Africans in Sydney, was a disturbing experience, even in the NSW captain, Miller, did pretend to soften the blow by saying: 'You fellas have first dig and get yourselves some runs. If you do, it will help you draw good gates.' As McGlew, too, had drawn his boot-leather along part of the wicket and noticed that it left a green, juicy smear, he had diagnosed the pitch as a greentop, so was not puzzled by the magnanimous invitation which would have taken a home captain's hospitality too far. The South African guests lost their first three wickets for three runs to Lindwall's and Davidson's pace. As they struggled dourly to retrieve their position a barracker on the Hill lost patience and shouted: 'Bring on the West Indies. At least they lend a bit of ——— colour to the game.'

Jackie McGlew and Jackie Grant (West Indies) are the youngest captains I have seen in big cricket, though records show that at the same age, 23, the Hon. Ivo Bligh led an English team in Australia and W. L. Murdoch captained Australia in England at 24. Percy Chapman, at 25, was England's youngest skipper at home until David Sheppard took over the leadership against Pakistan when seven months younger.

McGlew, a Pietermaritzburg accountant, first led Natal at 22 and from the start deployed a brilliant fielding side in attacking formations. He re-enacted one of these in Sydney to crowd the strong NSW batting side in which No. 10 was Lindwall, the all-rounder who has since scored the fastest fifty in Test cricket. The sight of two silly mid-ons and two silly mid-offs for Tayfield was enough to make onlookers wonder whether they were suffering from double vision or had underdone the pre-play session in the bar. The close fielders formed a menacing crescent near the middle of the pitch and stared at the batsman as implacably as the Four Just Men. Reading from left to right they were sturdy Hedley Keith, 25, a left-handed fitter from Natal, Russell Endean, 28, a Transvaal accountant, and little McGlew himself in the shadow of 6ft 2in. Anton Murray, 30, a schoolmaster and all-rounder from Eastern Province and the father of twins. At close range to batsmen who included two of the world's hardest drivers it looked a toss-up whether Murray would ever see the twins again.

NSW found the Four Just Men hard to shift. Again and again they won applause by unblenchingly standing up to the powerful drives of Miller and Benaud, who put 13 stone or more into their shots. With sudden dives Endean caught both low by the pitch's edge in the same

instant as the loud crack of the shot. At long-on Roy McLean, 22, of
Natal, was the only outfielder — good enough for two, as he proved by
running two dozen yards toward the fence, under a ball swaying in
the sky, to catch Morris. Sid Barnes, a man of experience and
assurance, tired of trying to slam the ball through the Four Just Men.
The only way he could disturb their unbroken rank was by skipping
forward and lifting the ball over them to unpopulated territory. That
made one silly mid-off migrate to block the gap but, throughout the
day, whenever a wicket fell all four would be back at the old address to
confront the new batsman facing Tayfield. The bowler and his
intrepid fieldsmen were rewarded with six more wickets in that
innings. When I congratulated Hugh on his success he said smilingly:
'They're catching 'em!'

When Cheetham was fit to take over the side again he did not use
more than three pitch-side fieldsmen. He had enough good men for
these positions to change the cast sometimes and proved that tall John
Watkins could catch almost as well in front of the bat as he could in
slips beside Percy Mansell, bespectacled yet sure-handed. The South
Africans blew the dust off the old truism that good catching makes
moderate bowling strong — like a stiffener of rum in weak coffee —
and good bowling better.

The men who post the names on the big Australian scoreboards
began to take things for granted. Once when Ken Funston, sprinting
out from mid-off, reached a chance with juggling fingers, the
Brisbane scorekeepers had already removed Harvey's name from the
board and had to restore it when the ball got away from the fieldsman.
Harvey made 33 more before he was run out. In the Adelaide Test a
ballooned on-drive by Hassett, 132, was dropped at mid-on by a
thickset man so like Endean that nobody could tell the difference, not
even scorers W. Ferguson and R. Hammond after rubbing up their
spectacles. Hassett, who boasted that he had cunningly applied
overspin to the catch, made 31 more. As if to reward the South
Africans' keenness, such occasional misses seldom cost many runs.

The Melbourne crowd at the second Test forgot the usual grievance
— the scoring rate — in relishing the finest day's catching by a visiting
international team for nearly a quarter of a century. It revived
memories of Chapman, Henderson, Hammond and Hobbs together in
England's XI. When catches are held, the scoring cannot get out of
hand either, so the Australians were dismissed for 243 on a good
wicket by a team that had two regular bowlers, Watkins and Murray,
absent on massage tables after lunch. When a drive by Morris hit
Cheetham's upflung hands at short mid-off, bowler Tayfield was
excitedly jumping in the air by the pitch. As the ball ricocheted from

the captain's hands Tayfield spun around, chased it several yards and dived to retrieve it as it fell near the mid-off position. That masterpiece of quick thought and action set the standard for the day. To remove the dangerous Harvey, Cheetham lunged to gather a drive just above grass level, causing the batsman to nod in admiration. Under a skied leg-hit by Ring, McGlew dashed twenty yards with his back to the wicket, keeping his head and his sense of direction until he sprawled in the mud with the catch. As a drive by Miller soared over the longfield the crowd in front of the concrete stand parted like the Red Sea to allow a sixer to land. His back to the iron pickets, Endean put up his hands — in a gesture of surrender, some thought. Instead he brought down a catch that will be talked about for years.

With Australia in dire trouble on the fourth afternoonn Hassett's batting science was receiving a great deal more acclaim than usual, as if the situation had changed the public's outlook toward the veteran's defensive skill. When a thunderous burst of applause rewarded one of his most guarded pushes to mid-on for none, it turned out that the excitement was engendered by portable radios proclaiming Ken McGregor's Davis Cup win against an American in faraway Adelaide.

With six wickets in the first innings and seven in the second, Tayfield enabled South Africa to down Australia for the first time since any player in the match was born (the oldest was Hassett, 39). His matchwinning bowling earned him the distinction of being the first South African to take 13 wickets in a Test. While his length threw a blanket over the scoring and the fieldsmen held it down by the edges, spokesmen for the crowd told the batsmen they would just as soon see members of the Board of Control at the wickets. Once Tayfield and his troupe pinned the Australians down for 77 balls without a run while he took three wickets. That was one of the occasions when batsmen, frustrated by having their carpet drives smothered, lost patience and tried to force runs in other ways. One of them attempted a sweep and lost his middle stump. Tayfield's 13 wickets cost him less than 13 runs apiece but a lot more in energy because he had to bowl 533 balls. In one afternoon he sent down 212 of them unchanged. Back in South Africa ex-captain Dudley Nourse looked at the bowling figures match after match and expressed concern lest the Durban off-spinner be burnt out.

Tayfield has the stamina of a Grand National winner, though only half the number of legs to keep him going. One of his secrets — as of many a hard-working bowler from Tate to Lindwall — is the faculty for relaxation immediately he leaves the field. The trials of the heaviest day are forgotten as he gossips over a sociable drink with his opponents or recovers enough energy to go to a dance.

Once the South Africans' anxiety to let no opportunity for advantage slip led to a boilover. After Lindwall and Miller demolished their first innings in the Sydney Test for 173 rain stopped play and the crowd squelched home, except for a few stragglers. Almost an hour later South Africa's captain entered the Australian room eight minutes before closing time for the day. He suggested that conditions had become fit for play to resume. 'You're joking!' said Hassett, who was barefooted. 'No, I think we should go out,' replied Cheetham.

Hassett: 'May I have time to put my boots on?' Cheetham: 'No — time is important.'

Hassett dragged on his boots without lacing them. With five minutes to go the tarpaulins were removed to enable the captains to inspect the pitch. Umpires Elphinston and McInnes went out to the wicket three minutes before time-up. A moment later Cheetham led ten players into the field (the eleventh, pre-occupied in the ladies' stand, was unable to return to base in time to take part in the sortie). The umpires made a detour to explain that they had come out to supervise the final two minutes' rolling of the pitch, because only five minutes of the seven minutes' rolling specified by Law 10 had been given before the wicket had been covered from rain. So the ruse to make the Australians bat for one uncomfortable over misfired. It was the most curious incident to the kind since the umpires in the Oval Test of 1930 decided to resume play for five minutes before time on the rainy third day.

Only bowlers young and brave put their hands to Miller's full-weight drives at point-blank range, as Tayfield kept doing during the powerful Australian's record fourth-wicket partnership of 168 with Harvey. Tayfield hopped in pain as one drive fractured a bone at the base of his left thumb but he pluckily continued with one hand to help his well-ironed flannel curtain of offside fieldsmen keep guard until Miller lost patience and his wicket simultaneously. After 11 days' use of a plaster splint, removable for physiotherapy to prevent the thumb stiffening, Tayfield gamely declared himself ready to bowl to the hard-driving Australians in the fourth Test. As central cog of South Africa's machine-like out-cricket he would have been worth playing even if his captain had to get Australian permission for a nurse to hold his hand behind the square-leg umpire between overs. He played with the base of the thumb bound and unflinchingly used both hands to catch a Harvey hook but his length was not as tight as usual.

Because of a fractured finger, Tayfield's ace offside fieldsman, McGlew, was missing from the line-up in the final Test and thereby lost the pleasure of opening the innings against a milder Australian attack lacking those men in the public eye, Lindwall and Miller, nursing injuries from the Adelaide Test. Tayfield's quick reflexes helped him to another ricochet catch when Benaud's on-drive bent Watkins' fingers back at silly mid-on. On the opposite side of the pitch the bowler dived to the falling ball. With it he scooped up a new record for a South African in a season's Tests against Australia by passing the 25 wickets taken by Llewellyn's left hand in 1903 and by Schwarz's googlies in 1910–11.

Despite the known perils of using the push-stroke instead of the drive on a worn pitch where the ball occasionally kept low or popped slightly, three other batsmen gently patted well-pitched spinning balls to short mid-on. A couple of these were accepted by Endean with almost casual ease after a season of handling drives of smoking muzzle velocity. This adaptable sportsman, a hockey star, was originally chosen as second wicketkeeper but it seems that he shall have catches wherever he goes. His fielding in gloveless positions was as important to South Africa as his dogged and heavy rungetting, 1496 in 17 matches in Australia and New Zealand. He held 27 catches on the tour and turfed only a couple.

In enabling the South Africans to square the rubber a fortnight after his twenty-fifth birthday, Tayfield made himself the youngest bowler from any country to have taken 30 wickets in a season's Tests in Australia since World War I. Before that, J. N. Crawford, 21, F. R. Foster, 23, and T. Richardson, 24, had reached the thirty mark for England in Australia and W. J. Whitty, 24, had done so for Australia against the first visiting South Africans in 1911.

Tayfield is the youngest visiting bowler ever to have taken 70 wickets in first-class matches in Australia. Only one man of any age from any country has exceeded that total, the super-bowler Maurice Tate, who at 29 flip-flopped his way to 77 wickets with 4018 balls for England (818 balls fewer than Tayfield).

By the time Hugh sailed home a round 100 wickets had fallen to him in all games in Australia and New Zealand, 84 of them in first-class matches. Of these, 54 were catches, 13 by Endean and seven by himself, bearing out the strategy he had adopted from the start. By the reckoning of Jack Fillis, who scores for South Africa as a hobby, the team took 294 wickets on the tour and fielding skill brought 196 of them (170 caught, five stumped, 21 run out). Only one-third fell to bowling unaided (63 bowled, 34 lbw, one hit-wicket). Midway through his twenties Tayfield was climbing into the higher branches of South African wicket-takers.

On his twenty-sixth birthday Tayfield excited Johannesburgers at Ellis Park in 1954 with a deadly spell against New Zealand, more demoralizing than his inspired hour at Melbourne. After the New

Zealanders had scored three runs off him he took five wickets in 32
balls before the next run and finished with six for 13 in 14 overs
(seven maidens). He developed a ball that went away slightly with his
arm, making a troublesome contrast with his stock off-break.

Tayfield is unique among cricketers in having reached a total of 78
wickets in 17 Tests without having bowled a ball against England.
Before South Africa's 1955 tour of Britain all his victims were
Australians (47) and New Zealanders (31). By the age of 27 he had
drawn within six wickets of the South African Test record, 84 in 25
Tests, by C. L. Vincent, the left-hander who played his last Test at 33.

21 Growing Pains

Had Bernard Shaw been living at the other end of the earth when he wrote *Androcles and the Lion*, he would have had a priceless opportunity to get the atmosphere for crowd scenes. Any day at a Test cricket match or football final in the Melbourne Cricket Ground is like a day in the Roman arena.

Ranged around the vast amphitheatre, the populace is worked up to a fever-pitch of deafening applause, exultant shouts, strained silences and bitter groans. Minor disparities are that their thumbs are always up (opening bottles), the Christians are mostly nominal and the only lions are social ones in the trustees' sanctuary.

But wait ... From a dungeon beneath towering rows of seats a little figure appears. Not Androcles, but at least a member of a Congregational Church younger set, carrying the hopes of all beholders. Admirers click snapshot cameras in his face as he threads his way through an aisle of excited humanity, mostly tiptoeing girls and back-slapping boys. As he steps through the iron gate into the area, newspaper and newsreel photographers train a whirring battery on him. He must feel like an island entirely surrounded by stares.

The biggest crowd of the season, 47,000, uncork a welcome of the kind Melburnians used to give Sir Donald Bradman. It is Ian Craig's first match in five weeks. Australian cricket followers have been impatient with the selectors for keeping the 17-year-old boy on the sidelines as twelfth man. It would be overdoing it to borrow a metaphor from Shakespearian circles and say that Craig's absence from the Australian XI had been like playing *Hamlet* without the Prince, but at least the Adelaide Test had looked like *Annie Get Your Gun* without Annie's little brother.

Now the Melbourne crowd can see that the newcomer is just a slip of a lad. His freckled face is shadowed by the big peak of a cap which looks as if it is the nearest that could be found to fit him. Tapping his bat on the ground, he walks with quick, short steps, straight-backed as a pupil coming forward to receive a prize on speech night. Applause follows him all the way to the middle of the field, because the lure of youth has brought many of the crowd in specially to see the youngest cricketer ever to play in a Test Match in Australia, 17 years 239 days.

All noises are hushed as the boy's turn comes to face the bowling. South Africa's captain, Cheetham, heightens the tension by taking time to place the field for Mansell's bowling. Cheetham's duty allows him no sentiment for Craig's tender years — and the South Africans have already felt the weight of his bat in matches against New South Wales. The captain waves mid-on up to silly-leg, a few yards from the waiting youngster. When Cheetham turns to motion gully in closer, the crowd, waking up to all this, emit angry rumbles and shouts of: 'Give the kid a fair go!' A woman in a sky-blue frock exclaims: 'They're not fair to the child.'

Another hush as, at last, Mansell begins his run-in toward the lad, whose shy, greenish eyes glance down twice to make sure that his bat is in the right place behind his right toecap. His grip is low, as if he were still a small boy trying to manage a bat too big for him. It lowers his back a fraction in an otherwise well-poised stance, nicely balanced on feet about six inches apart. As the bowler runs, Ian tilts his bat's short handle away from his legs toward point, then pulls it back — like a lever to open the gate to success.

Along comes Mansell's first ball, pitching on a length. Ian pushes a straight bat to it. The tense crowd applauds, though the ball rolls no farther than silly-leg. To two similar balls the batsman makes the same movement, giving notice that while the bowler keeps the ball there this is what he will do in reply.

The fourth ball has a flight a little more airy. While the wicketkeeper's gloves await a leg-break, Craig unhesitatingly skips a yard or more from his crease and drives it past cover to the pickets. The sight of the boy opening his Test career by jumping out for a boundary hit sends the crowd into a din of delight. Craig's mother and brown-eyed sister Helen unclench their fingers from the handkerchiefs they squeezed while Ian was undergoing an initiation which the setting made more than usually trying.

Of all the people in the ground the most unmoved is Craig himself. Young minds are as clear as young eyes. A ball is played on what it does, not what it might do or what the one before did. Add experience to youth and the mixture is a tonic to the game, a trial to the opposition. Ian's first 20 are the best I have ever seen by a batsman dipping his toe into the cold edge of Test cricket, granted that newcomers in Anglo-Australian Tests have often had to face more difficult bowling. Four times in his first half-hour cover-drives roll to the boundary, despite the presence of four fieldsmen in a row from mid-off to point.

For the first time Craig is batting with Neil Harvey. As runs mount at a rate exceeding 80 an hour this trimly-built pair's association looks the most ominous event for the world's bowlers since Bradman and Ponsford took up joint occupation of the wicket a quarter of a century before. Craig's cover-driving is distinguished by skilful placing which Ponsford himself could have admired (had he not been too busy totting up the turnstile takings). Even when a fifth man goes to extra cover to join the off-side company Ian still steers some shots through.

The 47,000 count every run as Craig nears 50 and obviously hope he will carry on to become the youngest centurymaker in Test history. A disappointed gasp like a hundred bus tyres going down is heard when, at 53, he tries to force Fuller's sixteenth delivery with a new ball and hits a sharp catch to Hedley Keith at cover. Applause follows him until his neat figure disappears into the lane of back-slappers.

Back in the dressing room, Bill Johnston asks him about the fatal stroke: 'You hit that rather well, didn't you?' Craig, like an urchin owning up to an orchard raid: 'Yes. I got tired of playing second fiddle — you don't get enough runs.'

By topping Australia's second innings with 47 when the pitch was less favourable, Ian made a round 100 in his first Test. His innings were not free from blemish but they gave deep satisfaction to selector E. A. Dwyer, a former captain of Mosman. Having been handsomely repaid for his faith in the teenaged McCabe before the war, 'Chappie' Dwyer remained politely unmoved by doubters who thought Craig was being thrown to the lions when he was promoted to the NSW XI at 16½, before he had completed a season in inter-district first-grade matches. The boy had come from North Sydney High School, a fruitful nursery for sportsmen and physicists. Preceded there by Graeme Hole and Olympic sprinter John Treloar, Ian had become the school's cricket vice-captain to Peter Philpott, who at 16 impressed the Bedser twins as the most promising leg-spin bowler in Australia.

In his first State match, against South Australia, Craig had played a few balls when a friend noticed Stan McCabe watching and asked: 'Do you think he'll make good?'

McCabe: 'I've seen enough already.'

Craig made 91 as an opening batsman, but next season his captain, Keith Miller, finding him not mature enough for this position in first-class cricket, gave him opportunities lower in the list. When he pulled on his tan gloves and walked to the wicket in his first match against the South Africans, umpire Herbert Mackinnon asked him: 'How are you feeling, Ian?'

Craig: 'All right now I'm out here, thanks — wasn't so good waiting inside.'

He looked as matter-of-fact facing international bowlers as when wrapping pills, phials and prophylactics in the Mosman pharmacy where he was apprenticed. After his first century against South Africa he hurried back to help in the shop. To my congratulations on this hundred, he said the only time he felt anxious was at 91 — the score at which he had twice fallen in his first seven matches.

Craig carried his first century on to 213 not out, his largest and luckiest score. It was lucky because he had a liberal share of a weakness common to all teenage batsmen — failure to cover balls outside the off stump properly. Making the ball go away late, Melle left Craig fanning empty air a dozen times. One such ball was tickled for a low, one-glove chance to the 'keeper. It takes more than good strokes to score 200 runs, and I doubt whether any batsman has done so without at least one chance of false shot, much less the youngest ever to score a double-century in a first-class match, at 17 years 207 days.

Apart from his luck against Melle, every shot against straight or leg balls rang true, whether the ball was well up or short, whether his answering stroke was forward or back, off toes, off knees, off hip but never off balance. Fastidiously, he lifted his size-seven boots out of the way of a near-yorker by the leg stump so that the bat could glide it around the corner. For the boundary that raised his 200 he knelt to sweep a Tayfield off-spinner off his middle stump. The nature of his innings is revealed in his having hit 22 fours and made two-thirds of the runs NSW scored in his 6¼ hours at the wicket.

Looking back to Bradman's and his own first match on Sydney Cricket Ground, W. J. O'Reilly said that Craig was a more developed batsman than Bradman had been at his debut, with more varied strokes, but he warned that it would be foolish to infer from this that Craig would become another Bradman. To my eye, Ian at 17 unmistakably had more poise and precision than the Don I first saw at 19, but there was nothing to indicate whether Craig would develop

Bradman's power and pugnacity. To say more would be like comparing a well-informed yearling with Tulloch, the champion stake-winner.

It was recalled that Ian's father, banker John Rochford Craig, had jokingly told friends in Yass on 12 June 1935: 'Australia's second Don Bradman has just been born.' As a point of interest, Ian's 213 was his thirteenth innings in first-class cricket; Don's first double-century had been his twenty-fifth innings (it was a triple-century at that). One headline hailed Craig as 'Another Bradman', another called him 'A New Don', and somebody described his as a reincarnation of that wonder-batsman. All this impelled Miller to come out with a timely plea against saddling Craig with the title of Second Bradman and putting the unassuming lad in the unenviable position of having to rip off massive scores in every innings.

Evidence that Craig's outlook differed from Bradman's (Don never seemed to tire of batting) came with Ian's double-century, which began after lunch and continued until tea interval next day. As the youngster was removing his cap at tea, unaware that the innings was being declared closed, his skipper motioned toward his pads and said: 'You may take them off now, Ian.' Craig: 'Thank goodness for that!'

Craig and Archer, 19, had each played only 10 first-class matches when they were chosen to tour England in 1953. Ian had scored 754 runs (90 more than Sid Barnes did in his eight first-class games before he was selected for the 1938 tour at the age of 21).

To the dogmatic assertion that a player is too young to tour abroad at 17, I believe the answer is that each case should be considered on its merits. Ian David Craig at 17 was a well-balanced lad of 5 ft 8 in. and 10 stone, with manly bearing and the intelligence to win a scholarship to Sydney University. News that he had been chosen for Australia — enough to send a teenager bounding upstairs three at a time — left him calmly dabbing ammonia on a little boy's arm to soothe hornet stings. Craig remained unblinkingly level-headed in a glare of camera-bulbs, thunderous applause, autograph signing and front-page interviews. In one, a girl reporter who thought he might have a regular girl-friend, spoke about the North Sydney Old Boys' Ball and asked him: 'Taking anyone special?' Ian played that one back along the wicket with a deep: 'No.'

When England welcomed the most youthful cricketer Australia had ever sent, he was 15 months younger than the Clem Hill of 1896 and two months younger than Jeffrey Stollmeyer, from the West Indies, in 1939. In the panelled hall of the Skinners' Company in the City of London, the finest after-dinner speaker Australian cricketers have heard in their travels, Lord Justice Birkett, predicted that, as Ian left the pavilion to bat, every mother in the land would pray for him, and the prayer might be: 'May the Lord bless thy going out and thy coming in!' Cricket Writers' Club chairman Charles Bray arranged a photograph of Sidney F. Barnes, 80, and Sir Jack Hobbs, 70, beside this youth of 17, not much more than a year out of high school.

On first acquaintance Craig liked English conditions. 'I was seeing the ball well,' he told me. 'After batting a couple of hours against Bedser, Laker and Lock in my third match I felt so happy about it that I walked in against Oxford University feeling ready for a century.'

Scottish left-hander James Allan was bowling. As Allan prepared to make his diagonal run behind the umpire, Miller asked: 'Which wicket is he going to bowl on?' Allan's riposte was to bowl Miller, whose bat allowed for break that wasn't there, and the word was passed to Craig that the left-hander was not turning at all. Sure enough, Allan's first two balls to him came straight on. Craig stepped out to drive the third to the ropes. It broke sharply and Rhodesian wicketkeeper Walshe stumped him for 0. It was the only ball that turned like that all day.

Next, a couple more setbacks from balls that pitched in bowler's footmarks left Craig uncertain what to expect from English wickets. The delicate mechanism of batsmanship was upset, the hairspring of confidence slipped.

At such a moment in any sport any defect in a player's style stabs him in the back. A serious flaw in Craig's footwork was his failure to use the depth of the crease in playing back. Habitually, he put his back foot across near the white line, not far enough over to get behind a ball veering late outside the off stump. Other times he began a tentative movement just inside the crease and finished with the back foot straying a yard farther forward than the left — like a cramped imitation of the change-of-mind stroke that has fattened Bill Johnston's batting average.

In forward play, instead of his left side leading into cover and off drives his shoulder was screwing out of line, leaving only the husk of the stroke. Balls he intended to play straight were dragged to the on-side, giving the impression that over-eagerness to use his on-shots was unbalancing his play. His unorthodox grip — back of the top hand almost square toward point — was shutting the face of the blade in mid-course.

His captain and seasoned team-mates diagnosed his footwork and grip troubles for him but to correct the deficiencies in time was another matter, even if he had worked on them from the start, before misfortune compelled him. For hours and hours he practised, staying in London during the Leeds Test so that he could have time at the nets. County teams arriving early at Lord's would see him at it with the dew on the grass. When the tour ended, his 27 innings in Britain had yielded 429 runs, highest score 71 not out.

Changing style in mid-season is only slightly easier than swapping horses in midstream. I doubt whether an older player would have made a better fist of it. Craig had to wait nearly 13 months and 40 innings for a century. It came in Hassett's testimonial match, but in that lighthearted game his four driven sixes in five balls from Ian Johnson revealed little more than a Bradmanlike power latent in his slight frame. A more satisfying sight was Craig playing the best innings for New South Wales in a hard-fought, low-scoring match against Victoria when he was on the verge of being dropped from his State's side. The growing pains of his batting were easing.

At last the winter of 1954 brought him the opportunity to concentrate on correcting his style without interruption, without having to break off the good work by going in to score runs. Putting down a pharmaceutical textbook he would go to a crease in the backyard of his Mosman home and practice taking his right leg back and across, swinging his short-handle bat through with the back of his top hand toward mid-off, as McCabe recommended.

Throughout his year in the wilderness those closest to him admired the way he swallowed bitter disappointments without a grimace. They recall the day when the Australian and Middlesex teams, ranged on the field in front of Lord's pavilion, were being introduced to the Queen. The Queen spoke longest of all to the freckled boy, and among the things she said was: 'I understand this is your first visit to England?' Craig: 'Yes, your Majesty, and unless my batting improves it probably will be my last.'

22 The 300-a-Day Men

Cricket-goers are fortunate if, once in a lifetime, they see a batsman make 300 runs in a day. This number is often beyond the combined efforts of 11 Test players, especially if they are skimped in the quota of balls bowled in a day.

Australia had to wait 44 years for Barry Richards' 325 in a day for South Australia at Perth in November, 1970, an innings bringing fresh evidence that at 25 he ranked as the most complete batsman in the world.

This is the kind of innings that makes a barracker's day, as it did when Bill Ponsford delighted a Melbourne crowd in 1926 by piling up 334 for Victoria against New South Wales at the rate of 60 runs an hour.

Ponsford's 334 stands as the highest one-day score by an opening batsman anywhere in the world, although hours of play are usually longer in England. Sir Donald Bradman's epic 309 in a day at Leeds in 1930 took 18 minutes longer, against Test bowling, but an explosive 345 by Charles Macartney, batting third, in 1921, reddened the Nottingham sky for 77 minutes less.

Seeing Ponsford playing pennant bowls on Alma Green, Caulfield, people find it hard to believe he is 70. He has yet to see Richards, the imported opening batsman who has come nearest to his three-storey feat. The fair-haired South African, 6 ft 1 in., stands confidently erect awaiting the bowler and bats with willowy grace. Bowlers tackling

Ponsford were confronted by a sturdy man of 5 ft 9 in. and almost 13 stone, his black hair hidden by a cap he constantly fiddled with — a habit carried on by Australian captain, Bill Lawry. Ponny's half-hunched shoulders, sometimes almost a crouch, always gave an impression of matchless concentration on reading the secrets of every ball.

Richards has the high back-lift that helps powerful hitters off the back foot. Ponsford's pick-up was controlled — close to his legs if he suspected a ball's intentions, fuller for his array of strokes on both sides of the wicket. Both gripped the handle higher than is the prevailing custom.

Richards' way of looking for runs from the start is more adventurously obvious. 'He gives the bowlers a chance,' they say, an illusion — or is it a delusion? — that saves them from becoming down-hearted dropouts. Barry defies convention by often lifting the ball over the top to unpopulated tracts of outfield, especially behind mid-off and cover. His 325 contained a six over the sightscreen into the members' stand.

Ponsford preferred along-the-carpet shots and made a science of placing the ball, as if his brown eyes had in-built protractors and his mind was a forerunner of today's computers. Exceptional footwork to get to the ball for strokes and get well behind it in defence meant as much to Bill as it does to the blue-eyed South African. They are alike in the faculty of reading the swing and cut pacemen are imparting.

These possessors of strokes to all points of the compass have both scored more to the on-side. Completing each shot, Barry leaves onlookers feeling that was how the ball ought to have been played. So did Ponsford, in spite of individual differences in style.

Asked to name a shot in which Richards outdoes Ponsford, I'd say the hook. Bill used it sparingly, and never with the raking force of Bradman, McCabe or Darling. He usually preferred turning shots he could keep down as part of his open-ended range of placements that made the on-side field look full of gaps. Australian bowlers and skippers anxiously searching for a vulnerable spot in Barry's technique have noticed that some of his hooks at bouncers have flown in the air.

Ponsford demoralized bowlers most with drives that scorched through the off-field or past the bowler or mid-on. Advancing along the pitch with crab-like mobility, he hunted the ball down with a bat weighing 2 lb. 10 oz. — six or seven ounces heavier than most batsmen carry. It was called Big Bertha after a German long-range gun that shelled Paris in World War I.

Behind this formidable weapon bowlers saw wide pads — wider, they alleged, than were necessary for adequate protection of even his substantial legs, as tireless as a marathon runner's. Yet in 51 Test innings he was never out leg-before-wicket.

In back-play he stepped into the crease to a depth where I don't see many boots tread today. His rare balance of forward and back strokes, with footwork that altered the bowlers' length, caused him to be hailed as the world's best player of slow bowling, in addition to one of the surest starters against pace.

Opening South Australia's innings in Perth with John Causby, Richards faced an attack with more than a whiff of Test quality: fast bowlers, Graham McKenzie and Dennis Lillee, medium-pace swinger, Ian Brayshaw, Tony Mann's leg-spin and boseys, left-hand spinners Tony Lock and John Inverarity. It was Richards' fourth match for his adopted State, and as early as Lillee's second over three faultless boundary hits showed he was on good terms with the WACA wicket.

Against the wily flight of Lock, who keeps Australian batsmen down to three runs an over, Barry sometimes began stepping along the track before the ball left the left-hander's fingers. He sent Tony's cost-rate up by one-third.

He scored his first 100 in 125 minutes from 110 balls. His second 100, raised in 83 minutes, included a chance at 169, a mis-hit on-drive off McKenzie, one of the season's unluckiest bowlers.

By making 129 as Richards put on 167, captain Ian Chappell not only provided a feast of footwork and strokes but blew out the candle-power theory that a prospering batsman's partner should confine himself to holding the other end intact. Lock could not separate the pair until Marsh's stumping ended a second-wicket stand of 308 in only 170 minutes.

Usually the fairest of all wickets, the WACA track was in its most quiescent mood for years. Perth onlookers are not used to seeing Lillee and McKenzie forced off the back foot from outside the off stump to wide of mid-on. Richards lifted the ground record from Bob Simpson (246 against the South Africans in 1963). Never one to 'play out time' (a strange ritual) he whipped on 25 in the last 13 minutes to reach 325 off 322 balls in 330 minutes.

Onlookers from the stands swarmed around the players' pavilion in a standing ovation for his 5½ hour innings against keen fielding that never flagged.

With stamina to match his talent, the genius from Natal did not get to bed until about an hour before midnight.

'I have never been a big scorer,' he told an interviewer Jerry Roberts. It was the third time in about 30 centuries that he had passed 200. 'Though this is by far my largest score I have played so much cricket now that it had no effect on me — no reaction when I resumed batting.'

Next morning Richards went on to 356 before a full toss from Mann succeeded where hundreds of length balls had failed. Trying to get it away to leg, Barry fell lbw, whereupon WA bowlers cleaned up six wickets for 24.

'I didn't throw my wicket away,' Barry said. 'I kept on the way I always play — to score as many runs as quickly as I can.'

Taking records as targets does not appeal to this graceful cricketer. As he has played continuously for Natal, South Africa, Hampshire, the Rest of the World and South Australia since 1968 it should not surprise us when he says he sometimes feels tired of cricket. Bonuses from his Adelaide employers, Coca-Cola, of $1 a run and $10 a wicket exceeded $1100 by his sixth first-class match, providing an incentive rather like a barrister's refreshers.

On a day when he can tear himself away from bowls and fishing, Bill Ponsford watches cricket at the Melbourne ground, which he once helped to run as an MCC official. In January he took two grandsons to the one-day knockout match.

It was as sunny as the December day in 1926 when Ponsford opened the innings with Victorian captain Bill Woodfull against NSW. When 26, he was playing his third game after his first tour of Britain. Playing on English turf had closed the last gaps in his batting — chinks so narrow that bowlers had been unable to prevent him from scoring 429 against Tasmania at 22. (He had to break a world record to convince obtuse selectors of his right to a place in Victoria's Sheffield Shield XI).

Play began three minutes late — in those leisurely days the rat-race was vaguely thought to be a circus stunt. In the first over Ponsford cut tall medium-paced Ray McNamee to the fence and in the second over hooked new fast-medium right-hander Harold McGuirk for an all-run four.

When I asked was that the way opening batsmen in the 1920s played themselves in, Bill made a characteristic reply: 'It was a beautiful wicket. They made some wonderful wickets in those days.'

In half an hour the two Bills had 54 up. Their brusque treatment of the new ball caused captain Alan Kippax to bring on his main bowler, Arthur Mailey, whose nine English wickets in a Test innings on this ground six years earlier have yet to be equalled. At 112 Norval Campbell joined Mailey in a two-way leg-spin attack, but by lunch Ponsford was 75 and Woodfull 50.

Returning from nibbling a little fruit, Ponny accelerated to a run a minute. Big Bertha was middling the ball so surely that not even an appeal was heard until at 211 wicketkeeper Andy Ratcliffe asked whether Mailey had him lbw to a wrong'un.

In two hours between lunch and tea Ponsford clapped on 158 (surpassed only once by an opening batsman, Colin Milburn's thunderous 181 for WA at Brisbane in 1966). Fours were more numerous than singles. It was a feast of crisp, vigorous batting, without slogging. Four medium-pacers, McNamee, McGuirk, Mick Morgan and Norman ('Pelter') Phillips, and three leg-spinners, Mailey, Campbell and Tom ('Tosser') Andrews could not make him give even a chance. Kippax had a try as eighth bowler in time to see him reach 300 in 285 minutes. Next milestone was Charles Gregory's 318 in a day for NSW at Brisbane in 1906–7.

Though Ponsford was tiring — that heavy bat and those pads were telling — he still added 107 in the last session, 105 minutes. When stumps were drawn with Bill 334 in 322 minutes he had averaged 3.3 runs an over off his own bat without losing a chip. Under unremitting punishment the NSW players were too sportsmanlike to stall by resorting to time-wasting dodges. They bowled 101 overs in less than 5½ hours — about 150 balls an hour. With all that action packed into the game, should we wonder that close to 23,000 watched this day of an interstate match?

'I was tired,' Bill recalls, 'but if anyone's feet had blisters they weren't mine. No, long innings never brought calluses or swollen finger joints on my hands.'

Next day they tried to keep him away from the strike and used deep fields to brake him back to 18 runs in 41 minutes. A misdirected leg shot turned a ball from Morgan against his toecap, whence it cannoned into his stumps. Out for 352, Ponsford shook his bat and muttered as he turned away, amid the crowd's deafening applause.

'One thing I remember well,' Bill says, 'is Kippax chipping me about this, saying: "Fancy going crook about getting out after making three hundred!" Probably he didn't know our fellows had urged me to go for Clem Hill's Shield record, 365, and that was why I looked disgusted.'

It was the 17th of 47 hundreds in first-class cricket by a man whose career average is 65. Hill's record had to wait until the next December for attention. It went when Ponsford piled up 437 against Queensland, the world record until Bradman's 452 not out against the Queenslanders in 1930 and Hanif Mohammad's 499 for Karachi in 1958.

And what happened to Big Bertha the bat? 'I sent it to Archie Smith when he asked for it to display in a cricket museum in England,' Ponsford says. 'I read later a fire broke out and the whole place went up in flames.' No bowler of the day mourned the loss.

23 Best 200 Against Australia

Looking for a double-century to compare to Gary Sobers' scintillating 254 for the World XI against Australia is like gazing at the Crown Jewels with the naked eye.

The glitter almost makes my eyes water.

Many say the matchless West Indian left-hander's batting delighted them more than any other innings they have watched. Test veterans of such standing as Sir Donald Bradman and W. J. O'Reilly had to go back 34 years to Stan McCabe's unique 232 against England at Nottingham to recall an innings outshining it.

Having seen the finest players of the last 50 years, Sir Donald said: 'I believe Sobers' innings was probably the greatest exhibition of batting seen in Australia. I have seen nothing to equal it in this country. Overseas, I still believe Stan McCabe's 232 at Nottingham was, in some respects, better'.

Figures reveal only a prosaic part of such inspired innings but they convey a lot when an effortless stroke-maker rescues a losing cause with 232 while eight partners go for 58, making McCabe's Nottingham achievement unparalleled in international cricket.

Bill O'Reilly said Sobers held the Melbourne crowd enthralled as McCabe had done Sydney people during his 187 not out in the first Bodyline Test, when illness kept Bradman out of the Australian XI.

Fellow-players generally rank that innings so highly not only because of Stan's breath-taking 187 while seven companions fell for fewer than 90, but for the courage needed against two fearsome speedmen, Harold Larwood and Bill Voce, using bouncers with a frequency which the rules have since tried to outlaw, while a large posse of leg-side fielders awaited a catch.

Bradman's own errorless 254 at Lord's in 1930 followed an opening stand of 162 by Woodfull and Ponsford but at Leeds he was practically an opening batsman, coming in at one for one to make the fastest Test double-century (214 minutes) and go on to 309 in a day. His 271 in a day at Leeds in 1934 came after Australia lost three for 39.

I believe Sobers' 254 shares the blue riband for the best double-century against Australia since the war and perhaps within living memory. It could be a photo-finish with Graeme Pollock's 274 for South Africa in the Durban Test, 1970. Whether they should be bracketed together or one awarded top place depends on what you think counts most in judging the merits of such wonderful innings.

Besides the state of the wicket, the team's position and the standard of bowling they overcame, we look for quality of batsmanship, power and range of strokes, matchwinning scoring rate, freedom from error and the imagination to take command of the game in a manner holding the crowd spellbound.

Both these illustrious left-handers play every shot. Each ruins bowler's length by driving powerfully off either foot, with Sobers' preference for the back foot as evident as Pollock's for the front. In quality of batsmanship, though they differ markedly, any cricket-goer is happy to watch either and enjoy every shot, even if played semi-defensively to keep the ball away from their stumps.

Both double-centuries were made on good, if dissimilar, wickets. No bowler as swift as Dennis Lillee opposed Pollock at Durban but he was up against a good attack in McKenzie, Connolly, Gleeson, Freeman, Walters and Stackpole.

In impact on the match and its effect on the series Sobers' 254 had more influence. The fielding captain at Durban, Bill Lawry, said Barry Richards was already tearing Australia's bowling to shreds when Pollock joined him at 126 for two wickets, putting South Africa on the way to become 2 to 0 in the series.

When Sobers entered in Melbourne the World XI were one down in the series and in danger of becoming two down, as they were only 45 ahead with Gavaskar, Ackerman and Zaheer Abbas out.

Batting as nobody else can, Sobers instantly took command. The captain's second shot was a hook and he sped to his first Melbourne 100 off 129 balls (23 fewer than Pollock's 100 at Durban). In almost every over before Gary's arrival Lillee had looked like taking a wicket. Cuts began scudding past point so rapidly that a third man posted almost square on the wide boundary could not intercept them.

When Ian Chappell brought Lillee back with the second new ball Sobers defused the fast bowler's explosive attack. What appeared to be a length ball was driven straight to hit the sightscreen almost before Dennis had completed his follow-through. Challenging shots like that struck 29 off three overs from Lillee.

In freedom from error Pollock's 274 takes precedence, as Australian fieldsmen can recall no chance. This is the main point against Sobers' 254 being awarded premier position. Gary gave a half-chance with a square-cut against Kerry O'Keefe at 55. From his bat's bottom edge the ball went down sharply to Rod Marsh's finger-ends; I wondered whether England's gloved genius, Alan Knott, could have made a catch of it. After adding one to his overnight 139 Sobers, playing forward to Terry Jenner's top-spinner, edged a chance, the only definite let-off in six and a quarter hours. Sobers was 150 before he rolled his sleeves a couple of turns from his wrists — an ominous sign for bowlers.

Heading for 274 in Durban, Pollock reached 200 quicker — five hours seven minutes, 23 minutes sooner than Sobers, who was slowed down for a while by a blow on the leg.

I wish I knew the progress count of Pollock's 250 for comparison with Sobers' 254 off 324 balls in 376 minutes with 33 fours and two driven sixes (off consecutive balls from O'Keefe). In scoring 20 more runs in 41 more minutes Pollock received 77 more balls before Stackpole held a return catch. Graeme hit 34 fours, one five.

In run-flow, an index to domination of the bowling, there is little between these two innings. Each averaged a boundary hit every 10 balls, but Gary's overall rate was 79 runs per 100 balls received, Graeme's 69 per 100 balls.

If anyone thinks Pollock's innings was superior because it was 20 runs higher, I would point out that Sobers could have gone on had a taller score been his aim. As soon as the World XI were 400 ahead the 35-year-old West Indian walked along the pitch to tell his partner, Peter Pollock, they had enough runs, so that his bowlers would have about nine hours to get Australia out. Both hit out and got out. When Walters caught him at deep mid-on off Greg Chappell Sobers had made 254 while five partners and extras added 105.

Gary's 33 fours travelled so swiftly that often he simply stood where he finished his follow-through. In Melbourne crowds totalling 133,000 I heard of only one not enraptured by this power and placing. Ian Glass, of Glen Waverley, told his mother: 'It was rather boring — he just kept hitting the ball and hardly ever ran'. At nine, playing a shot is tame compared with the excitement of scampering for a run.

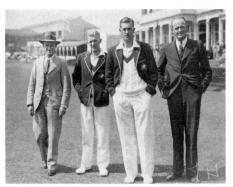

(Above left) Hans Ebeling, second from right, with Grimmett, Barnett and O'Reilly in 1934

(Above) Alf Valentine

(Below) Rod Marsh

(Below) Greg Chappell

Ian Craig

Hugh Tayfield, bowling in England

Sonny Ramadhin

Barry Richards with Tony Greig

On his imperturbable way to the record Test score against Australia, Sir Leonard Hutton's 200 took seven and three-quarter hours, compared with Sober's five and a half hours in Melbourne. Sir Leonard's 364 occupied 13¼ hours and contained 35 fours and a stumping chance at 40.

More in the vein of Sobers' and Pollock's batting was 240 at Lord's in 1938 by Walter Hammond, the only man who has made four double-centuries against Australia. On a day when Ernie McCormick's high-speed bowling had England three down for 31, Hammond produced his most majestic cover-driving in a chanceless innings lasting six hours.

Probably no eye-witness survives of R. E. Foster's 287 for England in Sydney, which has stood 69 years as the highest Test score by a visitor in Australia. In days of unsheltered turf, Foster began on a drying pitch on a day when seven Australian and English wickets had fallen for 99 runs. He made 73 on a Saturday and added 214 on Monday. Despite great changes in the game over so many years, this innings remains one of the greatest ever. Foster's 287 in seven hours 20 minutes took him only 23 minutes longer than Pollock's 274.

Ken Barrington's 256 in 11 hours 25 minutes at Old Trafford in 1964 was part of England's reply, 611, to Australia's 656 for eight (declared) of which captain Bob Simpson made 311 in 12 hours 42 minutes, the longest innings played against England.

Until Pollock's 274, Dudley Nourse held pride of place for South Africa against Australia with his spirited 231 that enabled the Springboks to draw at Johannesburg in 1935.

West Indies had lost six for 147 to Australia at Bridgetown in 1955 before Denis Atkinson made 219 in 351 minutes, including 29 fours and a chance off Lindwall at 195. Atkinson and wicketkeeper Clairmonte Depeiza kept the Australians out in the sun all day without a wicket in a record seventh-wicket stand of 348. By the time it finished matted hair was sticking to Denis' forehead, already reddened by exposure with his fishing fleet off the Barbados coast.

24 Richards v Bradman

Comparison of Vivian Richards with Sir Donald Bradman opens up a feast of memories that cannot be surpassed. Trying to find how closely the West Indian wonder approaches the all-time genius is a study that arrays the glorious with the magnificent and sheds lustre on each. Richards comes closest to the domination Bradman imposed on bowlers yet contrasts in their batting are as marked as in their build. The thing they have most in common is an inborn urge to attack, each in his own distinctive way. Each has made awesome bowling look awful.

Standing 9 centimetres taller and 10 kilograms heavier than Don, Viv clearly has greater power, especially as his exceptional shoulder development could be a model for sculpture of a bigger man. This shows up chiefly in driving. Both cut superbly. The frequency and force of their shots often put bowlers and fieldsmen in a whirl of quick changes and enforced field alterations.

In normal form each could skim the cream off the bowling, with Bradman less likely to skid off the rim. While Bradman stood side-on, Richards' toes are slightly open in a comfortable stance. Each watched the approaching bowler with eyes level. Bradman's grip, with the right wrist almost behind the handle of his lighter bat, facilitated a more regular roll of the wrists in hooking downward. Viv's grip, nearer normal, also favours on-shots, especially over mid-on and mid-wicket. Both are primarily back-foot shot players, with all the advantages that gives, provided there is an essential element of front-foot play.

One sector where Viv's stroke-play excells Bradman's is between cover and point. Circumstantial evidence, including his surer catching of the swiftest strokes, suggests that Richards has the sharper sight.

Don's percentage of double-centuries was twice as high as that of any other batsman. In 9 Test innings he batted longer than 6 hours, in 4 of them 7 hours. Viv's 2 innings longer than 7 hours were 291 at the Oval and 232 at Trent Bridge in 1976. Bradman seldom hit sixes, except after completing 100 or 200. It was habitual for Don to score quickly when Australia was in a favourable position, yet self-discipline under pressure made his innings at Trent Bridge in 1938 the slowest of his 29 Test hundreds. His 144 not out in 364 minutes was his lowest percentage of runs scored while he was in.

Watching Bradman, I used to get the impression that he could bring off shots with more certainty than could have been expected. Don surprised Yorkshire left-hand spinner Johnny Wardle at Sheffield by hitting a four behind square leg and in the same over forcing an identical ball through mid-wicket.

Once when New South Wales needed a heap of runs in a hurry in the last few hours Bradman was sent in first to face Victorian fast bowler Harry 'Bull' Alexander. Though 'Bull' pitched the first ball on a length Don hooked it for four with a shot that made the fieldsmen stare.

As Bradman's Test experience began at 20, he had already made 1889 runs (8 centuries) in 3 years before the age at which Viv began to contend with Test bowling. The former Antigua Grammar cricketer played for Leeward Islands before turning 20. Besides sharpening his reflexes, boxing won him the nickname 'Smokin' Joe' after heavyweight Joe Frazier.

At a time in 1975 when the West Indians were under extreme pressure from Dennis Lillee and Jeff Thomson, it affected him so much that he had to be lowered in the batting order because of vomiting caused by upset stomach nerves. Consulting Dr Arthur Jackson in Sydney about difficulties in concentration led to his regaining confidence to make the most of an abundance of natural talent. Dr Jackson told me Viv was an exceedingly good subject. The outcome was that re-established confidence launched him on the most successful stretch of his career. His 1710 in 19 innings in 11 Tests set a record for a calendar year (1976). He carried on to make his record 2181 in 24 innings in 14 Tests inside 12 months.

Since a single one-day game on England's 1975 visit to Australia, more than 20 such games a season have brought a pattern different from what Bradman knew in his time.

Exceptional quickness in picking up the line of the ball enables Richards to unleash shots that others do not attempt. As it cannot be intuition, it must be this genius' readiness to chance his luck that prompted the most imaginative shots I have ever seen.

To counter England's packed leg-field in the 1979 World Cup final Viv charged at an angle away toward mid-on before Phil Edmonds delivered. Swiftly passing his right foot behind his left, he twisted into position to drive past cover to the boundary. No other batsman since World War I has attempted such breathtaking shots and nothing of the kind was mentioned in earlier descriptions.

This marvellous cricketer risked his future in the game by playing on in 1979–80 despite an injury that could have ended his career. Before West Indies' First Test at Brisbane Richards was barely able to practise. After a few dozen balls he retired to the team's room and sat with his head bowed in his hands.

Yet as one of the selectors he put himself in the Test side, despite the precedent of 1930–31 when Everton Weekes persisted in trying to play with a torn hamstring. Australia is the only country the West Indians visit that was denied a sight of any of Weekes' 15 Test centuries. Viv said, 'I'll make a desperate attempt to get through this Test then take a couple of weeks off.' It involved the pain and mental stress of 5½ hours at the wicket for 140. Australian fieldsmen unsparingly returned the ball to the end that would prevent him from jogging between wickets.

When the agony of 19 hours batting and fielding rendered him unable to stay on longer, captain Greg Chappell raised no legal issue about his not being entitled to a substitute for an injury suffered before the game. After injections the hobbling hero flew to Melbourne and enthralled a one-day crowd with an innings even more sensational.

His 153 not out in 130 minutes contained every shot known to batsmanship and a number unknown until he brought them off. Though wincing at times, he grinned after stepping back to squeeze a leg-stump yorker from Thomson to the off boundary. A torn tendon in the right hip was blamed until just before the last match an X-ray disclosed a hairline fracture at the base of the spine.

I believe Viv's regular walkabout toward backward leg helps him relax after a scoreless stroke. While watching a bowler run up he continued chewing longer than Bradman used to. Viv has become so relaxed that at times he looks casual. He treats each day, each innings and each over as it comes, with composure I have seen ruffled only once. Being greeted by a bouncing no-ball close to his skull stirred him to give a fingers-up sign to Len Pascoe, who followed with three more. Captain Clive Lloyd said it was the first time he had seen such a reaction from him. Controlling his anger, Richards was smiling as he pounded the last of them down Adelaide Oval. If ever a drive could be called scorching it was this shot as it sped 113 yards (103 metres) to the cathedral end. Viv was still grinning as the ball was returned to the crestfallen bowler.

No other batsman smiles so often. Gordon Greenidge's best-timed contacts deal the ball some more stunning blows without rivalling the rapture evoked by Richards' fusion of artistry and authority.

Bradman apart, no Australian who has played more than 13 Tests has an average as high as Richards' 59. The closest are Greg Chappell (52), Harvey, Ponsford and McCabe (48), Walters and Lawry (47), Morris, Hassett and Woodfull (46), and O'Neill (45). But the changing pattern of cricket is making it much more difficult for players to pile up records than it was before the onset of one-day games and split series reduced the balance of Tests.

Playing off either foot, Viv hooks with much ease as his classic namesake, Barry, adding an effrontery that makes his innings as exhilarating as a ski-jump. His mastery of front-rank bowlers caused Ian Chappell to say we have been seeing the closest thing to Bradman's dominance.

Beginning by off-driving this first ball for four, he reached 3000 in his 33rd Test. He sped to 100 off 105 balls in 25 minutes, his tenth Test century. He hit 25 masterly fours and a six in 145 before he was caught at square-leg. Viv had taken 20 first-class matches to hustle past 15,000 in 118 games.

25 Calling All Sloggers

Judging by prizes on offer, you'd think the safest place in a Test cricket ground (safer than the armoured car collecting the gate-money) would be a seat close to the clock. $2000 from Melbourne Cricket Club for the Test batsman who can hit the pavilion clock ... $20,000 from the *Daily Telegraph* for one who can do it at Sydney Cricket Ground. The clocks remain calm. Neither offer has caused them to tick a little faster in apprehension — like the hearts of batsmen awaiting the next bouncer from John Snow.

For years, these clocks have looked down on cannonading by the longest hitters and wildest sloggers Australia and visiting teams have produced, without a crack marring their smooth expressions. If they could only speak, they would scoff at reports that the old Melbourne pavilion clock was broken by man-mountain George Bonnor in the 1880s and by 21 stone Warwick Armstrong in 1908. Historians of those days discredited both as myths. The Armstrong legend was said to have originated in two enormous drives off English spinner Len Braund which flew in the direction of a clock in the old pavilion but did not reach it.

The present pavilion's clock, set in the fascia of the top deck, certainly seems well out of range.

Could the club and the newspaper making the offers, cover their risk by insuring against such a hit? New South Wales ex-captain Warren Saunders, an insurance broker up with all the latest trends, told me: 'It is not the kind of thing Australian insurance companies have covered. I'll have to ask Lloyds of London.'

Despite the general impression that it can't be done, I believe a hit could reach the Sydney clock. The odds against this are astronomical and it would be something to boast about, even in an age when men have been put on the moon.

Of batsmen I have seen, I think several could have hit the ball far enough and high enough: left-handers Percy Chapman, Frank Woolley, Alan Davidson, Gary Sobers and Graeme Pollock, right-handers Keith Miller, Jack Ryder, Cecil Pepper, Walter Hammond, Ted Dexter and Pakistani slogger Farooq Hamid.

Everything would have to go perfectly: a ball suitably inviting, a clear eye, immense power, true impact, flawless timing — and the imagination to give it a go. Granted all that, it would still have to be a mighty fluke to home on the clock. Not even a cricketing gunlayer from the garrison artillery could achieve such pinpoint accuracy with a shot requiring such a whole-hearted heave.

If you are still sceptical, remember what Davidson did to a hip-high full toss from occasional leg-spinner Colin Cowdrey in a match for NSW in 1955. Pulled by Davidson, then 14½ stone, the ball was heading in the direction of the Blue Mountains when it was intercepted by the roof of the Brewongle Stand. Borrowing a steel tape from curator Athol Watkins, I found it hit the roof about 113 yards from the wicket and 40 feet above outfield level.

The longest drive to the pavilion end of the SCG since the war, was by Miller off Victorian all-rounder Sam Loxton, now a Test selector. The ball hurtled just under the cantilever upper deck of the Noble Stand. This is 120 yards from the striker's end and about 21 feet above outfield level. It penetrated deep under the cantilever deck, so carried much more than 120 yards — sufficient power but not enough elevation.

Farooq Hamid's wallop off left-hand spinner Johnny Martin in 1964 clanged high on the roof of the two-tier Ladies' Stand, 102 yards from the pitch and 54 feet above outfield level. It had close to the right altitude but the navigation was inaccurate.

On eye-witness descriptions, an off drive by Chapman between the wars got nearest the clock — suggesting that it is not beyond the range of human endeavour. Six years before he captained England in Australia in 1928, Chapman, 22, made 100 against NSW for an English team on the way to tour New Zealand. A fresh-faced, 6 ft 3 left-hander, Percy gripped his long-handled bat high, with bigger hands than Nature usually provides.

Test googly bowler Arthur Mailey had given tickets to two of the

Balmain boys he coached who later played for Australia — opening batsman Archie Jackson and left-hand spinner Bill Hunt. They saw Chapman step out to thrash a ball from the coach they worshipped. Up it soared like a homesick angel. Clearing the pavilion balcony roof it crashed against the base of the clocktower, then rolled back into the guttering.

After the Englishmen were out, Mailey asked his young proteges what they thought of the game. Gradually and diffidently, Archie and Bill got around to asking how it felt to be clouted by such a colossal hit.

'Oh, you have to learn to take these things,' Arthur replied. 'The ball deserved it. I overpitched it on to his strength.'

'But, Mr Mailey, to be hit so far and so high!'

Arthur: 'Well, while he was about it I'm sorry he didn't time the shot a fraction better and give it a little more carry ... then we'd both have gained immortality.'

Hammond's closest to the Sydney clock was an on-drive that hoisted another famous bowler, Bill O'Reilly, into the upper deck of the pavilion.

Compared with those hitters, Sir Donald Bradman was giving away several inches of reach and two or three stones of weight, yet he once lifted Victorian googly left-hander Fleetwood Smith into that deck.

The clock on Adelaide Oval's scoreboard is much safer. The furthest hits in that direction in my time, were Sobers' on-drives off Davidson and Martin, estimated to have travelled 140 yards on to the terrace in front of the scoreboard bar.

Barrackers seem pessimistic about the chance of some latter-day Chapman having the luck to find the target on an Australian ground. 'Hit the clock!' one Melbourne fan grumbled. 'Why, this mob don't even look like breaking the umpires' watches!'

Part III
Cricket Mayhem

26 Be England
What She Will . . .

Schoolboys reading of what the Crusaders did in Palestine and what
Henry the Fifth said to his troops before Harfleur and how Edward
the First earned the title of Hammer of the Scots must be curious
when they turn to cricket history. After noting the Duke of
Wellington's inside opinion that the Battle of Waterloo was won on
the playing fields of Eton they are entitled to wonder what has
happened to the combative spirit of the English, as evidenced in those
who go to cricket matches.

Can the weather's coolness, if that is the word, be the reason why
onlookers endure passively upsets of a sort that in warmer climes
have brought bottles and objects of mineral and vegetable nature over
the boundary fences, sometimes followed by the irate throwers in
person?

To time of writing, not one of 267 Test Matches on seven grounds
in Britain has been halted by an invasion of Englishmen. Though no
English ground figures among the place-getters in the riot stakes the
citizens of Manchester deserve mention for a good try, in which a
crowd did hold up a Test at Old Trafford.

It was after a riot abroad that a British fan wrote to *Playfair* editor
Gordon Ross suggesting that, if a disturbance prevented a team
winning, the International Cricket Conference should award the Test
to the deprived side. He thought inclusion of such a provision in the
laws might be a deterrent to potential rioters; if framed so that

hooliganism could cause disqualification of the demonstrators' national team such incidents might cease.

The time lost in the 1921 Test at Old Trafford, about half an hour, was to England's disadvantage. It balked a move by the Hon. Lionel Tennyson, the poet's grandson, to press on from the first good start England had made after three losses to the most powerful Australian side England had seen. About 6000 people waited through Saturday while recurring showers kept the wet wicket too soft for play to begin. Several times small groups of people walked out to the pitch to test the turf with fingers, feet or prod its edges with umbrellas. Each time police quietly escorted them off. About 4.30 p.m. captains Tennyson and Armstrong gave up hope of play. Abandonment of the day without a ball bowled annoyed some of the crowd and hundreds invaded the field. They were tactfully ushered off by Manchester police and placated by the issue of rain-passes for Monday, suggested by Australian manager Sydney Smith although a notice outside had warned people that they entered at their own risk.

That blank day reduced the Test to a two-day match in which the pitched rolled out so placidly on Monday that batsmen could face the dreaded fast pair, Gregory and McDonald, without alarm. Essex right-hander A. C. ('Jack') Russell, 101 with two chances in four hours, and Kent left-hander Frank Woolley, 41, tried to score at the rapid rate England needed, but Hampshire left-hander Philip Mead's 47 took 2¼ hours. With dash like that Dexter showed here 40 years later, Lancashire right-hander Ernest Tyldesley, 78 not out, and hard-hitting Surrey captain Percy Fender, 44, did their best to make up for that slow rate by rattling runs on to the board at almost three a minute.

The fifth-wicket pair had made 81 and the total was 260 when Tennyson entered the field at 5.40 p.m. and waved the batsmen off. His closure was designed to get the Australians in for the last 40 minutes of the day. In the pavilion Archie MacLaren exclaimed: 'Hello, there's Sammy Carter pointing to the clock. I'll bet an even pound we've made a mistake.' Primed by Halifax-born wicketkeeper Hanson Carter (the only Yorkshireman in the match) Armstrong challenged the legality of the closure. Reference to the laws proved that the attempted declaration was 50 minutes too late for the first day of a two-day match — a point overlooked by several ex-captains who had been advising Tennyson. Meanwhile players and umpires left the field and the Australians enjoyed 20 minutes' rest.

Mystified, the crowd greeted the Australians' reappearance with a storm of hooting from all around the ground. No doubt most of the hooters were not sure why they came back but felt that 20 unexplained minutes off the field when England might at last have a chance deserved censure. Hooting as Armstrong took the ball to bowl caused him to sit down until it eased. As he had bowled the last over before the stoppage it was illegal for him to deliver the next but amid the din neither the players nor the umpires noticed.

Ever-sportsmanlike, the debonair Tennyson went around the boundary to explain the position and clear the Australians from blame. Umpire Street also spoke to the noisiest section of the crowd. Play was resumed and Tyldesley and Fender carried their partnership to 102 in a total of 362 for the day (5 hours 33 minutes). This tally and the Australians' average of 130 balls an hour (21½ overs) illustrate how much more cricket crowds used to get for their money. There were two fast bowlers, medium-pacer Hunter Hendry, leg-spinner Armstrong and left-hand spinner Charlie Macartney.

After overnight rain the prospect that England might bowl the Australians out twice in a day on a drying wicket attracted 25,000 to Old Trafford on Tuesday. One man stood in the way, vice-captain Herbert Collins. His was not the sort of batting the crowd had come to see, all defence with strokes a secondary consideration. Few except players on the field or watching could fully appreciate his care and concentration on a pitch responding to the spin of Cecil Parkin, left-handers Woolley and Charles Parker and leg-spinner Fender. Collins saw six partners come and go for low scores before he was joined at 125 by all-rounder Jack Gregory. With almost three hours to go the game could still be lost. By the time Collins fell leg-before-wicket to Parkin only 90 minutes were left and England's chance had been smothered. While holding out for four hours 49 minutes he had inconspicuously put together 40 runs.

This innings was brought to life, so to say, two years before Trevor Bailey was born. Though most of the crowd had long tired of the sight of Collins, 14 fellow Australians in the dressing room applauded heartily enough for double their number, well aware that his patient bat had averted a real danger of defeat. In keeping the bowlers out for five hours 18 minutes, the Australians made only 141 off the bat from 117 overs. England's four spinners and one medium-pace swinger, Johnny Douglas, had made them play an average of 132 balls an hour. Six of the 10 batsmen had their stumps hit, and the pitch was awkward enough for 22 byes to get past George Brown and swell the extras to 34. The Australians were 187 behind but, as there was time for only 13 overs, Tennyson did not order them to follow on.

For an English crowd's invasion halting a touring team's play we have to go back to a lesser match than a Test in Queen Victoria's reign, the 1884 visit by W. L. Murdoch's Australians. In a game at the Oval, where scarcity of runs gives clues to the state of the wicket, F. R. Spofforth took eight for 62 and six for 34 in dismissing Players of England for 107 and 71. As they had made 151 the Australians needed fewer than 30 to win, but a complication arose when Edmund Peate (who had taken five for 50 in the first innings) bowled giant batsman George Bonnor. I am grateful to historian Irving Rosenwater for unearthing this gem from *Cricket*, 1884:

The Australians were left with only 28 to win, and just as two o'clock arrived Bonnor was bowled with the score at 17. It was generally thought that, as there were only 11 left to win, the game would be completed before lunch. The bell rang, though, and this gave rise to a very disorderly scene. The Players remained in the field but, Emmett's application to the Australian captain for the continuance of the game being met with a negative, there was no other course for them but to retire.

For some time a certain section of the crowd remained in front of the pavilion, behaving in a very disorderly manner. When the bell rang for a renewal at half-past two their attitude became still more hostile, and the middle of the ground was not only occupied but the stumps were sent flying.

Seeing the mob pull up the stumps, some of the Australians went out to explain that they left the field not to get more gate-money from people coming in after lunch but to save the caterers heavy loss. No charge would be made after lunch.

A Surrey official asked some of the players to join in trying to persuade the invaders to leave. Tufty-haired Edmund Peate, the skilful slow left-hander from Leeds, replied: 'Naw, sir. Ah didn't coomere t'quell riot, Ah coom to play crickit.'

At last, after the arrival of a reinforcement of police, and on Murdoch and McDonnell proceeding to the wickets, the crowd gradually cleared away from the centre and the game was resumed at half-past three. The 11 runs wanted were quickly got and the match ended in favour of the Australians by nine wickets. The two batsmen were loudly cheered at the finish and there was no sign of renewal of the disturbance.

27 The Battle of Adelaide

In the year 2010, I wonder, will Wesley Hall and Frank Tyson be remembered with the awe evoked by the name Harold Larwood 40 years after his bowling demoralized Australia's batting in the Bodyline Tests of 1932-3? Why, it seemed to take almost that long for batsmen's nerves to settle down again!

Men who faced one of these high-speed bowlers find it hard to credit that either of the other two was faster. It is rather like an argument whether the north, south or west wind can blow hardest. Facing these human cyclones, merely to take block was rather an act of bravado before three ashen stumps.

What was the secret of Larwood's ability to bowl at terrifying speed when he stood only 174cm (5 feet 8½ inches) and weighed less than 80kg (175 pounds)? Harold has since revealed that, through his 14-stride run-up, he felt relaxed right up to the high lift of his forward foot which gave batsmen a last warning of the wrath to come. The gift of co-ordinating balanced momentum and sudden muscular thrust into an explosive climax was his to a degree nobody has equalled, though Ray Lindwall got too close to it for batsmen's peace of mind. Harold was the smallest of captain D. R. Jardine's ballistic battery. Yet the perfection of his side-on delivery, the torque from an ex-miner's strong back and the downthrust of a high arm enabled the one-time pit-boy to make the ball rear from the earth more abruptly than his taller and stronger allies, Bill Voce, 185cm (6 feet 1 inch), and Bill

Bowes, 193cm (6 feet 4 inches), each around 91kg (200 pounds).

The Adelaide match was the third of five Tests in which Larwood totalled 33 wickets, an unsurpassed feat for a fast bowler anywhere until Rodney Hogg sliced through the Englishmen for 40 in his first five Tests in 1978–9.

When Jardine won the toss from W. M. Woodfull at Adelaide Oval on 13 January 1933, the happiest faces were in the Englishmen's room, as batting last had cost them the second Test by enabling O'Reilly and Ironmonger's spin to equalize the rubber. Soon the happiest expressions were worn by Australia's fieldsmen. Pleasure at capture of four good wickets for 37 in 90 minutes before lunch was exceeded by relief at being spared having to stand up to Larwood, Allen and Voce on a responsive wicket. 'Luckiest toss we ever lost,' one Australian told me.

Australia's sole fast bowler, Tim Wall, a 182cm (6 feet) Adelaide schoolmaster went into action and bowled like a man sensing a chance to take five wickets, if the catches would stick. Douglas Jardine's mastery of defensive batting could not save his leg stump from a break-back.

England's finest batsman, Walter Hammond, made only two before a jumping outswinger edged from his bat into the gloves of Oldfield, one of the central figures in the most bitter Test Match ever played, if played is the word.

After 45 minutes, a fleeting stay for him, Herbert Sutcliffe (9) fell to a one-hand catch at silly-leg by Wall off Bill O'Reilly, an even taller schoolmaster, 189cm (6 feet 3 inches). O'Reilly was a bowler of genius so versatile that he could be called on to help open the attack, though it was his artifice with spin that caused Sir Donald Bradman to rank him as the greatest bowler he ever faced. Tilting back the middle stump of Leslie Ames (3), left-hand spinner Bert Ironmonger lowered the fourth wicket at 30.

To halt the inroads, England had Yorkshire left-hand Maurice Leyland, a commonsense batsman if ever there was one, solidly supported by studious Bob Wyatt. Leyland counter-attacked as soon as the sun removed residual moisture from the pitch. His compact strokes made Wall's bowling look tamer. With well-muscled forearms he off-drove O'Reilly, Ironmonger and Grimmett in a manner to which they were not accustomed. In his chanceless 83 of a 156 stand in three hours Maurice hit 13 fours before O'Reilly bowled him off the inside edge. On his way to 78 Wyatt survived a low slip chance. He picked the safest direction — over the narrow side boundaries — for a hook off Wall and two sweeps off Grimmett to make himself the only Englishman who has hit three sixes in a Test innings in Australia.

Artful flight brought Grimmett revenge when a mishit was caught by Richardson.

Seven out for 236 on the day (98 eight-ball overs) left Eddie Paynter only tail-enders for company in his first Test innings against Australia. Jardine had chosen the Lancashire left-hander to replace the Nawab of Pataudi, although a few weeks earlier the Indian prince had scored 102 on his five-hour Test debut. Pataudi later joked: 'It's a dangerous thing to score a century in our team — you'll get yourself dropped.' Some thought Jardine felt the Nawab too slow a scorer (a fine distinction!) or it might have been because of another witticism. To maintain maximum pressure in the leg-trap wing of the Bodyline attack Jardine had directed that, if a batsman hit a ball hard to leg, there must be no flinching among the arc of close fieldsmen. Once Jardine himself had involuntarily flinched, causing Pataudi to say: 'Skipper, you seem to have forgotten your own instructions!' Such an undiplomatic shaft was not good for the discipline the iron-willed captain thought necessary to carry through his strategy in the face of resentment from the batsmen, tirades from several critics and vituperation from crowds enraged by the frequency of bouncers.

Paynter carried England to 341, and the match was almost eight hours old before anything caused an outbreak of ill-feeling that had been festering for two months since the first trial of Bodyline — which had been primarily designed to bring Bradman's excessive scoring back to a more reasonable level. In a Melbourne match in November five fielders had been posted behind the batsmen's legs before bouncers struck Woodfull's chest and rattled Bradman. Don looked as if he thought Larwood and Bowes were trying to skewer him to the sightscreen.

The word Bodyline had been coined in December in an attempt to label a type of direct attack as different from traditional leg-theory as an inter-continental missile from a boy's paper dart. At practice two days before the Adelaide Test the sight of Bowes skittling Jardine's stumps brought a loud cheer from watchers behind the nets, followed by heckling and jeering. As the noise upset concentration, the captain curtailed the spoilt practice and complained to the Board of Control. Next day locked gates and police guards kept out all 'except officials whose presence was indispensable'. So fuel was heaped on smouldering acrimony! All around Australia on the morning of the match, reports about locked gates and police guards pushed into the background what normally would have been the barred reporters' Test previews.

After his first over toward the cathedral end Larwood saw Fingleton touch Allen's third ball into Ames' gloves. As spearhead of the Bodyline attack, Larwood's pattern was to bowl to four slips while the shiny ball would swing out for him. When it lost its gloss he would run wide of the stumps to deliver shorter break-backs that leapt at right-hand batsmen trying to protect their bodies without popping catches to five leg-trap fieldsmen, backed by two leg-outfields.

The fifth ball of Larwood's second over bounced inches from Woodfull's head. Moving across for back-foot defence as the next pitched short outside the off stump, the captain was struck over the heart when the ball broke in. The bat fell from his hands and he clutched his chest as he doubled up in pain. An angry hoot exploded from the outer crowd, most of whom had seen photographs of Woodfull suffering a similar blow in Melbourne. Allen, Jardine and other fieldsmen ran to offer sympathy to the stricken skipper and booing continued for three minutes before he recovered enough to resume. Meanwhile Jardine had walked down to Larwood, whom Hammond was encouraging to take no notice of the trouble brewing at the ringside.

In his book *The Larwood Story* the bowler recalls that Jardine said to him: 'Well bowled, Harold!' Larwood knew what this meant, as Bradman was standing only a few feet away and Jardine was trying to unsettle him by making him believe the ball was being bowled intentionally to hit the man. The roar the blow caused was mild compared with the sequel when, as Larwood began to run up for his next over, Jardine clapped his hands to stop him and motioned slip-fielders across to the leg-trap, leaving Voce alone at deep backward point. At the sight of the hateful Bodyline field-setting being used against a batsman who had just been shaken by a severe knock a thunderous bellow burst from the crowd, not only those on the open green mounds but many in the shaded stands lining the western side of the oval. The noise, growing louder as Larwood ran to the crease, doubled when the next ball, a bouncer, knocked the bat from Woodfull's hands.

Everyone who knows the Notts speedman is aware that the combative side of his nature contains nothing vindictive or spiteful. Somebody even said he wouldn't hurt a fly. Perhaps so, but he wasn't bowling against flies, and barrackers' howls spurred him to a high pitch of hostility. Savage roars started up every time he bowled. Seeing Bradman evade several bumpers in the seven balls after Woodfull was hit, Larwood bustled Don (8) into spooning a catch to silly-leg, Allen. McCabe (8) uneasily deflected the last ball of his seventh over to fine leg, Jardine. His dominance disturbingly asserted on a now-dull pitch, Larwood was rested after eight overs.

Several shortish balls from the three fast bowlers rapped Woodfull around the haunches — an occupational risk against pacemen — while he hung on for three-quarters of an hour before Allen bowled him via the bat for 22. Four were down for 51 but England missed Voce's left-hand skip-bombing when an ankle strain put him off the field for the last hour of the second day. A loudspeaker call for a doctor set the crowd thinking aid was needed for Woodfull, instead of Voce. Fresh taunts were hurled at Larwood. Whenever his captain fielded near the boundary jeers came from some of the crowd. The politest remarks heard were: 'Do you call this sport?' and 'Why don't you play cricket, Jardine?'

Woodfull, who to that stage had not resorted to newly-created anti-Bodyline chest pads, was lying on a massage table receiving treatment for a livid bruise on the breast when MCC manager P. F. Warner walked in to express sympathy. Woodfull replied: 'I do not wish to discuss it, Mr Warner.'

Warner: 'Why, what is the matter?'

Woodfull: 'There are two sides out there. One is playing cricket and the other is not. The game is too good to be spoilt. It is time some people got out of the game. Good afternoon.'

From later talks with Woodfull I gathered that he felt his words might bring home to the team managers the necessity for them to do something about tactics that threatened to ruin the game. In this his utterance was ineffective, but news of it had an impact on public opinion like a flour-bomb on a university chairman. Half-a-dozen players had heard their skipper's words. When these became known outside, 'Plum' Warner jumped to the conclusion that they had been divulged by Fingleton, a journalist. This deduction by Sir Pelham (as he became three years later) ran counter to a well-founded belief in the Australian team that another batsman with quick perception, realizing the full significance of his captain's reproof, thought it would be a mistake if the truth were hushed up. The players heard that the news was imparted next day at a rendezvous in a car on North Terrace with a pressman he could trust to keep the source confidential. So as not to leave an obvious trail, Claude Corbett did not keep the facts for a scoop in his own paper alone but shared some of them with other writers when they returned from Sunday cricket in the hills.

Numbers of people who had not seen the tactics had, like the folk at home, regarded it as inconceivable that an English team could resort to the methods reported. That such an eminently fair-minded man of Woodfull's high principles should have been moved to speak so, caused many of them to take a closer look, among them Sir Robert Menzies.

As Bill Ponsford walked from the stand stairway to the arena gate a friend in the crowd, wishing to know the name of his hotel, called: 'Where are you staying, Ponny?' The sturdy Victorian answered: 'Out in the middle for as long as I can'. Three and a half hours he stayed. His 85 contained a few chances but eight fours came from the middle of his heavy bat and he endured punishment in a manner that gave the attackers no encouragement. In Larwood's words, Ponsford suffered more than anybody in the match and showed he could take a hiding. On his doings in the heat of the battle, Harold could have been barred for life from the Anti-Vivisection Society!

Ponsford wore no extra protection except a thigh pad. When players at an interval commented on ten bruises on his body, he muttered: 'I'd take ten more if I could get a hundred'. (A newcomer under a shower in a later match, seeing purple blotches with yellow haloes on Bill's side, back and hip, wondered was he suffering from some strange disease!) Australia's hopes of matching England's 341 faded when Ponsford, trying to glance Voce, was bowled behind his well-nourished calves after lunch on the third day.

Six were down for 194 but Oldfield produced his most stylish strokes for 41 before he was accidentally knocked out by a ball from Larwood. Here is the dapper player's recollection of how it happened: 'After I glanced a ball to the boundary Larwood dropped the next one short, almost a foot outside the off stump. I think I could have hit it to the off for maybe two but — as an admirer of Charlie Macartney, who influenced my outlook on batting — I was not satisfied to score fewer than the maximum number of runs from any ball. So I decided to step across and hook it for four. You may wonder how Larwood's pace allowed time for this but the definitive speed of the brain is something wonderful.

'I hooked a fraction too soon and the ball struck me here' — with a wicketkeeper's gnarled fingers he touched the right side of his forehead, just below the hairline. 'How lucky I was! Had it struck me here' (fingering his temple a couple of inches lower) 'it would have been the end of me. By good fortune it hit the thickest part of my cranium. These are all afterthoughts, of course. The blow knocked me over and for a while I lay stunned.

'Billy Woodfull came hurrying out in civvies to where I lay. Though naturally a mild-mannered, scholastic type of man he came out in a way clearly indicating that one of his men had been hurt and he was going to take over. He helped me up, saying, "Come along, Bertie". With his arm supporting me I was able to walk off, although still dazed and shaken by the shock.'

Larwood was not bowling to a Bodyline field-setting as all the recognized batsmen were out. But Oldfield was going along so well that, soon after taking a new ball at 200, he dropped one short to unsettle him. 'All hell broke loose when the ball hit Oldfield,' the bowler says. 'Critics and spectators had been prophesying that Bodyline would kill someone sooner or later. It now seemed that dark moment had arrived. Bert dropped his bat, clutched his head in both hands, staggered away from the wicket and fell to his knees. As a low rumble of hooting and rage swelled from the crowd I ran to the crumpled figure and said "I'm sorry, Bertie". "It's not your fault, Harold," Oldfield mumbled as soon as he was able to speak. The scene that followed was one that had never erupted on any other cricket field and it is difficult to imagine it ever being repeated.'

Thousands of infuriated onlookers began counting Larwood and Jardine out. From the mound they beefed: 'One, two, three, four, five, six, seven, eight, nine, OUT, you b_____!' Others bellowed: 'Go home, you Pommy b_____s!' Barrackers untiringly repeated a noun that, in the cussword vocabulary of the time, had more offensive personal connotations than its surface aspersion on the chastity of the recipient's mother. The word carried more sting than it does in today's permissive society or it did in William the Conqueror's day. Occasionally amid the hubbub a few coarser hecklers rang in other improper nouns, one of which Sir Alan Herbert has called a short and unattractive word. If Napoleon, who labelled the British a nation of shopkeepers, had been resurrected to watch this day he could have called South Australians a nation of bullock-drivers.

The blow made Adelaide Oval like one huge hornets' nest. As Allen brought a jug and towel to bathe Oldfield's head many in the crowd worked themselves into a frenzy. Maurice Tate, watching from in front of England's dressing room, said in his low voice: 'I'm getting out of here,' and went inside. Larwood thought that if one man jumped the fence the whole mob would go for the English team. He and others moved toward the stumps, ready to grab them if a mob rushed the field (as happened in 1879 when barrackers' invasions after a run-out dispute stopped play at Sydney and A. N. Hornby seized and marched off a larrikin who menaced Lord Harris with a stick).

The whole ground was in uproar for five minutes. It seemed longer. The next batsman, O'Reilly, took some time to get on to the field as he had to force his way down crowded steps between rows of incensed members standing on their seats as they gave vent to their indignation. The members were restrained by comparison with the outer crowd. On the mound near the scoreboard bar men were jumping in the air shaking their fists and even the mounted troopers' horses seemed restive.

Unwilling to bowl amid such din, Larwood lay on the grass, tossing the ball in his hand. The 32,500 present were making as much noise as almost 51,000 had on Saturday. When Oval officials appealed for police reinforcements constables were hurriedly mustered at Angas Street headquarters on the other side of town. When Hammond ended Australia's innings at 222, a deficit of 119, not a clap was heard as the Englishmen left the field, their faces set in resentment of the crowd's rancour. They could scarcely have expected three hearty British cheers! As they mounted the stairs, wrathful members stood enfilading them with insulting crossfire.

Whatever the merits and demerits of Jardine's captaincy, his courage, like his success, was beyond question. With the risk that some inflammatory incident might touch off a mob incursion, it might have seemed politic for him to bat later but between-innings rumblings, audible in the dressing room, not only failed to deter him from again opening the innings but provoked him into putting away his true-blue England cap and hauling out his longest-peaked and loudest multi-coloured Harlequin cap — one that might almost make itself heard above the din. Amid hoots he pointedly took strike instead of Sutcliffe, but there were some counter-cheers from the stands. In the evening a mob waited to boo the Englishmen leaving the ground. Constables stood near them and one policeman walked close behind Larwood. More abuse was heard but no attempt was made to molest him.

As no arc of short-leg fielders had been associated with the two most damaging balls of the match pitching outside the off stump, neither could properly be called Bodyline delivery. The demonstrators, indelicately ignoring that scrupulous distinction, read them into the general context of events which rendered the intimidated batsmen jittery. The Board of Control had failed to heed Bradman's suggestion for action while the series stood one-all in Melbourne but the impassioned Adelaide demonstrators forced the hand of Board members attending the match. Interviewing the MCC co-managers, they suggested that the controversial bowling be called off. Replying that they had no power to interfere with the captain's control on the field, the managers fobbed them off by hinting that a cablegram to the Marylebone CC might meet the case. Hence the pyramids, as the saying goes. It was not foreseen that a message drafted while Oldfield's wound was covered with plaster would have a tone that shocked MCC committeemen, who had no evidence of what was really happening.

The undiplomatic cable read: 'Bodyline bowling has assumed such proportions as to menace the best interests of the game, making protection of the body by the batsmen the main consideration. This is causing intensely bitter feeling between the players as well as injury. In our opinion it is unsportsmanlike. Unless stopped at once it is likely to upset the friendly relations existing between Australia and England.'

Though without foundation, reports of dissension in the England side were taken seriously enough for a night team meeting to be called to vote confidence in Jardine.

The match went on, with one eye fluttering between the wireless counter and the skipper's cap, flaunting bold quarters of deep crimson, indigo blue and a light yellow ochre. It made a showy contrast with the dark, glistening hair of Victor Richardson, keeping wicket because a lineal fracture of the frontal bone had put Oldfield out of the match (and the following Test).

Disdainful of barrackers' jibes — some exhorted Wall to give him a dose of his own medicine by knocking him over — the angular captain took no more notice of noises than if they had come from Adelaide Zoo. Picture Lawry in a Harlequin cap and cream choker, sternly guarding his wicket right-handed, and you have the nearest thing to Jardine that day: 187cm (6 foot 2 inches) of fleshless concentration, but with a nose more like Julius Caesar's.

Jardine owned the straightest bat in captivity. Captivity is right; he kept it in close custody while 56 runs accrued to him at the rate of 13 an hour. No doubt his intention was to wear down the bowling but he wore the barrackers' tempers raw. When a shoulder of his bat broke and he sent for another bat hecklers advised him: 'You won't need it, you b____!'

Immobile periods made it easier for flies to settle on him. Once as he swished them off a voice called: 'Don't swat those flies, Jardine — they're the only friends you've got in Australia.' (Douglas himself thought that less funny than a remark from the Sydney Hill as he was being handed a drink on the field: 'Don't give the b____ a drink! Let him die of thirst!')

If anyone expected the stir about the Board's cable, on top of the first-innings scenes, to cause Jardine to modify Bodyline in the last innings they underestimated the character and inflexibility of purpose of England's captain, a Scot of unbending backbone. Though the only time he left his team on tour was to go trout fishing, the stork-like angler was not swayed by a Victorian's contention that bouncers to batsmen hemmed in by leg-trap fieldsmen were tantamount to putting a rainbow trout in a pail of water and fishing for him with a rod and line.

Jardine's 13-an-hour rate was the chief reason why England averaged only 2.1 runs an eight-ball over. The side's stylemaster,

Hammond, was making the bowlers feel his wicket was little larger than a postcard. Toward the day's end Woodfull tossed the ball to Bradman, causing Hammond and Ames to confer, as they had never seen him bowl. After Ames cracked a long-hop for four and a full-flopper for a single, Hammond called to him: 'There are only two overs to go, so don't try to make a meal of Braddles. We don't want to lose another wicket tonight.'

Wally played the next ball quietly but it was followed by another full pitch. It was too tempting for Hammond who tried to hit it too far — by the look of it a mile, when 100 metres would have done. His head came up, he missed the ball and it was straight enough to bowl him for 85. Even a player of such unemotional mien as Hammond was upset by missing 100 with an out-of-control shot at a ball that deserved anything except a wicket. His swarthy face looked livid as he walked away. Perhaps such untoward Fate made Wally regret not having asserted himself a little more in the last hour of his 221-minute innings.

Hobbling on an ankle wrenched in a fielding mishap, Paynter tried to bat. He was left not out when England finished with 412 midway through the fifth day, unassailably ahead by 531.

On the fifth afternoon, as Larwood had Fingleton and Ponsford out with only 12 on the board, a Wednesday crowd of 24,500 cheered him in six sizzling overs to a slipfield. Cheers turned to boos when he switched to Bodyline. To make the most of Larwood and Allen's rest period Bradman tore into the other bowlers, racing past 50 in little more than an hour. After on-driving Verity for six he was out next ball for 66 when the Yorkshire left-hander held a hot drive intended to be Don's eleventh four.

No partner could build on Woodfull's anchor-man foundations (he scarcely averaged one run an over). Watching his side crumple for 193, the Melbourne High School master looked ready to defend Australia to the last rabbit-burrow. When Allen's eighth wicket of the match brought England victory, Woodfull, 73 without a chance, carried his bat through a completed Test innings. He was the only man to do so a second time, the first having been for 30 of Australia's 66 at Brisbane in 1928 when two injured batsmen were absent.

England's Adelaide win was by 338 runs, the widest margin gained there since W. G. Grace was captain in 1892. Several larger crowds have since watched Tests at Melbourne, Sydney and some Indian grounds but the six-day total of 174,452 in 1933 still stands as an Adelaide record in which unprecedented publicity played a considerable part.

Before playing (and winning) the remaining Tests at Brisbane and

Sydney, Jardine insisted on withdrawal of the imputation that his sort of leg-theory was unsportsmanlike. Several days of tension and much buzzing of wireless messages were needed to wring this reluctant retraction from the Board, put on the spot by MCC's offer to permit the rest of the tour to be cancelled.

28 Meckiff's Last Test

Few close followers of cricket could have been staggered by the no-balling of Ian Meckiff in the First Test against South Africa at Brisbane, but I have yet to find one who was not astonished by his sudden recall to a Test Match after the selectors had virtually outlawed him from any kind of international side for almost three years.

Since Meckiff fell out of the Test team with a foot injury early in 1961 they had left him in discard. His breakdown put him out of the running for the 1961 tour of England. Though no umpire had no-balled his action before E. R. Dexter's Englishmen played their first match on his home ground, Melbourne, against An Australian XI in November 1962, nothing could have been more pointed than the way he was omitted.

To open the bowling, the selectors invited down from Sydney the fast right-arm bowler Frank Misson, who then had to fly back to Sydney to 'saddle-up' against the Englishmen in the next match. Many Victorians regarded this as a snub to Meckiff. (An official assurance was given that the Australian Board of Control had no secret pact with MCC not to choose bowlers with controversial actions.)

Similarly, for the South Africans' first match in Melbourne last November, the selectors found no place for Meckiff, though he had been the most destructive wicket-taker in the previous Australian season (58 wickets in 10 matches for Victoria). Changes had occurred. On his last appearance in Adelaide last January (1963) square-leg umpire Jack Kierse had called one ball, and in March, Brisbane umpire Bill Priem called one delivery for Victoria against Queensland. Before the present season the Board of Control and the Interstate Cricket Conference notified umpires that they would have full official backing in enforcing Law 26's provisions against throwing and dragging.

When South African captain Trevor Goddard mentioned in Sydney that he had a hunch Meckiff might be chosen in the Test team, a Board member offered him odds of 33 to 1 against such a happening. Retired all-rounder Alan Davidson said he was willing to lay 1000 to 1 — generous odds for a man now giving most of his time to banking. These offers found no takers.

Yet, after all, the selectors found Meckiff room at the top. Elbow room? Ian himself gasped in surprise when told he was in the team, a few hours after the South Africans' innings victory over New South Wales — that powerful State's first loss to a touring team in 33 years.

Richie Benaud, the Australian captain, was at third slip when the eight-minute drama began with umpire Colin Egar at square leg watching Meckiff's first ball pass outside Goddard's off stump. After Egar's ringing calls of 'No-ball' as the second and third balls left Meckiff's hand, Benaud ran to the bowler's end calling, 'Hold it!' Changing places with Lawry at mid-off, Benaud said to Meckiff, 'I think we've got a problem here, Dad' (Meckiff's team nickname). Meckiff: 'I think you're right.' Benaud: 'Well, look, in view of what's happened, you've got to try to keep your arm straight and not be called again.' Meckiff: 'All right.'

When the fourth ball, which Egar passed, was driven to the boundary by Goddard, Benaud chased it to the fence. Calling of the fifth delivery caused captain and bowler to confer and similar remarks were exchanged. As Egar called the ninth ball, a full toss, Goddard turned it off his thigh to the leg boundary. Egar allowed the last three slower deliveries to pass to complete the over.

Cheers followed Meckiff as he walked to mid-on to field for the other bowler, Graham McKenzie. In mid-over Goddard complained about noise from portable radios and umpire Lou Rowan ran towards the pavilion, calling a request for radios to be turned off. During this delay, Benaud walked to Meckiff and said, 'I'm afraid this is the finish, Dad'. Meckiff: 'Well, if that's it, OK.'

Thousands shouted angry protests when Meckiff's end was taken over by Alan Connolly, playing his first Test. Cheers broke out every time Meckiff fielded a ball. They were redoubled when he held a catch to take South Africa's first wicket (Goddard 52) off Benaud's bowling. Later, hundreds in the crowd repeatedly chanted, 'We want Meckiff!' Among those who rushed the field were a number of men who hoisted Ian shoulder-high and carried him to the pavilion gate.

Benaud is being criticized for not having brought Meckiff on at the other end, to obtain the additional opinion of umpire Rowan from square leg. There would have been nothing new in switching a called bowler to the opposite end. Before South Africa's innings began I expected that, if the issue arose, Benaud would follow such a course. Of those not present at the Test, Melbourne people are most puzzled that this was not done, to give Ian whatever benefit would have resulted from a second opinion.

Had Egar made one call, as a sign that Meckiff's action was unacceptable, I should have continued to expect the bowler to be tried at the other end, as soon as McKenzie was due to be rested. Hooting began with umpire Egar's second call and the noise swelled into a babel of protesting cries, such as, 'Give him a go!' By the fourth call, most males of all ages in the outer and grandstand sections appeared to be joining in the angry demonstration. In this atmosphere, Benaud no doubt had to consider whether switching Meckiff to the south end would provoke a worse storm, whatever Rowan did.

If Rowan, at square leg, passed Meckiff's delivery, it could not have been assumed that the issue would be left there, with the umpires 'one-all', as it were. Law 26 empowers either umpire to act, if not entirely satisfied of the absolute fairness of a delivery. Egar would not have been exceeding his duty had he stepped back from the bowler's wicket, disregarded Meckiff's footsteps in delivery and called him from that end — as he did twice with Brian Quigley (South Australia) in 1960 and as Rhodesian umpire John Fletcher did with Griffin at Salisbury in 1962. Had events taken this turn there is no knowing what hotheads in the 10,000 crowd might have done.

Under reporters' questioning, Benaud said, 'I bowled Meckiff for hundreds of overs before umpires who approved his delivery, and I have accepted their decision. Now that an umpire does not accept Meckiff's delivery I accept that decision, too. I will not bowl him again.'

To other questions, he replied: 'It just was not possible to bowl him again. After so much publicity about the possibility of Meckiff being called, it was impossible to pack it in the back of your mind. Yet it still came as a tremendous shock on the field.'

In his newspaper column five days later Benaud wrote: 'It defies description — the feeling that hits players when there is a no-ball called for throwing ... One can only assume that the game was carried on by instinct for a while, for the Australian players were not, as one might say in the modern idiom, "with it". You could count the number of words spoken on the field on the fingers of both hands . . . It was an experience no one would wish to go through again.'

In a television interview a fortnight after the Test, Meckiff said Benaud was right in not allowing him a second over. He said: 'If Richie had given me another over he would have made a fool of Colin Egar, and if Lou Rowan hadn't called me he would have made a complete farce of the game. I know that Richie did the right thing, because he is behind every player.'

29 Woe, Calcutta

Calcutta is no place for those who want a quiet life. It is down at the opposite end of society's seesaw from the Buckinghamshire churchyard where Thomas Gray penned his lines far from the madding crowd's ignoble strife. Take five million loins, bind up many of them with dhotis and you have the Bengalis, crowded in an industrial metropolis as populous as Sydney and Melbourne combined. You don't have to be a sharp-eared student of current affairs to hear rumblings of West Bengal's political volcano. They open up deep fissures. The raw nerve of the time is exposed here, painfully. Extremists commit political murders. In periods of legislative impasse the State has come under Federal Government control.

In December 1969, Communist propagandists plastered posters in the city, thickest near the Eden Gardens cricket ground, claiming that Doug Walters had taken part in the forces that fought in South Vietnam. 'Go home Walters!' the posters blared. This lie about a well-liked young sportsman staggered the Australian players. Two years of compulsory service in the Army had not taken Walters outside Australia. The only weapon Doug had borne outside his homeland was a cricket bat, never guilty of anything more vicious than a square-cut. The lie was nauseating to a team from a country largely unaware of what most of the outside world thought of Australia's involvement as America's ally in war in South-East Asia.

To the shocked Australian players it was inexplicable that untrue posters and a misleading newspaper report could prompt 3000 protest marchers to demonstrate outside their hotel, the Great Eastern, and that in the morning the team should find the front windows boarded up. Travelling sportsmen often know little about political ferments. Even consciousness that they were visiting a State where pro-Peking candidates had polled well at elections would hardly have helped the Australians feel less hurt by signs of public antagonism. Since incidents at Bombay, newspapers were increasingly critical of captain Bill Lawry and his demeanour on the field. In the preceding Test umpire I. Gopalakrishnan had told him to stop running on the Delhi pitch in the second innings and the crowd had jeeringly accused him of using unnecessary force with his bat in flattening spots on the wicket.

Memories of the Test holocaust at Eden Gardens three years earlier spurred the authorities into extraordinary precautions for the Australians' Test match. Chief Minister Ajoy Mukherjee called in units of the Eastern Frontier Rifles, a conference of police and Army chiefs arranged for them to be on standby in the Eden Gardens area and the Home Ministry rostered nine extra magistrates for duty in Calcutta. India's Delhi victory by seven wickets, squaring the rubber one-all, encouraged hopes of another win against the redoubtable Aussies. When over-enthusiastic Calcutta crowds pressed close, hindering practice, police dispersing them beat them with long staves. In this inflammable atmosphere team manager Fred Bennett demanded full protection for his players and was assured that 3000 police would be placed around the ground. Hessian awnings that normally shade sections of the crowd from the sun's heat were abolished as a potential fire risk — a precaution that contributed to trouble on the fourth day. As players reached the ground scalpers were demanding 40 rupees (about $6) for passes officially sold at eight rupees.

The weight of things on his mind did not impair Lawry's judgement of the wicket. Winning the toss from the Nawab of Pataudi, he became the first visiting captain to send India in. The Indians never really recovered from having Farokh Engineer and Ajit Wadekar smartly caught in McKenzie's first 13 balls on a misty morning. Five slip-fielders were watching expectantly as Garth seamed the ball and made it lift from a moistish track.

In an hour the athletic West Australian's three for 11 off eight overs justified his skipper's decision before the first drinks brought a rest for Garth and relief for the batsmen. It was the deadliest opening spell Bengalis had ever seen in a Test. How much catching counts had seldom been better demonstrated than by Stackpole's holding of both opening batsmen at second slip (Keith finished with four in the match) and footballer-cricketer Eric Freeman's high interception of Wadekar's glance. On the opposite flank from his normal spot Chappell picked up Pataudi at leg-gully off Mallett's off-break. Taber's three catches included the wicket that mattered most, Viswanath, at 20 already the finest batsman in the side.

Only 168cm (5 feet 4½ inches), Viswanath looked like a prep boy among prefects when, with two out before a run came, he entered to face McKenzie bowling at his top. Stunned by India's opening disasters, the crowd found their voices when the midget twice proved that McKenzie could be driven to the boundary; the first stroke of the bow tells of a master fiddler's presence. The gifted Bangalore college student is smaller than Lindsay Hassett and Hanif Mohammad who had shown earlier generations of bowlers that size isn't everything and that timing can achieve more than tonnage — as gifted Sunil Gavaskar reaffirmed later. It was evident in Viswanath's wristy square-drives and on-drives, his cuts late or square, his hooks, his glances and his sweeps. He shaped like repeating his Kanpur century — first player to make 100 for India in his first Test against Australia and the only one to score a Test 100 against Lawry's team. Left-handers scoop up a disproportionate share of cricket's honours but the boy from Bangalore is almost as tiny as the smallest southpaw batsmen, Alvin Kallicharran and Roy Fredericks (161 cm, 5 feet 4 inches).

Viswanath had made 54 out of 103 when Taber's gloves closed on his attempt to cut Mallett's straight ball. Touched bumpers ended at the same destination when vigorous Ambar Roy cut at one and left-hander Eknath Solkar, 42, swung at another on the leg-side. The same gloves collected Freeman's accurate throw from square leg to run out Prasanna, 26, and end India's innings for 212. All-rounder Sreeni Venkataraghavan had yet to emerge as the man to be chosen vice-captain in the next series at the age of 25. Bowling more than one-third of Australia's 97 overs, McKenzie beat bat and stumps more often than he took wickets, six for 67, best supported by Mallett, three for 55. For the 16th time Garth dismissed at least half a Test side.

The ball was still rather smooth for spinning when Prasanna and Bedi took over India's attack soon after lunch on the second day. Lawry swept Prasanna for six and, chastened by that indiscretion, left the main burden of scoring on Stackpole's substantial shoulders. Undertaking this with pleasure, Keith drove a six over long-on and hit five fours in his 41 of Australia's first 65. Stackpole's freely-used square-cut looked to be the most devastating blow seen in 1969 except for Mohammed Ali's left jab. When Keith attempted a single for an off

Graeme Pollock, with Alan Knott behind the stumps

Oldfield struck trying to hook Larwood

Viv Richards

Gary Sobers

"The troops are coming out to inspect the crowd...!"

(Right) Ian Meckiff in action

Clem Hill *(below left)* and Peter McAlister *(below right)*: 'their fighting and wrestling spattered the room with blood'

drive, Ashok Mankad nipped across from mid-wicket and threw down the stumps. Stackpole's surprise at being adjudged run out was understandable when a photographer developed a film of the incident. Keith had to wait a year to have a similar appeal answered the other way at Brisbane — one more incident at the bowler's end, bearing out that an umpire's eyes cannot be as unerring as a camera.

Heartened by the disappearance of Stackpole, the Indians applied pressure to Lawry. Three fielders crouched not far from his lean haunches, ready for any misjudgment of Bedi's left-hand spin. When the Sikh switched from over-the-wicket to around it Lawry, 35, was snapped up low by the middle man of the three, Solkar. A batsman can expect the worst if he puts a ball above grass-height anywhere near this left-hander. Solkar made 10 catches in the series and earlier had caught seven men in one match for Bombay.

Newlywed Bedi's Australian wife, Glenith, was looking on admiringly from near the pavilion, roughly square leg. Her presence seemed to inspire him. When Bishan first met Glen, a Commonwealth Bank girl, at a Melbourne party in 1968 they talked about banking until the conversation took a more engrossing turn for a couple in their early twenties. Before going to live in India, Glen made a five-month visit to obtain an insight into ways and customs. (Sixteen months after this Test she figured in a cross-world Stork Derby with Gary Sobers' Australian wife Prue; each had a son, while their husbands were opposed in a Test at Port of Spain in April, 1971.)

On the third morning Walters and Chappell made a holiday crowd glad they had packed in early. Walters swung the third six of the innings over the leg boundary and gave two chances in boldly trying to snap the web being woven by Bedi and Prasanna, founders of the world's best finger-spin attack as the 1970s dawned. Though not as young as Ramadhin and Valentine when the West Indians humbled England's batting as 20-year-olds, Prasanna and Bedi took only a couple of years from their first Test together in 1967 to begin overtaking Gibbs and Sobers as the top pair of finger-spinners in international cricket. Back from Pakistan in 1979 their total stood at 439 wickets. They had snared 319 in 40 Tests as more regular confederates than Laker and Lock (173 wickets in 23 Tests together).

India's pair offer as much contrast in themselves as their bowling does. While a patka covers the Sikh left-hander's scalp, sweat sticks strands of hair to the Hindu off-spinner's capless forehead. As Erapalli Prasanna spins the ball into the breeze a silver medal jiggles on a neckchain — not so much evidence of depth of religious devotion, I believe, as a token of good fortune, a Hindu equivalent of a St Christopher safe-journey medal. Puckers between his eyebrows are signs of the thought going on inside as he tries to outwit batsmen with variations of spin, pace, flight and drift — sometimes even a round-arm delivery.

Round-faced Prasanna, six years older than his junior partner, is shorter, looks busier, turns the ball more and usually delivers from over-the-wicket. Subtlety makes him less obviously hostile than Lance Gibbs yet batsmen find he can turn as much as the great Guyanese did; both incur pain from worn forefingers. Even batsmen with the footwork of a Chappell find it difficult to get to Prasanna and drive with the middle of the bat. When he took his 100th wicket he was the first Indian to do so in 20 Tests, two fewer than leg-spinner Subhash Gupte and three fewer than left-armer Vinoo Mankad, that overworked all-rounder. Prasanna passed 100 wickets in seven fewer Tests than Jim Laker and five fewer than Ramadhin and Gibbs, who made himself the first off-spinner to top 200 victims and went on to lift the world record to 309 in 79 Tests.

Bishan Singh Bedi does everything the other way around. After he has rubbed his hand on the earth and pushed a Sikh steel bangle up his right forearm, seven dainty steps bring him on tiptoe around the wicket to deliver from wide out. Compared with Prasanna, his movements are leisurely. The ball loops lazily from his hand, at first sight invitingly. Yet would-be hitters find it hard to draw a bead on Bedi. On its way the ball curls and drifts, and when it pitches nobody except perhaps the wicketkeeper knows whether it will turn or not.

Bedi's easy-going habit of calling everyone Phaji (meaning elder brother in his native tongue, Punjabi) has caused team-mates to make this his nickname. His off-field urbanity gives way to unemotional perseverance as he bowls. It takes a lot to change the facial expression visible between the whiskers and the turban. Whatever Phaji is thinking he keeps well behind wraps.

Absorbing cricket was seen as, against high-quality spin bowling from this pair and Venkat, Walters and Chappell added 101 at a rate of 51 an hour. Then Bedi swung the pendulum of play the other way by getting Walters, 56, and Redpath in one over, amid appropriate acclamation. Making a habit of getting Walters, the left-hander was chiefly the bowler who kept Doug waiting until the last Test for a century. Engineer's leg-side stumping of Walters to break the Calcutta partnership was a gem of wicketkeeping art. When Wadekar dived with one hand stretching for Redpath's low snick, the batsman awaited a decision. All the while Shambu Pan was consulting square-leg umpire J. Reuben crowd noises suggested it was a foregone conclusion. Some of the choicest batting of the year kept the crowd happy after lunch as Chappell and Sheahan lifted the total from 185 to

257 for the fifth wicket. Sheahan began as if his eye was still tuned from the 114 that charmed Kanpur. Excepting Barry Richards, and with Greg Chappell to come, no right-hander since Graveney batted more handsomely than this 188cm (6 foot 2 inch) Victorian in true form. Paul's classic straight-drive, on-drive and square-cut soon attested his touch this day.

Sheahan's graceful reach and power and Ian Chappell's range of mobile shots subjected the bowlers to continuous pressure from both ends: loyal Indian critics admitted that for the first time in seven Tests their country's bowling looked beaten, weary, almost bedraggled. Fortune came to their rescue. Sheahan cut Guha to third man, ran one and sprinted off for a second without noticing that his partner was not returning. As he scrambled back he was beaten to the bowler's end when Prasanna's throw was relayed by wicketkeeper Engineer. Exit Sheahan when a high score appeared to lie ahead of him. Run-outs have been a factor against his achieving the eminence promised when his 81 at Adelaide in 1967 signalled the advent of no ordinary batsman. Not all were his fault but in trying to steal a second run against England at Perth in 1970 his imprudent underestimation of D'Oliveira's throwing arm lost him his place in the Australian XI for the rest of the series.

'Chappelli', the Australians' Italian-style nickname for Ian, was playing the most outstanding innings of the match and probably one of the five best of his career. He showed the Bengalis a complete example of building an innings: a patient first hour on a pitch new to him, merging into swift footwork to take the initiative against good bowling. Two-thirds of his runs came from 16 boundary hits, of which the crowd most admired his cut. On a pitch where a wicket fell for every 10½ overs and nobody else in either side reached 65, he made 99 without a chance — nothing to encourage the bowlers except one lifted pull of Venkataraghavan that fell safely.

Noises anticipating 100 were being heard when Ian identified the ball Bedi brings in with his arm and moved to play it. Unaccountably, this one turned toward the off and was edged to slipfielder Wadekar. Chappell instantly walked toward the gate showing no sign of inner disappointment at missing a 25th century at the age of 26. The crowd's long applause probably expressed commiseration as well as appreciation. Following Chappell's 138 on a Delhi track with which few batsmen coped, his Calcutta 99 was one of the innings that caused Lawry to nominate Ian as the world's best batsman on all wickets. Several Indians were willing to accept this, though they had not seen Richards or Graeme Pollock and it was almost three years since Sobers had batted in India.

The one thing Eric Freeman and Geoffrey Boycott have in common while batting is that both wear contact lenses. Freeman's set seemingly make more balls look like half-volleys, judging by his hard-hit 29 before he was caught in the gully off Bedi.

Long regarded as incapable of batting any better than any other last man, big Alan Connolly (known as 'Al-pal' to his mates) felt the day had come to correct that misapprehension. The 188cm (6 feet 3½ inch) seam bowler blasted three sixes off Prasanna and a fourth off Bedi, all over long-on or mid-wicket. Could they have been there to see Alan make 31 in 18 minutes I wonder what would have been the reaction of a group of young men in Melbourne who used to laugh their heads off every time he scored a run. Lala Amarnath said he came like thunder and went like lightning. Connolly's unheralded onslaught lifted Australia to a count of seven sixes in an innings of 335. The only like spectacle I have seen in a Test innings was seven sixes in four hours from the bats of Sam Loxton and Keith Miller off the bowling of Jim Laker, Dick Pollard and Ken Cranston on a July day at Headingley in 1948. Walter Hammond alone hit 10 sixes in his 336 not out at Auckland in 1933.

As they followed Connolly's four soaring hits into the crowd Prasanna's eyes lost their usual happy expression: Australians could not restrain chortles at the sight of half a dozen sixes in an innings off the bowler who had done most to beat them at Delhi. Simpson ranked him the best spinner he faced.

Until Guha caught the last man off Solkar, India's only wicket-taker at Calcutta was Bedi, seven for 98 off 50 overs in a total of 355 off 143 overs. With grateful eyes, matching the pride in his wife's, his team-mates watched the left-hander earn his best Test reward on a day when the Australians took the measure of everyone else. Batsmen in attacking mood could scarcely average two runs an over off Asia's subtlest flighter of the ball. Unable to partner him at their usual level, Prasanna was having his only blank match against the Aussies, though he totalled 51 wickets in his other eight Tests against them.

On the third consecutive cloudy evening poor light curtailed play by 14 minutes. As on the first day, the umpires allowed two more overs before granting the Indians' appeal. India's batsmen found the umpires less compliant than the Australians, whose appeal on the second evening had been upheld instantly, 75 minutes before time. The holiday crowd streamed from Eden Gardens, noisy with animated chatter. Fascinated by eventful cricket, they had cheerfully endured daylong discomforts in the crush. Their behaviour was all that could have been asked. They were in lively mood, although their national team had been headed by 123. After all, the Indians had been

67 behind at Delhi yet won with seven wickets to spare. Throughout Monday's rest expectations of another enthralling day ran high.

Tragedy struck before the players could reach the ground. Through the night 20,000 had lined up outside in the hope of buying the day's quota of 6-rupee tickets on sale at booths — only 8000, as all other tickets had been bought in advance by members of cricket clubs. Later arrivals desperately tried to snatch tickets from fortunate buyers. As the hour for play drew near, those at the back impatiently pressed forward. A stampede began. People knocked down screamed and groaned as the mob trampled over them. Police tried to drag some of the fallen from under the milling feet. In an attempt to stop the stampede they charged into the crowd with lathis and burst several tear-gas grenades. Infuriated, the mob threw stones and soda-water bottles in a pitched battle with the police. Six people were trampled to death and 100 injured; 30 were admitted to hospital and 70 allowed to leave after treatment. It was in no way the players' fault, yet an aggrieved mob stoned the teams' hotel and broke a few windows before police dispersed them.

On behalf of the shocked Australians, manager Bennett drew up a message of sympathy. Many believe that the loss of life, injuries and the resentment of those who bore the brunt of the police action unsettled a number of the spectators who again strained the ground's capacity and that this contributed to later trouble inside.

Everything continued to go wrong for India. While the batsmen were giving McKenzie due respect Australia's second and third pacemen, Connolly and Freeman, took over as the main destroyers of Indian hopes. With the build and belligerence to walk unchallenged into any military academy 'Fritz' Freeman was a fast-medium bowler of high-voltage energy and determination. After having Engineer caught, cutting, in the gully, the Port Adelaide footballer bustled Viswanath into error. As the little student shaped to cut an off ball it ducked back under a bat he desperately tried to switch to defence. The side could not rally from the double setback of losing Viswanath for five and Pataudi for one, again to off-spinner Mallett. In the hope of breaking up a close leg-field of three, the captain swept hard but was caught on the boundary. Disappointed patriots who might have condoned such a shot at Kanpur seemed to brand it a miscalculated risk at Calcutta. Half the side had slumped for 93. Ambar Roy stuck with Wadekar for a stubborn hour and a half until Sheahan's electrifying dash in from cover to make a full-stretch catch that only a man with his speed and reach could bring off.

Ever since his Melbourne 99 I have been unable to guess why the bats Ajit Wadekar handles with natural ease did not stack up more than 2000 runs in his 37 Tests. This time the quick-sighted Bombay left-hander so curbed his strokes in a dutiful attempt to give the innings backbone that 32 of his 62 runs came in singles. Wadekar saw seven partners fall for 68 before he was ninth out at 159, lbw to the indefatigable Freeman, who shared eight wickets with Connolly.

With Gleeson an onlooker and Mallett the only spinner, Australia's bowling rate slipped back to 95 balls an hour, a long way short of India's 113 balls an hour, but the Aussies batted more like winners by averaging 42 runs per 100 balls to India's 36. So in every way except catching the cricket most worth watching came when the home players were in the field.

India's slump for 161 dismayed a crowd for whom the day had begun sadly with loss of life outside. In the 10 minutes between innings feeling against Pataudi bubbled up like tar on a blistering day, as if the team's leader were somehow to blame. Since his 95 at Bombay in the first innings of the series the Nawab's scoring had dwindled to 0, 38, 0, 8, 15 and 1. As the Indians began fielding, hoots and chants of 'Shame, Pataudi!' came from sections of the crowd. The cries rang discordantly in the ears of Australians who remembered — had the hooters forgotten? — 'Tiger' gamely limping on to the field at Melbourne, Brisbane and Sydney with a torn hamstring as well as one damaged eye, how he knelt at slip between balls, how he batted bravely almost on one leg for more than 330 runs in successive Tests, so that Frank Tyson likened him to Long John Silver.

In the Ranji Stadium section of the stands — this time without the usual hessian sunscreens on the two decks — the occupants downstairs had no protection from anything dropped from the gallery. After desultory potshots, volleys of bottles, stones, and refuse made the downstairs crowd escape on the field. Nobody knew whether the pelting was prompted by an unreasoning boil-over of disappointment, enmity over some local issue or whether there was more than one cause.

Lawry had hit opening bowler Subroto Guha's fourth ball to the boundary when the refugees from the Ranji Stadium swarmed on the field. Police stationed around the boundary shepherded them along the edge of the field. Lawry and Stackpole waited by the pitch like sentries. In that period an incident occurred that resulted in scathing criticism of Lawry and a chain of events that led to the Australians' bus being stoned in the most alarming scare any cricketers had suffered anywhere.

Versions differ but readers of most Indian newspapers next morning read that Lawry had attacked an Indian photographer. In Calcutta, *The Statesman*, a leading English-language daily said:

'Lawry did something that, to say the least, could be termed disgraceful. A photographer who had wanted to get a close shot of Stackpole and Lawry side by side brought upon himself the wrath of the Australian Pinnochio. Lawry, presumably irritated, could not keep his temper in check and knocked over the poor photographer and struck him with his bat. It was a horrible sight, and one was led to wonder what Lawry thought himself to be. Would he have done the same in England or South Africa? Lawry, not quite the most popular of captains, exceeded himself and should be asked to apologize ...' (Another Calcutta paper's report of an apology was a fabrication, Lawry said.)

Pictures of the photographer lying on the field appeared in *The Statesman* and in the *Amrita Bazar Patrika*, in which secretary Shyamal Bose stated the Press Photographers' Association's regret and resentment of Lawry having 'hit a photographer without provocation and abused another while they were taking pictures of him'. The photographer was identified as Miran Adhikary of the Bengali daily *Basumati*. In his account of the incident in the *Sun*, Melbourne, Lawry said that in trying to protect the wicket he pushed the photographer with his open hand. In the picture of the fallen man Lawry was not holding his bat, but stooping as if to pick it up from the ground.

Nearest witness was Stackpole, and here are his recollections: 'I think it great to play in front of such enthusiastic crowds as those in India and on such a fine ground as Eden Gardens, one of the best I have played on anywhere. This makes it more of a pity that anything should have happened to cause friction before the end of the Test. When bottles and debris were dropped on them, the people had nowhere to go except forward on to the field. Police came across to check the invasion but none of these people came within 50 yards of the wicket. As police were ushering them around the edge of the field, about 20 yards in, the Indian players walked two-thirds of the way toward the dressing room at the other end of the ground and looked ready to make a bolt for it if things got out of control.

'Twelve or fifteen photographers ran on to the field, each trying to get a scoop angle. Lawry and I tried to get them to leave but they took no notice. Some of them were pestering us to stand in the foreground of pictures of the crowd scene. We thought that a bit much, seeing that by coming on the field they added to confusion already caused with hunted-out spectators and police all over the place. We kept telling them to get off the ground. In his concern about the wicket Lawry took exception to one of the most intrusive of them. After taking a couple of sneak photos this fellow walked away. He was still hanging around so the Phantom went to chase him away. The chap started running, so Bill followed him, prodded him on the backside with his bat and said: "Now get off!" The photographer stumbled and fell. He had a press camera and when he fell I think it dug into his ribs. A couple of others helped him up. Lawry seemed to think he was playing a part but I think he was in pain, not putting on an act.'

Keith paused, then went on: 'At a time like this it's a bit lonely out there, but you realize that the only way to enable the game to be resumed is to stay. I'm sure that if we had gone off and the fieldsmen and umpires had left the field, the police would have been content to quieten things down. Their immediate task was to restore order and they weren't looking any further than that. By staying, we were a reminder that there was an interrupted game to be resumed. When things quietened down we asked the police could they get the people back over the boundary line, so we could play again. In some places they were sitting over the boundary line, the best that police could do with them. We were keen to finish the match that day. Though another day was scheduled, the disturbances raised a doubt whether the match could be resumed then. There was a possibility that masses of demonstrators or other crowds might block the approaches and the team's bus might not be able to get through.'

After 13 minutes the opening pair resumed seeking the 39 runs needed to win. The disturbance had left tension and nobody wished to prolong the game pointlessly. Only five overs in about 20 minutes were needed. When the totals were equal, Lawry said to Stackpole: 'Guha is going to bowl a full toss to end the match. Don't hit it for four, a single will do.' But Keith could not resist such an offering and his stroke sent the ball rolling to the crowd-fringed boundary.

In the moment of defeat sections of the crowd singled out Pataudi as target for a bitter demonstration. As the players walked off Lawry said to Stackpole: 'We'd better protect Pat.' Turning to the Nawab he said: 'Come with us.' Besides being two of the biggest men on the field, the Australians had bats. They walked each side of Pataudi, who was outwardly calm, although he had ample reason to be terrified by the mob's bitterness. A couple of wicker chairs were dropped on the group and nearby demonstrators spat betel-juice at India's captain before he reached sanctuary in the dressing room.

'None of the demonstration was against us,' Stackpole said. 'It was against their own side. I think they were most upset because they felt a couple of their batsmen got out to rash strokes, especially Pat's sweep off Mallett which Connolly caught.'

Far-reaching implications of the midfield clash with the photographer and another incident in the Great Eastern Hotel that night were not realized until the Australian team read the newspapers next morning. Reports that McKenzie and Redpath had assaulted Indian pressmen after the team's celebration dinner caused incredulous derision all the way from Melbourne to Perth and back. Two men less likely than good-natured Garth and gentlemanly Redders to lay a finger on anything except bat and ball could not be found in the touring fifteen or, for that matter, on the whole Australian continent. News that they were away from the hotel at the time quickly cleared their names in Australia — where their reputations made it least necessary — but thousands of Indians misled by the first report saw no correction and may still misjudge these two sportsmen.

With Australian touring sides a private team dinner to celebrate winning a series is a regular thing — as regular as match results allow, anyway — whereas it seems India's custom is for a formal dinner, with high officials making speeches well into the night. This chasm between customs added disastrously to the day's antagonisms because there was no one to bridge it. Lawry was feeling the lack of Australian reporters a severe handicap — a barrier to getting the team's viewpoint known to Indian pressmen. The absence of liaison in the Press box resulted in more than 20 Indian newspapermen turning up and having to be told to leave because the dinner was private. They retired to the hotel's liquor permit room but later men with cameras knocked and entered a bedroom shared by Freeman and Mallett. When they failed to heed the tired bowlers' request that they go, 81kg (14 stone) Freeman forcibly put them out and telephoned to have them removed from the hotel.

Coming on top of assorted versions about the Bombay riot, and Lawry's brush with the photographers, it would be hard to imagine anything more cumulatively damaging to the team's image than for people to read that Australian players had assaulted Indian pressmen. Lawry must have felt he was carrying more weight than an Everest expedition Sherpa.

Police had escorted the Australians everywhere but no escort was considered necessary on the six-mile bus ride from the hotel to Dum Dum airport. As the bus climbed a hill outside Calcutta the players were taking little notice of their surroundings when a loud noise like an explosion shocked them. Stones were crashing against the sides of the bus, cracking and starring the windows. Through one partly-open window came a stone bigger than an orange. It missed Gleeson, who was sitting on the opposite side of the bus, by a hand's span.

'We were badly scared,' players said, 'and we dived for cover to the floor of the bus, wondering what would happen next. The most frightening thought was that stones might break through the driver's window, knock him out, and leave the bus to career out of control. Fortunately, little or no glass flew about inside the bus, as the windows did not shatter. We have no idea who the throwers were, except that we had passed a ricefield. When the bus passed out of range and we looked back from the top of the hill we saw about 100 Indians waving their arms. At the airport we saw the police chief. He was astonished when we told him the bus had been stoned.'

After the Press Photographers' Association threatened a protest strike about the pitch incident, members wore black armbands while taking pictures at the next game at Bangalore. Here the Australians ran into a different kind of trouble — a danger of becoming the first international side to be beaten by a zone team. Led by Jaisimha, who declared both innings, South Zone had a side of almost Test strength, with exceptionally good bowlers in leg-spinner Chandrasekhar and off-spinner Prasanna. Jai's second closure, 249 ahead, left only 170 minutes to get Australia out. By taking six wickets for nine in eight overs Prasanna brought about the fall of the eighth wicket at 53, and the crowd of about 20,000 were dwelling on victory. Lawry was no longer thinking about runs — and who can put them out of mind more completely? — as he and Gleeson resorted to every ruse and stratagem to get through the last hour. Even a woman in a gay sari walking by the sightscreen gave the captain an excuse to step back from the wicket as the bowler approached. He told the umpire the sari was distracting him.

With only 10 minutes to go, the disappointed crowd began pelting coconut husks, orange peel and apple cores at the South Zone fieldsmen. So much debris was falling on the field that umpires Nagaraj Rao and N. S. Rishi called off play five minutes before time and the players ran into the pavilion.

The uneasiness of the team, scarcely knowing what to expect next after the stoning of the bus, was equalled by alarm caused in Australia by reports of riots and rock-throwing. Several ex-players supported a suggestion to cancel the remaining Test, in the belief that it would expose the team to undue risks. Photographers boycotted the Australians' arrival in Madras for this match but manager Bennett's on-the-spot assessment was borne out when the Test was played and won without cause for anxiety.

30 Besieged at Bourda

The most alarming ordeal endured by cricketers anywhere was undergone by the Australian and West Indian teams at Bourda ground, Guyana, targets of missiles flung by thousands infuriated by delay in the start of World Series Cricket's fourth Supertest in 1979.

Huddled in their dressing rooms, the players were besieged for more than two hours by rampaging spectators who hurled bottles through shattered windows and banged on doors with pieces of timber. The riot was so frightening that half the Australians voted to leave Guyana before captain Ian Chappell and his brother Greg persuaded them to remain.

The Georgetown riot followed bottle-throwing stoppages at preceding Supertests in Barbados and Trinidad. Play in Barbados was abandoned after three such incidents about controversial dismissals of opening batsmen Gordon Greenidge and Roy Fredericks.

When umpire Douglas Sang Hue ruled Greenidge caught by wicketkeeper Rod Marsh on the leg-side off fast bowler Len Pascoe, the batsman waved his fist and tore off his gloves so angrily that spectators in the stand gestured menacingly toward the Australians. As the players walked off from the first bombardment fast bowler Dennis Lillee put a protective arm around Sang Hue's shoulder and light-heartedly pretended to kiss him.

Given out lbw to Pascoe, Fredericks stared in disbelief at umpire Ralph Gosein. The bowler chipped Fredericks who, after an angry exchange with the wicketkeeper, walked off slapping bat against pad to indicate he had snicked the ball. Abandonment of the match after more bottle-throwing deprived the Australians of a win, as in the 1978 Test in Jamaica.

WSC officials 'deplored the action of certain players inciting the crowd and of other players not accepting the umpire's decision'. The captains agreed that any player showing undue dissatisfaction with a decision should be sent home immediately. Lillee, Greenidge and Fredericks were cited to appear in Australia before WSC's governing committee, who had power to recommend the management to revoke their contracts.

On the day the Australians squared the Supertest series in Trinidad Chappell asked for police protection for his fieldsmen. Onlookers throwing bottles held up play 23 minutes after Gosein gave a run-out of Deryck Murray, who doubted whether Laird had the ball when he broke the wicket.

It was the first tour on which demonstrators strewed three grounds with bottles and other debris — Kensington Oval, Barbados, Queen's Park Oval, Trinidad and Bourda, Guyana. Hitherto Barbadians had been the best-versed and least volatile of the lot. While waiting they had heard radio descriptions of a military take-over in Grenada. Barbados and Trinidad added two to the usual cause of outbursts, an umpiring decision against a West Indian batsman when his side was in trouble.

After drenching rain delayed the Bourda start from Friday, Guyanese read an assurance that the Supertest, trimmed to four days, would begin on time on Sunday. A capacity crowd, 13,000, began packing the ground at 7 a.m.

Over-cautious umpires and players reluctant to play on a damp outfield caused a predictable and understandable reaction. After a loudspeaker announcement that the umpires would inspect again at noon, players in street clothes prodded the surface, shrugging their shoulders. After a third inspection at 2 p.m., 40 minutes elapsed before an announcement that play would begin at 3.40.

By the time the announcement had been made people had begun hurling bottles, chairs and benches, demolishing fences and hurling hundreds of metal seats on the field. Others toppled heavy seats from two-tier stands. Some wrenched pieces of wood from stands. Smashing down a gate, some pushed a heavy roller toward the pitch. Wire-mesh fence barriers were dragged aside and thousands swarmed on the field. Broadcasters fled as the mob broke every pane of glass in their booths and wrecked equipment inside worth thousands of dollars. Rioters dragged turnstiles from entrances and tipped them in the dark waters of the moat surrounding the ground.

Police in midfield helplessly watched thousands surge across the playing arena to storm the pavilion. Marauders grabbed bottles of beer and stout and threw them on the field. Others smashed trophies and photographs. A man in another stand was reported to have been shot.

Missiles smashed eight windows in the Australians' room. Broken glass covered the floor. Bruce Laird said: 'We just put on helmets, grabbed bats and sat there hoping like hell.' Several rioters tried to force their way in through a broken window. Players armed with bats kept them out.

Bottles flung from an adjoining stand crashed through a broken louvre into the West Indians' room. Two of them bruised elbows of Vivian Richards, who shielded his face just in time, and team manager David Holford.

Channel Nine cameraman Greg Cameron was about to take a picture when a bottle hit him on the chest. Except for a bottle having stunned Gleeson at Bombay this was the first time rioters' missiles had injured players. The West Indian players took refuge in the bathroom and toilets. Swing bowler Mick Malone said: 'I wouldn't care if I were being paid $100,000 a year, I have three children at home.'

Australian team manager Richie Robinson said: 'We were very frightened because all we had was one thin timber wall separating us from the crowd. At the height of the riot we feared for our lives. We did not appear to be getting a lot of protection for all we had was one police sergeant in the room. Two police officers came in later but they were not armed and I think we were better equipped for the situation.'

Riot police who arrived after an hour wore gas masks as they used smoke-bombs to drive vandals from the pavilion and dispersed a wild crowd of 10,000. After about 600 police cleared the field a riot-squad bus escorted the players' cars back to their hotel.

Police with guard dogs in the hotel grounds were reinforced that night. The Australians' first vote on whether to leave or stay was tied, eight-all. Ian Chappell said he had been through a similar riot in Bombay in 1969 'but we felt pretty vulnerable here when the crowd came into the pavilion'.

Before the next day, Chappell set out the situation with firmness characteristic of his leadership: 'This is not a war and I will not ask any of our players to walk out on the field if he does not want to play. I am not asking any player to put his life on the line. But I feel we have to go back there just to show them that we will not allow mob rule to take over and stop us playing cricket. Before each day I will go to the ground and ensure that there is adequate security for the players. If I consider there are not enough police we will simply not play.'

The West Indies' top broadcaster and critic, Tony Cozier, wrote: 'As in every outburst, cramped, uncomfortable grounds, with their appalling lack of basic amenities, aggravate an angry crowd. A long wait may be bearable at Lord's or the MCG but not in sweltering heat on a seat shared with at least one other backside. Prices up to 50 per cent higher than usual and lack of communication for those running the match further exacerbate the situation.

'Caribbean Labour Congress president Frank Walcott, a former umpire, said: "This regional explosion is more than discontent with an umpiring or administrative decision. It is a growing sign of discontent in the area".

'WSC also had its image tarnished by an incident involving Ian Chappell whom a magistrate fined 150 Guyana dollars (A$39) for having assaulted a local WSC official and used unseemly language.'

So that play could begin as a three-day match, the club obtained 50 national servicemen to work all night under pressure-gas lamps. They repaired damage estimated at $88,000 and cleared away wreckage. Engineers set up generators for the messiest job of retrieving the sunken turnstiles. They could not be seen and had to be found by trailing grappling hooks. Team finance manager Bruce McDonald, a former Sydney umpire, said: 'They made such a transformation that I couldn't believe it was the same ground. Not a paling out of place.'

Clive Lloyd sent the Australians in. His battery of four fast bowlers, drawn from Holding, Roberts, Croft, Garner and Daniel, formed the most formidable firepower batsmen ever faced.

Mike Holding, 24, who took his 28 wickets in the season at the cheapest average, 20, has perfected his style since his open-chested action on his first tour in 1975 to Australia. Power from his swing of the shoulders in his model delivery adds two yards to his speed. The 192cm (6 feet 5½ inches) Jamaican delivers some balls off a short run.

At his most rhythmic, the exceptional speed of Andy Roberts is electrifying. Colin Croft, 26, built in proportion to his height, 193cm (6 feet 4 inches), took most wickets in the season, 33 (average 24). Batsmen would rather he had fulfilled his parents' wish when they also named him Everton Hunte after two famous Barbadian batsmen. After the longest run-up he brings his arm over the back of his head at the point of delivery. Tallest of all cricketers, 203cm (6 feet 8 inches) Joel Garner, 26, is nicknamed 'Big Bird'. At less speed, he extracts awkward lift.

The frequency of bouncers in World Series Cricket caused all the Australians to bat in skullcaps. So did the West Indians, excepting

Richards, King, Holding and Garner. Haynes, nicknamed 'Hammer' for his power batting, wore a helmet fielding at close-leg. Protection had saved Rowe from grave injury in the first Supertest. The blow put him out for three weeks.

Both Australian openers at Bourda fell to catches by wicketkeeper Deryck Murray—Laird, 6, off Croft and Trevor Chappell, 5, off Holding. With two out for 25, Greg Chappell joined Martin Kent for the most important stand of the match. They prevented further inroads of the sort that fired the side out for 106 and 194 in the Kingston loss. Repetition would have threatened a second defeat, even within three days.

Kent's promotion to first drop in the strongest Australian team rewarded him for developing his best form after averaging only 16 in WSC's first season. At 25 he had mastered over-venturesome impulses. Yet he was still recognizable as the gifted stroke-maker who made the first century before lunch for his State — 104 off 102 balls against the Pakistanis in 1976, though nine balls had been bowled in the two-hour session before he came in. It was a dazzling feat that fitted his nickname, 'Superman'.

At Bourda he made 51 of his 86 stand with Greg. This is the best partnership by players from Queensland for Australia in international cricket. Their stand before Murray caught Kent off Garner enabled the side to bear the loss of Ian Chappell's prize wicket for 9 to Holding's speed and left-hander David Hookes, 28, to Croft.

Emerging from steadfast defence, Greg turned the match around, as he had done in Trinidad a week earlier. At 90, three successive boundaries lifted him past 100 in 290 minutes. Seeking quicker runs, Chappell hit five boundaries in his last 24 before he edged whippy medium-pacer Collis King for Murray's fourth catch.

Throughout his five-hour 113, memories of Chappell's century against Guyana in 1972 enriched the appreciation of many of the 12,000 for his batting. When Greg said: 'Guyanese are the warmest crowds I have played before', he did not mean their solar-heated state. This timely century followed his 90 in the second Supertest and 150 in the third.

Marsh, 49, and nightwatchman Ray Bright, 29 not out, carried the first-day 161 on toward 341 off 112.1 overs.

Exceeding a run a minute, the West Indians scored almost 4½ runs an over. Only Fredericks, 12, and Greenidge, 52, were out as Rowe, 64, and Richards, 54, hurried the total to 200. With an old ball on a slow wicket, fast bowler Jeff Thomson astonished 14,000 spectators by having Rowe lbw and Richards caught off the third and sixth balls of his ninth over.

Lloyd, whose chanceless six-hour 165 made him Man-of-the-Match in the first Supertest, was 31 when he edged Len Pascoe to the youngest Chappell.

Though later to come to the fore than most West Indians, King, 27, is one of their top batsmen, a hard hitter who won the Man-of-the-Match award. He cracked three sixes and 16 fours in 110 in 150 minutes. Murray made 29 while sticking with Collis in a sixth-wicket stand that put them 38 ahead. With 476 off 113.6 overs, the West Indians led by 135.

Croft and Roberts dismissed three Australians for 117 in 33 overs before the umpires ended play an hour early because a decision was impossible. An unfinished match in Antigua left the series one-all.

Outstanding run-getter in Supertests, Greg Chappell totalled 631 in 10 innings and alone averaged over 50. Next came Fredericks 363, Richards 303, Lloyd 309, and Ian Chappell 300. Lillee took most wickets, 23, followed by Holding 19, Croft 17 and Thomson 16. Laird and Hookes played on all 37 days. The tour did better than pay its way, aided by a WSC grant of A$60,000 to the West Indies' Board and a Trinidad company underwriting the series with A$87,000. Greg Chappell won Ovaltine's Man-of-the-Series award, $2000.

The West Indians' scoring in the Guyana Supertest is the fastest, 96 per 100 balls, of any in the 18 international matches interrupted by crowds.

Of the sides in the last two series in the West Indies only one put the ball into play 100 times an hour. Kallicharran's Test XI averaged 103 balls hourly. This was achieved at Sabina Park only because four spinners bowled more than half the balls and the two pacemen's run-ups were of moderate length. Although three spinners did two-thirds of Australia's bowling there the average rate was only 93 an hour.

Thomson's long walkback before running up was the chief visible cause of the poorer rate. He was the only bowler who played in the WSC series as well as the 1978 Tests and for each bowled about one-fifth of the balls. When he joined Lillee and Pascoe in the WSC attack fast bowlers and a seamer delivered roughly four-fifths of the balls and Australia's rate fell back to 83 an hour, the slowest of any of these sides.

Yet Marsh is one of the wicketkeepers who runs from end to end between overs, often accompanied by slipfielders, and fieldsmen and umpires take a fast bowler's cap as he comes up to save unnecessary steps. Progress will be difficult to make until pacemen can recover the technique that enabled some of the swiftest bowlers to work up momentum in not more than 17 strides, like Pascoe and Hurst, and perfect it in 15 (Roberts and Tyson), 14 (Larwood), 12 (Lindwall) or even nine or 10 (Miller and McKenzie).

In Sydney WSC managing director Lynton Taylor said: 'Riots are threatening the future of international cricket in the West Indies. All national cricket authorities must be questioning the wisdom of going there. Inevitably, the players who now have lucrative careers to consider will be reluctant to risk serious injury or even the possibility of death.'

31 Internal Strife

To understand how and why the Australian Board of Control came to veto its Test selectors' choice of opening batsman, Sidney George Barnes, in 1951 we have to trace cricket history back to days before most of us were born.

The roots of the Board's troubles run back through a series of episodes which could be entitled:

Selector's KO punch.
Sacking of the Big Six.
Faces on the bar-room floor.
Deposed skipper's comeback.
Record-holder rung out.
Champion fined £50.
A trier penalized.
Test stars carpeted.
Barnes v the Board.
Chief State rebuffed.

The Board had a stormy birth after 13 English teams had visited Australia, 14 Australian sides (one Aboriginal) had toured Britain and 76 Test Matches had been played.

At that time the Melbourne Cricket Club handled this end of English visits to Australia and the Australian players organized their own tours of Britain, sharing the profits.

When the Cricket Associations of the States tried to found the Board to take control in 1905 England refused to send a team until differences were settled.

South Australia would not join until the founders issued this definition of control of finance in 1906: 'The Board shall have complete control of all financial matters — that is, the Board shall provide the necessary funds to send teams away ... The Board has no intention of interfering in any way with the profits earned by the players on tour.'

In addition to that safeguard of financial benefits, the players' enterprise had built up; Regulation 9 of the Board's constitution upheld the players' right to appoint their manager and submit his name to the Board for confirmation.

Friction occurred when the Board handled a tour of England for the first time in 1909. Going back on its financial definition, the Board decided to take five per cent from the profits of the first £6000 earned by the team and 12½ per cent of any balance.

The players objected that they had been double-crossed — that they had given up their entire control of tours abroad on a different basis of agreement — but the Board asserted its authority and carried its point.

In between his managerial duties, Frank Laver, 39, found time to take 70 wickets with late swingers. This tall Victorian was called on to play in four Tests and took eight wickets for 31 in England's first innings at Manchester.

On return, trouble began to brew when Board members could not get all the information they wanted from the treasurer's book which a Victorian batsman, P. A. McAlister, 40, kept for them on tour. So the Board asked Laver for some books he had kept.

Laver said his books contained many private entries of his own and other players' affairs. He offered to attend a Board meeting to answer any questions about receipts and expenditure. Some Board members wanted Laver to attend but the majority accused him of neglect.

An English Test team was playing in Australia (1911–12) and at the end of the season Australia's team was to be chosen for the triangular Test tournament with England and South Africa in Britain in 1912.

After a sitting in private (then, as now) the Board announced on 30 December 1911 that the only matter of importance was the appointment of the selection committee to act in England.

Secrecy failed to bottle up the news that G. Mostyn Evans (South Australia) had moved that the players appoint a manager on the same financial terms as themselves.

H. R. Rush (Victoria) then moved that 'as the Board has already decided to send a Board representative with the team, the players be informed, as soon as the team is selected, that it will be unnecessary for them to appoint a manager.'

When chairman W. P. McElhone (NSW) disapproved several amendments proposed by J. F. G. Foxton (Queensland), Foxton remarked, 'But under Regulation 9 the players have the right to appoint a manager.'

Rush: 'Oh, we swept Regulation 9 away last night.'

Rush's amendment was carried by seven votes to four.

Critics assailed the Board majority's action as a second double-cross and a gross repudiation of an honourable agreement with the players.

Making a stand for the last of their rights, six of Australia's finest cricketers wrote to the Board objecting that costs of a Board representative on tour could not fairly be chargeable against their earnings and stating that if the Board did not comply with their request for appointment of their own manager none would be available for selection to tour Britain.

The six were Australian captain Clem Hill, 35, (SA), wonder-bat Victor Trumper, 34, fast bowler Albert Cotter, 28, wicketkeeper Hanson Carter, 24, (NSW), all-rounder Warwick Armstrong, 32, and left-hand batsman Vernon Ransford, 27 (Victoria).

The Board majority broke its silence by announcing that:

- As governing body taking the responsibility for the tour, the Board had entered an agreement with England's Marylebone Cricket Club and the players had nothing to do with the arrangements.
- On selection, each player would be told the Board's terms and would have an opportunity to decline the invitation if not satisfied.
- The Board would not permit any number of cricketers to dictate the terms and conditions of a tour or appointment of a manager, if one were appointed.

A sensational climax occurred on 3 February 1912, when, after the Board majority appointed a Board representative for the tour of Britain, two Australian selectors fought in the NSW Cricket Association's office.

Peter McAlister was involved in both incidents, as candidate for Board representative and a participant in the fight.

In a last-minute plea for a settlement that would rebound to the Board's credit, Dr Ramsay Mailer, (Vic), suggested that the players' legal right to appoint their own manager be respected and that the Board then bind the manager by agreement to carry out its wishes.

When the majority turned this down, Mailer and the three South Australian members asked that the minutes record their refusal to take part in an illegal appointment of a Board representative.

In the ballot by the remaining eight members McAlister received only two votes (from Ernest Bean and Harry Rush, two hatchet-men whose tomahawk was kept whetted in the feud between the Victorian Cricket Association and the Melbourne Cricket Club). So McAlister was discarded and in the second ballot Bean and Rush supported a Queensland nominee, G. S. Crouch. This defeated by five to three a Sydney man, E. Hume, who was supported by the Board chairman, W. P. McElhone.

By letter, Test captain Clem Hill complained to the Board that, in reply to his telegraphed suggestion for Australia's XI in the third Test at Adelaide, McAlister had wired back, 'If you want Macartney in, leave yourself out'.

Some Board members proposed that the Board express regret that such a message should have been sent, but the majority held that this act by one of its selectors had nothing to do with the Board.

That night, when selectors Hill, McAlister and Frank Iredale (NSW) met to choose Australia's team for the fourth Test the following week, McAlister severely criticized Hill's captaincy.

Hill: 'The Australians wouldn't have gone to England under you.'

McAlister: 'I'm a better captain than you and Trumper put together. You are the worst captain I've ever seen.'

Hill: 'If you keep on insulting me I'll pull your nose.'

McAlister repeated: 'You are the worst captain I have ever seen.'

Angrily, Hill leaned across the table and slapped McAlister's face.

McAlister: 'You hit me when my hands were down.'

Hill (putting his hands behind his back): 'My hands are down now.'

McAlister rushed around the table and grappled with Hill. Locked together, they swayed around the room, crashing against the table and walls. Their fighting and wrestling spattered the room with blood, which stained their clothes and the clothing of Iredale and Board secretary Sydney Smith.

After 10 minutes McAlister was on his back on the floor, with Hill standing over him.

When Hill left the room McAlister rose, called out, 'Coward!' and made to follow, but Iredale and Smith shut the door. McAlister's nose and face were cut and there was a bruise under his left eye. Hill bore no marks.

Hill told Smith he could no longer act as a selector with McAlister. A hurriedly-called meeting of available Board members accepted his resignation that night.

I knew both men years later, when time had so mellowed them that it was difficult to imagine them fighting. Hill was open-mannered and companionable, ready to forgive and forget, McAlister tall and reserved, with a smile that could melt his Scottish dourness.

Their outlook on the game then was still as different as when they quarrelled. Hill judged cricketers by their play and temperament, while McAlister set much more store by the figures of their performances.

After Hill's resignation, McAlister and Iredale chose the fourth Test team and 10 certainties for the 1912 tour — the six who had written to the Board about their rights, (Hill, Trumper, Carter, Cotter, Armstrong and Ransford), NSW googly bowler H. V. Hordern, (who had announced he was not available), plus NSW batsmen Warren Bardsley and Roy Minnett and Victorian wicketkeeper William Carkeek.

Carter said, 'When the whole team is selected and meets, we six will abide by the majority's decision about a manager. We don't want to see Laver persecuted and we are prepared to place the facts before any independent arbitrator ... We will abide by the arbitrator's decision and the Board should be prepared to do likewise'.

The Board outsmarted them by requiring them to answer in 10 days — before a full team was selected which could hold a meeting about the managership.

The six accepted, subject to the right to withdraw should the managerial question not be satisfactorily adjusted.

Australia's ex-captain M. A. Noble commented that he was a strong supporter of the principle of having a Board of Control but the majority of present Board members had failed to be credited with a single act of conciliation and forbearance. They had held a pistol at the heads of the players and gradually taken from them all their privileges.

Noble added, 'No doubt the cricketers have made mistakes and used faulty tactics, but the Board has adopted unjust, dishonest methods to evade the rules and take away the only privilege left to the players'.

Former Test player Tom Horan called the Board majority 'wreckers of Australian cricket'.

In the end only three of the first-chosen 10 were in the 15 to tour England. In the final Test before the side sailed, the Sydney crowd cheered Hill all the way to the wicket.

Before the makeshift team departed with the Board representative G. S. Crouch, Mailer said:

'Without the six, as well as Noble, Laver and Hordern, the nine players best known to the English public will be absentees. I think there will be a loss.'

The Board's team won only nine matches in a wet English season, lost eight and left 20 unfinished. Macartney's brilliant batting was one of the few bright spots in an ill-fated tour. Mayne found fault with English umpires.

Wisden's editor wrote: 'In the special circumstances I think personal considerations should have been put aside and made subordinate to the prime need to send over Australia's best team for the Triangular Tournament ... The Board of Control carried its point, but as regards the prestige of Australian cricket the victory was dearly won ...'

The tour resulted in a loss to the Board of £1286, to enable 11 players on a profit-sharing basis to receive £190 each and to pay four players and the manager, who were guaranteed lump sums of £400 each.

In the following passage from manager Crouch's report to the Board, heavy type shows the suggestion which led the Board to take unto itself the power by which a 9–to–3 majority vetoed Barnes' last season:

'The conduct of the team on the whole was good, but from experience gained on the recent tour I feel it absolutely necessary, in the interests of Australian cricket, to say that it is my firm opinion that, **in the selection of future teams to visit England or South Africa, qualifications of candidates other than individual cricket ability should be weighed.**

'Further, I would remind you that the members of the Australian XI come prominently before the public eye in England, and from a national point of view it is desirable that you shall send men who will realize the responsibilities of their position and be a credit to their country.'

Wisden's version of this included, 'The tour did not pass off without unpleasantness, manager Crouch lodged a scathing complaint with the Board, stating that some of the players had conducted themselves so badly in England as to lead to the team being socially ostracized ... It may be added that some of the players were not at all satisfied with Mr Crouch as manager.'

When the Board received Crouch's report in Melbourne a critic wrote, 'Members of the Board are faced with a report which bears out all that the rejected senior players had told them. The members do not wonder now that players, who for years have been in the forefront of Australian cricket, should have insisted on their right to appoint their own manager, to see that they were looked after by a man with experience, and that men who could not appreciate the social conditions under which an Australian team lives in England should not be selected...'

The Board appointed a committee early in December, 1912, to investigate the conduct of some members of the team in England.

Crouch's complaints were reported to contain a statement that when the team was crossing to England from Ireland after a match at Bray the skipper of the steamer had to issue orders that no more liquor be sold that night.

Wild rumours circulated in Australian cities dragging in the names of players against whom Crouch made no complaint.

The committee was criticized for delay in its investigation because it was unfair that innocent players should for a single day be allowed to remain under suspicion and be at the mercy of scandalmongers.

(Note the similarity to the Barnes case. Barrister J. W. Shand, QC, told the court that, because of the Board's extraordinary decision to keep secret its reasons for disapproving players, the only inference people could draw from Barnes' exclusion was that he had been guilty of crimes and serious offences, such as theft and offering insult to the Royal Family.)

Nearly two months after appointment to investigate Crouch's report, the committee called on four of the 1912 team to explain incidents on the tour. They were skipper Syd Gregory, 42, of Sydney, a veteran of five trips to Britain, and three Victorians, wicketkeeper Barlow Carkeek, 34, slow bowler T. J. Matthews, 28 (who took two hat-tricks in one Test, the only bowler ever to do so), and batsman Dave Smith, 28.

The first three attended, with other members of the team, but Dave Smith wrote from Melbourne that he was too ill to travel to Sydney.

After deliberating two days the committee handed out a statement that the inquiry was private and evidence and statements were not for publication, but would be submitted to the Board in due course.

The hand-out said many of the outside statements being circulated were gross and unfair exaggerations, and the committee regretted sensational cries by newsboys using the name of the captain, as they were unjustified and uncalled for, especially at the termination of a long and honourable career.

It took cricket a long time to get the smell of those seven years out of its nostrils. There were more feuds than those carried on by the Martins and the Coys, those reckless mountain boys.

Attempts were made to depose Warwick Armstrong as skipper of Victoria. The giant all-rounder's autocratic captaincy made enemies, but officials' moves to drum him out of the game failed. Cricketers 40 years ago had not been deprived of the democratic right (still held by most club teams) of electing their own captains. One Victorian bowler, J. Kyle, revealed that two VCA executive members had constantly been urging him to propose another player for skipper instead of Armstrong, but he said Warwick had always handled him well as a bowler and led the side satisfactorily.

Kyle added, 'If this is the sort of thing that's going on in big cricket I don't care whether I ever play for Victoria again.'

One of those who temporarily displaced Armstrong as State skipper was a Rhodes Scholar and Oxford Blue, J. Arnold Seitz (later Victorian Director of Education and now VCA president). Feeling ran so high that Dr A. E. V. Hartkopf was not allowed to vote for Armstrong, on the ground that he was 12th man and not in the final eleven.

The third attempt was just after World War I. It fizzled after thousands of cricket-lovers held a mass protest meeting in Yarra Park. Discomfited officials reinstated Armstrong. 'The Big Ship', as he was called, went on to captain Australia in an unbeaten series of 10 Tests against England before he voluntarily furled his sails at the age of 42.

Most of the officials who provoked the 1912 squabble had passed out of office before the retirement from big cricket in 1928 of Arthur Mailey, NSW googly bowler who tickled the crowds with his tricky flight and spin and with his sketches and articles as a cartoonist-writer.

But officials were not amused sometimes when his writings contained criticism of the administration, especially his opinion that office-bearers with little or no experience as cricketers were not qualified to decide matters affecting the play — such as whether bowlers should be denied the use of resin, or have a smaller ball to handle.

Mailey took 110 wickets in 24 Tests before he went out of the game holding two records which still stand — only man to take nine wickets in a Test innings and only Australian to capture 36 Test wickets in one season against England.

Also still standing is his record of being the outstanding Test player of his generation who has never been given a testimonial match. Every year that passes without this being rectified reflects the pettiness of officialdom's thin-skinned reaction to frank criticism.

When the Australians triumphed over England to regain the Ashes in 1930, vice-captain Victor Richardson asked for a few weeks' leave to avail himself of a chance to gain experience in the London headquarters of the company he represented in Adelaide. Manager W. L. Kelly realized that this would mean a lot to Richardson, but said he could not grant the request because of the Board's definite rule that all players must return as a team in the same ship to their home ports.

Yet when the liner was halfway across the Indian Ocean members of the Board in Australia (without reference to manager Kelly) granted permission for Don Bradman to leave the ship in Western

Australia and be flown ahead of the team to Sydney for presentation with a motor car as an advertising stunt by a company which did not employ him.

Bradman's record-breaking batting and C. V. Grimmett's great bowling had been the chief match-winning factors for Australia in 1930. Both were brought before the Board, not for congratulations on their fine cricket, but to answer charges that they had broken their contracts not to write for the Press.

The Board fined Bradman £50, though he pleaded that not he but his publishers had sold the serial version of his book which appeared in English papers during the tour.

Grimmett was let off with a caution for having written a book about cricket (not serialized at the forbidden time).

In my opinion, officialdom has shown no poorer spirit in the past 20 years than in 1935. The Board had been unable to accede to India's requests for an Australian team, so Frank Tarrant organized an unofficial team to play in India while Australia's Test side toured South Africa.

Among the players Tarrant invited was NSW googly bowler Hugh Chilvers, 34, a keen and tireless cricketer, who had given years of wholehearted service to Northern District Club since its inception. He had taken about 100 wickets for NSW and twice had been on the brink of Australian selection without the luck to get an overseas tour.

Chilvers was not allowed to go to India, on the ground that he might be wanted for his State.

The sight of Chilvers continuing to play for Northern District until last season, when he turned 50, should have been an annual reproach to officials who denied this honest toiler his only chance for a trip abroad.

The Barnes libel case in Sydney District Court last August included this passage:

Barrister Shand: 'Do you remember in the middle of a Test Match, O'Reilly, McCabe and Fleetwood-Smith being summoned before the Board?'

Board member K. O. E. Johnson: 'I think they were.'

'And it was suggested they had had too much beer?'

'I don't recollect that.'

In a later reference to this, Shand said, 'Never was any charge made. I merely mentioned the matter for the purpose of cross-examination and to draw attention to the trivial attitude of the Board'.

Judge Lloyd: 'Everybody took it that way. There was no reflection against them.'

The inside story was that England had routed Australia on storm-damaged wickets in Sir Donald Bradman's first two Tests as captain in 1936, and the new skipper had made two of his rare ducks. Besides taking six wickets in these games, bowler W. J. O'Reilly topped Australia's score in the first innings of the second Test and vice-captain S. J. McCabe topped the second.

After that match a whisper went around that trouble with the Board was looming for a couple of Australian players. One mentioned this to Bradman, who waved the rumour aside, saying, 'Don't be silly.'

The day Australia won the third Test in Melbourne some of the team were invited to VCA rooms at 3 p.m. The players found that only four of them were wanted — McCabe, O'Reilly, left-hand googly bowler Leslie Fleetwood-Smith (who had just finished his first Test and was one of Bradman's closest friends in the team) and left-hand batsman L. P. J. O'Brien (who had opened the innings in the second Test, but was not in the third Test eleven).

At the VCA rooms they were welcomed with handshakes by Dr Allen Robertson (Board chairman) and three other Board members, R. A. Oxlade (NSW), R. Hartigan (Qld), and H. W. Hodgetts (the stockbroker who had taken Bradman to Adelaide from Sydney).

Dr Robertson read from two sheets of foolscap a kind of abstract essay about unnamed players who did not give full support to their captain, or who kept late hours, or drank too much liquor or were not in the best condition.

One of the mystified players then asked, 'Dr Robertson, does this mean that we four are accused of these things?'

Dr Robertson: 'I assure you there are no accusations whatever.'

A player: 'In that case, sir, this is just tiggy-touchwood and we all might as well go.'

The gathering broke up. As the players left, Hodgetts shook their hands at the door, saying, 'Don't say anything about this.'

But in the street the players saw news posters proclaiming: Board Carpets Four Test Men.

Unaware of the nature of the interview, the public could only guess why the players had been called in. By its action, the Board needlessly exposed four fine sportsmen to the risk of their reputations being damaged and their livelihoods affected by unfounded rumours.

When Australia's selectors chose 13 players before the final Test of 1937, instead of 12, England's captain G. O. Allen told Bradman and Board members of his batsmen's fears that the addition of fast bowler L. J. Nash to the usual opening bowler E. L. McCormick might portend an onslaught of bumpers. Allen, a peacemaker after Bodyline, said he was anxious lest this mar the season.

The Board ordered the selectors to reduce the list to 12, apparently in the belief that newcomer Nash would be squeezed out.

Feeling that it would be a slur to drop any announced player before the match, selectors Don Bradman, E. A. Dwyer and W. J. Johnson refused to do so. Dr Robertson insisted — until they threatened to resign.

In September 1937, this remark by Dr Robertson went around the world: 'I doubt whether England will ever produce a team to make an even go with Australian cricketers ... In my lifetime they are not going to produce a team equal to ours.'

Before the next September came around, England gave Bradman's Australian team the biggest trouncing in Test history, in the last prewar Test, at Kennington Oval.

Since the war, the Board has twice failed to gain for its players the best conditions available for tours.

After the Australians toured New Zealand in 1946 on 30 shillings a day, it was proposed their pay should be augmented out of tour profits, but the Board let this slide, when a member said, 'Why give them any more? It would only go to the Tax Department.'

After England lost to Australia in 1948, South Africa paid English players an allowance of about £600 for their 1948–49 tour, and was reported to be willing to give at least as much to the members of the world's top team, Australia, in 1949–50. But the Board settled for a £450 allowance, and Barnes said he could not afford to go on such terms.

That was the trip when the Board's selectors, by omitting all-rounder Keith Miller, risked the loss of Test cricket's greatest drawcard to tempting offers from Lancashire League.

Officialdom affronted English ex-captain C. B. Fry, a distinguished MCC member, by refusing him entry to Brisbane members' reserve because he was a journalist. Next was a rumpus there with the visiting Indians, followed by an attempt to keep England's famous fast bowler Harold Larwood out of the ground — '20 years too late', as Neville Cardus remarked.

Ruler of Queensland cricket, lawyer J. S. Hutcheon, QC, (now nicknamed Czar-Czar) has been a Board member for 33 years; no one has done more to make the Board what it is.

It was Hutcheon who moved the notorious hush-hush resolution to omit from the minutes any reference to selected players, and who advised Board secretary W. H. Jeanes to refuse to produce the Board's book in the Barnes court case. Judge Lloyd immediately canned that.

Paradoxically, members who have often mishandled relations with the players have mostly believed that they were doing the right thing. Several members are well-meaning men who, separately, would take pains not to embarrass others or cast a shadow on their reputations. Yet, collectively, the Board, swayed by an influential kernel, has failed to shake off the old practice of ponderously imposing its will in ways that could do individuals lifelong harm.

The Board has done some good work, chiefly by ploughing most of the profits back into cricket. Perhaps it has done other good things, but nobody knows, because of its habit of concealment behind a cloak of secrecy — a cloak that trips it up.

With the petty removal of Test selector E. A. Dwyer (NSW), silencing the most populous State's voice, the Board's prestige has sunk to a low ebb.

The Board has a lot to live down and if the present members do not achieve this, club cricketers who elect delegates to the State Associations should direct them unmistakably to appoint members who will.